Praise for

CHANGEMAKER PLAYBOOK

"*Changemaker Playbook* is filled with stories of everyday changemakers who have the courage to act on their empathy. This book is a true blueprint for how we rise above our differences, come together, and fix real problems."
—Van Jones, CNN political contributor, host of
The Van Jones Show, and best-selling author

"The game has changed, so how do you respond? *Changemaker Playbook* offers a new game plan on leadership that everyone needs for a world in which change is the only constant."
—Pete Souza, #1 *New York Times* best-selling author, former director
of the White House Photography Office, Chief Official White
House Photographer for President Obama, and Official
White House Photographer for President Reagan

"In today's world of rapid change, our systems and institutions must be continuously renewed and reinvented to ensure peace and sustainability. De Sio's examination of leading and emerging innovators in business, civil society, education, media, and other fields offers both a framework of understanding and invaluable advice to thrive in this world—and change it for the better."
—David Bornstein, best-selling author of *How to Change
the World: Social Entrepreneurs and the Power of New Ideas*,
New York Times columnist, and founder of Solutions Journalism

"This book confirms all I have seen during my years growing and nurturing a network of thousands of entrepreneurs: that empathy and courage, combined with proximity to urgent challenges, can fuel solutions that address persistent community needs. As we consider our rapidly changing world of work, it is more important than ever that we equip individuals and institutions to shift culture, policy, and resources to the changemakers who are making lives better in their communities. This book offers the models and stories we need to build an inclusive, flourishing future."
—Alfa Demmellash, co-founder and CEO at Rising Tide
Capital, co-founder at Future Tide Partners, and World
Economic Forum Young Global Leader

"*Changemaker Playbook* is a powerful new leadership framework and organizational model for working in teams of teams, powered by the idea that when we put ourselves in the shoes of those who are struggling or are on the margins—if we can genuinely understand the world from their perspective—then we can take care of business and solve society's most urgent and pressing issues."

—Jostein Solheim, former CEO of Ben & Jerry's
and senior business executive at Unilever

"As a student leader, ours is the generation that will lead us into the new, complex, ever-changing game. *Changemaker Playbook* is an essential tool that every student leader needs to read in order to thrive and excel in this elaborate world we live in today."

—Anna Counihan, student body vice president at
University of Minnesota Duluth and student leader
at the National Campus Leadership Council

"If ever there was a time in which strengthening our communities, supporting fresh leadership approaches, building trust, and taking care of each other were paramount, it's now. *Changemaker Playbook* shows us that when everyday people channel our creative energies to issues we are passionate about that affect our lives and then galvanize others who share those passions, we can truly make better communities for everyone."

—David Simas, former Assistant to the President
in the Obama White House

"*Changemaker Playbook* is hopeful and bound to inspire. We all need a guiding light. And in this book Henry shows us so many guiding lights. For all of us who strive for the world as it should be, this is a roadmap for how we can make it happen."

—Johanna Maska, host of *Pod is a Woman* and CEO
at The Global Situation Room, Inc.

"Because entrepreneurship is an important driver for improving livelihoods, *Changemaker Playbook* is the case for why every young person must be equipped and supported as a changemaker. Recognizing the power of young changemakers is the way forward for global development."

—Per Heggenes, CEO at IKEA Foundation

"Change and disruption define our present and foreseeable business operating climate. *Changemaker Playbook* offers readers a leadership-paradigm-shifting and thought-provoking way forward to achieving successful business engagement."

—Ertharin Cousin, former US Ambassador to the United Nations Agencies for Food and Agriculture, *Forbes'* The World's 100 Most Powerful Women, and *TIME's* 100 Most Influential People in the World

"Henry De Sio understands and unearths an essential truth in his latest book: empowering everyone as a leader is what the modern workforce demands and what solving the big problems of the day requires. This is a must-read for anyone thinking about how to build flourishing teams and leaders."

—Eric Waldo, executive director at Michelle Obama's Reach Higher initiative

"De Sio reveals the new paradigm of leadership and teams that are operating, now, in front of our eyes. As he states with clarity, spirit, momentum, and affirmation, the new game of everyone a changemaker only requires of us that we abandon the former, hierarchical relationships of the past and build impact and innovation that taps into everyone's insight and potential."

—Torey Malatia, radio executive and co-creator of the long-running radio program *This American Life*

"*Changemaker Playbook* is the perfect guide for people who want to better their communities and themselves in today's fast-changing world by fostering empathy, following our creative passions, and solving problems through teamwork."

—Mimi Goss, author of *What Is Your One Sentence?*

"The pace of change in our world is accelerating, and regardless of your profession, you need to adjust your approach to face the challenges of this new terrain. Drawing on his transformative work leading a winning presidential campaign and later, working with remarkable social entrepreneurs across the globe, Henry De Sio shows us how everyday people can come together to do extraordinary things. *Changemaker Playbook* is the new leadership handbook for today's world."

—Chris Lu, political commentator and former Deputy Secretary of Labor

"This is the story only Henry can tell. For more than a decade, he has been the global ambassador for changemakers, bringing this powerful framework to leaders across sectors all over the world. This is the definitive playbook for the new game of living in complexity, with a clear roadmap for preparing our children to thrive and for lifting each other above the challenges before us."

—Maja Frankel, secretary-general at Friends: United Against Bullying

"Audacious visions of BIGness, innovation, and 'change on steroids' have crowded my imagination since being exposed to the ideas in this book. In this fast-changing world, today's young people are trying to make sense of the new reality of careers and the economy. Henry gives original language and insights to help us understand a dramatic new world."

—Amy Morrill Bijeau, director of Experiential Education at American University

"Henry De Sio captures beautifully how technology has democratized leadership, and he provides a compelling framework for unleashing a generation of distributed change agents who can chart a new course for our society... from anywhere. His focus on empathy, agency, and innovating for the good of community will be core to rebuilding the American fabric and provides a key strategy for bridging the rural-urban divide our nation is facing."

—Matt Dunne, founder of the Center on Rural Innovation and former Googler

"*Changemaker Playbook* offers a clear picture and a powerful vision for commanding today's world. This is a must read for business and social-sector professionals advancing mission-led organizations."

—Christoffer Omberg, CEO and co-founder of Oslo Business Forum

"As the Chief Operating Officer (COO) of Obama for America, Henry was an indispensable member of the management team that built the campaign from a startup in the earliest days into the impressive organization that was the foundation for our candidate's success. His management approach, interpersonal skills, and ability to think strategically were integral to the establishment of the foundation of the Obama White House. Having worked closely with Henry as he performed in both roles, I rate him as one of the best managers of a large organization I have had the privilege of observing an action."

—Peter Rouse, former Counselor to President Barack Obama and Chief White House Aide

CHANGEMAKER PLAYBOOK

The New Physics of Leadership in a World of Explosive Change

HENRY F. DE SIO, JR.

JOHN
MURRAY
BUSINESS

First published by Nicholas Brealey Publishing in 2021
(from September 2024 known as John Murray Business)

An imprint of John Murray Press

This paperback edition published by John Murray Business in 2024

An Hachette UK company

SRD

A CIP catalogue record for this title is available from the British Library

Library of Congress Control Number: 2020941848

Hardback ISBN 978 1 529 33019 9
Paperback ISBN 978 1 529 33021 2
US ebook ISBN 978 1 529 35582 6
UK ebook ISBN 978 1 529 35582 6

Typeset in 10.12/13.8pt Minion Pro-Regular by Jouve (UK), Milton Keynes.

Printed and bound in India by Manipal Technologies Limited, Manipal

John Murray Press policy is to use papers that are natural, renewable and
recyclable products and made from wood grown in sustainable forests. The logging
and manufacturing processes are expected to conform to the environmental
regulations of the country of origin.

John Murray Press
Carmelite House
50 Victoria Embankment
London EC4Y 0DZ

John Murray Business
123 S. Broad St., Ste 2750
Philadelphia, PA 19109

John Murray Press, part of Hodder & Stoughton Limited
An Hachette UK company

MIX
Paper | Supporting
responsible forestry
FSC™ C104740

To the strong, courageous women who have shaped me
   and the boys:
Grandma Giovanna modeled bravery, leaving her home to
   make America our home;
Grandma Fireman passed on to us the gift of our faith,
   and the opportunity for a life's walk with Christ;
My mother taught me to care about what others care about;
Farmor, Grandma Darlene, Aunt Mary, Mother Mary—
   always there for us;
And my wife, Sine, the blessing in my life.

CONTENTS

The New Game

CHAPTER ONE

The New Nature of Change

I T'S GAME TIME.

Alone in the locker room, the football player is making his final preparations before heading out onto the field for the big game. He sits on the bench, head down. His breathing is deep and steady, evidence of his purposeful focus.

His is a sport for gladiators, requiring heavy protective gear. He begins to stir. His movements are slow and decisive. The muscular athlete lifts a large set of pads into the air with both hands and slides them over his head to fit them perfectly on his shoulders. Next, he grabs the oversized jersey with large numbers and lettering, and he pulls it over the bulky armor that frames him. Finally, he places a gleaming, thickly padded helmet onto his head and carefully fastens the strap across his chin. Now ready, the competitor gives the hard, protective shell a slap with both hands, leaps to his feet, and charges out of the locker room to join his teammates out on the field.

His stride is steady as he glides through the dark tunnel toward the light at the end. As he nears it, the hum of the fans grows. It escalates to a loud buzz. His pace quickens. Then he bursts through to the other side of the tunnel and he charges into the stadium at full speed. Spotting the other players, he quickly adjusts his course toward the deep green playing field that is awash in the warm glow of a bright spotlight. Adrenaline is pumping. He is excited.

This is the moment for which he has prepared his whole life.

Then, suddenly, his pace starts to slow. Something is clearly wrong. He grows more uncertain with every step. The steel spires that typically mark each end of the field are gone. In their places are two large nets. The brown pigskin football he knows—uniquely designed to cut through the air when thrown—has been replaced with a round ball that spins out a black-and-white pattern as it skips across the ground. The players warming up on the field are unfamiliar. They don't sport the same heavy gear he does. Instead, their hair flies freely in the wind, and they are wearing shorts and light clothing that supports their nimble movement.

The game has changed.

What do you do when the game for which you've prepared your whole life has changed? There are three likely reactions we can expect from our athlete in this situation. The first would be to freeze in place, watching in fear and confusion as this strange new activity plays out before him. It is a helpless feeling that will force him to the sidelines, where he will feel dismissed and irrelevant. This might cause great distress and perhaps trigger unruly behavior on the part of the young man. After all, he has been wired to play.

The second possibility is for the athlete to dig in stubbornly and double down on what he knows. This is a familiar response to uncertainty. In this particular instance, it might compel the football player to lower his helmet and run full steam into those unsuspecting players in the light clothing and flowing hair, tackling them to the ground. Of course, that would make him dangerous and worrisome, forcing a response from the others—and he would again be pushed to the sidelines.

The third option would be for the athlete to see differently and then respond differently. Playing in the new game must begin with a personal recalibration based on one's environment or circumstance. In this case, the daunting prospect is made less intimidating once it's understood that the new game demands new skills, the use of new muscles, new methods of training, and a fresh new outlook. The old rules don't apply, and a wholly different playbook is required.

The old playbook will not work in the new game.

It's a New Game

The game has changed for us, too. The world is undergoing a dramatic shift socially, politically, and culturally. The difference for us—unlike our athlete—is that making sense of the exact change before us isn't as clear. To fully comprehend the stark shift that has occurred, it is important to focus on one key element: the new nature of change. This isn't simply the kind of disruptive change made by advances in technology or innovations in science, though we do see those developments all around us. Nor is this about the increasing pace of change, a complaint that sounds increasingly cliché. Even King Henry VIII grumbled about the speed of change in his sixteenth-century world. Besides, isn't humankind wired to evolve and change?

I am talking about a full societal transition to the era we are in, which is characterized by:

- rising individual agency;
- powerful technology at the fingertips of the many that was once available to the few; and
- the democratization of leadership.

Today, nearly everyone can make and lead change. The capacity for specialized problem solving and access to mass communications, once the domain of a few elite leaders, are now the domain of the many. This has enabled more of us to contribute and play more fully in virtually every aspect of society, and it is changing everything we know about change.

This new reality is a stark departure from our history. For millennia, society fiercely pursued the perfection of efficiency through organized repetition. Work was largely clustered by skills and specialties governed by hierarchies that were powered with a centuries-old, one-leader-at-a-time mindset. It was a way of working that reached its zenith with the advent of the assembly line in the early 1900s, and the rise of the white-collar professional in the mid-twentieth century, who enforced the bureaucratic systems meant to maintain order and production through repetitive processes.

That system is now breaking apart. The top-down knowledge and leadership structures that have long supported society's dogged pursuit of efficiency in repetition are collapsing. Technology and the organized movements that have torn down the walls of society have transformed the complexion and complexity of the global strategic landscape— flattening hierarchies, bulldozing silos, and dramatically lowering barriers to citizen participation as a result. Emerging from the debris is a world that is fast, fluid, and hybrid in nature.

Everyday citizens are embracing our newfound power. We no longer need an intermediary to facilitate our civic engagement. We have a plethora of online gateways to express our opinions and activism. A well-timed hashtag on Twitter helped fuel the rise of the grassroots #MeToo movement, which trained a spotlight on the widespread prevalence of sexual assault and harassment, particularly in the workplace. After another deadly school shooting, this time in Florida, the hashtag #NeverAgain became a rallying cry both online and in youth-led public protests across the country. Within weeks, student leaders organized a march numbering in the hundreds of thousands on the National Mall in Washington, D.C. After the separate murders of George Floyd and Ahmaud Arbery, thousands took to the streets for weeks behind #BlackLivesMatter, and a global movement was unleashed. Today, it is commonplace to see a crowdfunding page created by a neighbor generate funds to bring relief to those displaced by fire or natural disaster, or to see food and clothing assistance mobilized using Facebook.

Our *one-leader-at-a-time* past has given way to a present reality in which everyone has the potential to lead in every aspect of our lives. Any individual with a reliable Internet connection and a computer, or a smartphone, can become his or her own news organization or entertainment broadcaster, easily creating images and video footage for distribution on Instagram and YouTube. We all have printing presses at our fingertips, which means we can be pundits and content creators, and our ideas are available to the world as soon as we hit *Send*. Where we once had to scramble to find a public phone to dial 911 and have emergency personnel dispatched to a scene, citizens are now a vital and anticipated element of the first-responder equation.

We can home in on a possible health diagnosis in advance of a visit to the doctor. We can investigate investment options and then meet with our financial advisor without ever having to leave the confines of our home, thanks to the widespread adoption of videoconferencing technology. Our kids can be schooled on Zoom. The knowledge that is immediately available to the individual will only continue to empower us further as stewards of our own well-being.

We are the first generation to navigate this reordered world. When change was a game for a few leaders, keeping up with the speed of change was a challenge for the rest of us. Now, change is a game of the many, and that is causing explosive disruption on a constant basis. There have been major societal paradigm shifts before, but what we are experiencing now is the transition from hundreds of years of repetition-making, to an everyone-empowered present in which disruptive change is the only constant. Change is no longer linear and faster. It's explosive and omnidirectional, and it's bouncing off of all the other change forces ricocheting all around us.

This decisive shift is changing the face of the global strategic landscape. It has paved the way for new patterns in social organization and behavior that are disrupting whole industries. New technology and a new mindset have made it so that our private cars can be turned into taxis, our homes into hostels, and our things into commodities for trade or sale in the online marketplace. Powerful innovations have us at the precipice of self-driving cars on our roads and robots in our homes and at work.

Forty years ago, it would have been hard to imagine the possibilities of this transformed environment. We have the ability to command and create in once-unimaginable ways and to solve problems once deemed unsolvable.

The Old Playbook Won't Work in the New Game

The promise that comes with this transformed environment also brings complex societal and institutional challenges. The continuous generalized disruption we are experiencing increasingly affects us all, and high-tech advances will result in millions of jobs lost.[1] A White House report in 2016 anticipated that 83 percent of workers making less than $20 an hour would come under pressure from artificial intelligence (AI) technology.[2] Repetition-based jobs are becoming obsolete—for example, customer kiosks in fast-food restaurants require fewer service workers to take food orders, even as algorithmic-driven lending is transforming the financial services industry—while difficult-to-automate jobs with varying tasks and responsibilities are on the rise.[3] Self-driving automation threatens the truck-driving profession, which would impact the truck-stop employees waiting tables or perched behind mini-mart registers, as well as far-away mechanics, warehouse workers, and auto-insurance providers.[4]

Some are comfortable with disruptive change as the new societal norm, while others want to control it because they don't feel equipped for the amount of change we are experiencing. This is the social tension we feel between those who want to corral change versus those who want to drive into it—fear of change versus hope in change.

Just like our football player, old playbook in hand, many of us are struggling to find our way. This is contributing to an outbreak of unhappiness in a world where everyone must show up and step into our full agency and leadership. It opens a troubling, yet unnoticed, new divide in society requiring immediate attention. It isn't Red versus Blue or rich versus poor—it's the emerging gap between the few who have the mindset and capabilities to thrive in this fire hose of technology-driven social change, versus the many who don't. Our old systems and institutions that were built for repetition can't keep up. The rule-makers in our society can't respond quickly enough. The skills we were taught for an old game won't work in the new game.

Our iEverything world requires a new playbook.

If you are reading this book, then you want in. You want the new playbook because you are looking for an edge in this new game with its many dimensions—at work and at home—as a parent, as a neighbor, and as a citizen. The insights presented here will give you the corrective lens and the how-tos that you can apply to every aspect of your life so that you can clearly see and confidently play.

But this brings us to an obvious first question: If the new game is so radically different from the old game, why don't we all see it? The answer is that we see what we expect to see. We look for what we were trained to look for. Our mindsets, our behaviors, and the tools we work with are oriented to the world as it was. We have been prepared for an obsolete game using an old playbook that's been passed forward through the generations. Consider, too, that we see societal change as an evolutionary process, even if what is happening in the world right now is revolutionary. In general, there is an unconscious bias toward viewing the world through the old-game lens we have known.

By the end of this book, you'll see the new game as clearly as our football player came to see his. And like him, once you see the new game, you will know that you can't play it like the old game. You'll have to take off that heavy armor. You'll have to train differently, work new muscles, add new players, and bring your old teammates along with you into the new game using different development approaches. And yes, you'll need the new playbook.

This prospect might feel overwhelming at first. It was for me. I didn't quite see the new game. I stumbled upon it when the large sprawling organization I managed, the 2008 Obama presidential campaign, made the extraordinary transition from the traditionally hierarchical *one-leader-at-a-time* structure to something decisively different—what I called an *everyone-leading-in-every-moment* organizational system. We didn't plan it. It wasn't even all that evident to us as we went through it. And note that while it happened with a campaign as the backdrop, there isn't a political point to be made here. I made a discovery of new leadership that can benefit everyone.

Standing the two models side by side, I could see *one-leader-at-a-time* and *everyone-leading-in-every-moment* are polar opposites. The *one-leader-at-a-time* model was based on one person being big and everyone else being small in any given moment. The *everyone-leads* system relies on everyone being big and playing big, stepping into their full capacity. I like to say that in the new game, there is no room for small; everyone has to step into their BIGness.

In the old game, teams were fixed and organized around functional roles. The new game is about fluid teams that form organically around a problem or opportunity. In the old hierarchical system, credibility was based on expertise and authoritative voice, while credibility in the new system is built on authenticity and the ability to learn and adapt. Where hard skills once trumped soft skills, empathy and collaborative teamwork are the new premium. You can't play the new *everyone-leads* game and the old *one-leader-at-a-time* game the same way. For us in the campaign, transitioning from the old game to the new game flipped the physics of leadership on its head; it was as if life for us had become opposite day, every day.

Initially, I thought I had a new management framework that business and other organizational executives needed. But as I reentered daily life after nearly two years in an all-absorbing presidential campaign and two-and-a-half years in the White House, I immediately recognized that the same shift that had occurred in my campaign ecosystem was happening in the world at large. Society had transitioned from a *one-leader-at-time* to an *everyone-leads* world.

It set me on a path to find the exemplars for playing in this new and very different game.

Meet the New-Game Players

I was introduced to some of the new-game players through Bill Drayton, whom I'd met in fall 2011. Widely credited with creating and defining the field of social entrepreneurship over the past four decades, Bill introduced the world to the notion that there is nothing more powerful than a bold new idea in the hands of an exceptional entrepreneur innovating for the good of all. The organization he founded, Ashoka Innovators for the Public, boasts a fellowship of the world's leading social entrepreneurs, with some 4,000 high-impact innovators having a presence in more than 100 countries. These are individuals who tirelessly devote their entrepreneurial capacities to creating broad systemic social change through their own initiatives and citizen-sector startup organizations. The social entrepreneurs affiliated with Ashoka are particularly impressive. A recent survey showed 93 percent have altered market systems in at least one way after their election to the fellowship, and 74 percent have changed legislation or significantly influenced policy. Additionally, 90 percent have had their innovations replicated by independent groups.[5]

Bill says that over 1,300—roughly one in three—focus primarily on kids. I've gotten to know many of them and have become acquainted with their work advancing powerful ideas and approaches aimed at giving agency to a generation of confident contributors in the world. Jürgen Griesbeck created Street Football World in 2002, after the murder of a Columbian national soccer player in connection with the goal he unintentionally scored for the opposing United States team that eliminated his own team from the 1994 World Cup competition. Jürgen wanted to show another side of soccer as a transformative tool for communities. The organization he founded supports a network of community-based organizations that use football to enable and accelerate social change where they are, including developing safe spaces and pitches for youth play, reaching more than 2 million young people each year.[6] Also in 2002, Arnoud Raskin launched Mobile School in Belgium to reintegrate street kids into mainstream society using his "box on wheels" with customizable educational games and content, behind a mission to help these young people value the qualities they exhibit of positivity, creativity, perseverance, and entrepreneurial skills.[7]

Many in the Ashoka Fellowship are also focused on issues of social inclusion and full economic citizenship in society. Sascha Haselmayer has brought new innovations to more than 130 global cities through Citymart, a platform for engaging the public in finding solutions to community challenges and exchanging innovation best practices.[8] For example, in 2017, Citymart worked with the City of New Orleans to launch a contest to close the city's digital divide, sourcing an idea for an innovative creative arts program that lowers barriers to access for hard-to-reach teenagers by baking digital skill-building elements into arts and cultural pursuits they love.[9] By taking procurement out of the back room and putting it in front of the public consciousness, Citymart is changing how cities solve increasingly complex and pressing challenges. In Sweden, recognizing the difficulties of integrating into a new country and building a new life from scratch, Sofia Appelgren launched Mitt Liv to help immigrants find jobs in companies that would value their motivation, skills, and experience. Mitt Liv matches educated, entrepreneurial people with foreign backgrounds to mentors in leading companies in Sweden as a way to assist with work integration.[10] And in the UK, Mark Johnson, a social entrepreneur and best-selling author who'd personally experienced crime, addiction, and homelessness, created User Voice to give people in prisons and on probation a voice in the system at the policy level—punishment should not silence. His flagship program, User Voice Councils, also enlists ex-offenders to lead the process for directly engaging decision makers on systemic issues that affect "users". This approach enables individual change, as people feel heard and get a stake in their rehabilitation and recovery journeys, while also reframing public perceptions about ex-offenders as contributors in society.[11]

I immediately understood the important insights that could be gleaned from this community of big-time social-impact leaders. These are the new-game players!

I'll introduce you to some of these extraordinary individuals throughout this book. You'll also get to know Bill. But this is not a book about social entrepreneurship, and it's not a book about how you can become a social entrepreneur. This is a book about what we can learn from the world's most highly effective changemakers so that we can thrive and confidently command this new game as parents, professionals, and fully contributing citizens. We will also meet everyday changemakers outside of this special community of social entrepreneurs who show us how this new game is played—civic leaders, educators, parents, and young people from all over the world and all walks of life. Together, they offer powerful insights that I have gathered and fully explored.

You'll learn leadership lessons from a clown—no joke—a Brazilian man who comes across as an everyday guy until he puts on a red nose and joins the medical teams of terminally ill children in hospital operating rooms.

You'll witness unusual bravery in a North Carolina mom who laces up her running shoes and becomes a superhero in the lives of the young women she's helping to make their way in a complex world.

You'll be taught how to fight by a petite Spanish woman with a big smile whom society once labeled "a victim." Her weapon of choice is radical inclusion, which she has used to build a global network of abuse survivors who are stepping out of the shadows of shame and into lives in the light.

Finally, you'll be schooled in empathy—one of the core foundational skills necessary for playing the new game—by a 6-month-old baby.

Along the way, we'll look to historical figures like Florence Nightingale for clues on how to play in the new game from those who were way ahead of their time. We will also explore how we can prepare youth to confidently play, not just because it is critical for their success, but because we learn best for ourselves when we teach the young people in our lives. You will see many examples of how I have practiced being a changemaker through my children.

In the end, you'll see the world in very different terms. It might initially intimidate you and cause you to freeze in your tracks, just like our football player, because it will challenge everything you understand about how to thrive in life. You will be forced to change. But I promise, it'll be okay. Changing your view of the world will change your view of yourself in the world. And then you'll have all the information you need to act.

Changemaker Playbook is quite simply the playbook for our new reality. We are already living in a world that requires every person to confront the new nature of change and to possess the skills to navigate and lead through it. As this twenty-first-century reality comes into sharper focus, you'll want the important principles revealed in this book to help you and the people you care about play the new game. Holding up a more precise lens on the world offers a better perspective to discern the qualities everyone must have to thrive and to fully contribute: an innovative mind, a service heart, an entrepreneurial spirit, and a collaborative outlook.

Let's play!

CHAPTER TWO

The Physics of Leadership
Are Flipped

EVERY GOOD DISCOVERY needs a laboratory, but mine wasn't what you'd have imagined. There weren't test tubes sitting on open tables or mice scurrying around in cages. The people around me didn't wear lab coats. There weren't shelves of library books surrounding me, or indecipherable formulas scribbled onto wall-length chalkboards.

My laboratory was the headquarters of Barack Obama's 2008 presidential campaign on the eleventh floor of a Chicago high-rise crammed full of smart, driven, and sometimes competitive staff. What I unexpectedly discovered about *leadership* in this frenetic setting was so profound, it was paradigm changing. In other words, it flipped everything I'd known and understood about the concept completely on its head.

When I joined the Obama campaign, I would have described myself as an empowering leader and a mentoring leader—someone who encouraged others around me to lead. Looking back, I now see that my orientation was still very much rooted in the *one-leader-at-a-time* framework that most of us carry. We've been taught to believe that someone has to be in charge at any given moment and that person is the leader. This was the lens of the world I'd been given in grade school. It was the dominant lesson I'd gleaned from my history books. It was the foremost parental guidance drilled into me throughout my youth: be a leader, not a follower. You were either one or the other. I may have been an enlightened leader, but this was still my bias.

Over the course of my 21 months as a member of the senior management team in the Obama campaign, my outlook changed dramatically. Inside the hothouse of this historic presidential campaign, I came to embrace the idea that *everyone leads in every moment.*

What caused this shift? For the answer, I'll have to take you inside this curious laboratory. There I can share a few of the most poignant lessons I gleaned through building this extraordinary organization, starting it from scratch and then growing it to mammoth dimensions over a nearly two-year period. I liken it to taking a mom-and-pop shop and scaling it into Walmart in less than two years.

Hope and Chaos

"Stop the spending."

That was the subject line of an email glowing on my BlackBerry when I woke up one morning in early April 2007. Since joining Sen. Barack Obama's presidential campaign six weeks earlier, I'd taken up a new ritual of rummaging for my campaign-issued phone as soon as I emerged from an abbreviated night's sleep. This particular early-morning message abruptly interrupted my foggy state, given that the plea came from Campaign Manager David Plouffe, who was alarmed about our new campaign's unrestrained spending.

These were still the first days of our startup organization, and I had the responsibility of getting this beast up and running. In those early days, my role as a member of the senior leadership team was to get people and systems in place. We had only about 100 staff at that point, most of whom were located at our headquarters in Chicago. We were also beginning to open offices and staff up in the states with the first contests ten months out in Iowa, New Hampshire, Nevada, and South Carolina.

I'd known David for just a few weeks, and while my 44 years made me almost twice the age of most of my new co-workers, David was probably five years younger than me. My impression of him was positive. He was a warm person but seriously introverted, and his steely gaze was both intimidating and engaging, depending on the situation at hand. Plouffe is sometimes described as a man of mystery. I found he was definitely a man of few words. On this particular day, our campaign manager wanted to ensure my team was getting an expenditure-approval system in place. This would go with the hiring, office-opening, technology, and procurement processes we were racing to get finalized.

Growing Up Siloed

From its earliest days, our campaign organization projected a tech-cool image that seemed a natural match with the candidate's youthful, energetic persona. Our staff was young, innovative, and hungry. In addition to our data-obsessed campaign manager, our ranks also included a former co-founder of Facebook, and a twenty-something prodigy who was charged with overseeing a first-of-its-kind department in a political operation, we called New Media. It housed the teams that worked on email communications, grassroots fundraising, online community activities, and our interactive website equipped with a suite of innovative networking and engagement tools. Establishing New Media as its own department was a calculated embrace of the emergent digital media space we relied on to bypass traditional media and communicate directly to voters, while also reinforcing our cutting-edge image. We would later be branded "The iPhone Campaign" by those in the media attempting to find a label that captured our Silicon Valley startup character. Ironically, our staff were outfitted with BlackBerry phones for the life of the campaign, as iPhones were not yet really out when we got started. While BlackBerry still held a large market share, it quickly became the marker at the other end of the innovation spectrum.

Fronting our organization was Barack Obama, a fresh-faced candidate who projected a hopeful outlook behind his confident demeanor and warm, dashing smile. A former community organizer who broke the mold of the typical seasoned white-male candidate profile, Barack was youthful, African American, and relatively new to the national political scene. With only two years in the US Senate, he was surprisingly at ease in front of crowds both large and small.

The man I later came to know was upbeat, easy to talk to, and comfortable in his own skin, as the saying goes. Whether strolling through headquarters dressed in black sweats that matched his White Sox baseball cap or sporting his trademark look on the campaign trail— a buttoned white shirt with rolled-up sleeves and a tie hanging off the collar—Barack Obama's easy demeanor embodied the no-drama ethos he publicly trumpeted.

Despite the innovative character our campaign projected from the earliest days, our organization actually grew up traditionally siloed and hierarchical, not unlike most organizations. Political campaigns are particularly noteworthy for having a command-and-control architecture, partly because candidates and the managers of these organizations are risk-averse. Our leadership intentionally wanted to break that mold to meet the candidate's desire to "build it from the bottom up." Also, the highly entrepreneurial staff we'd attracted wasn't suited to the stifling atmosphere of an antiquated structure. Still, we didn't immediately succeed in achieving our intended objective.

Our campaign's old-school organizational structure was mostly the result of having hastily constructed our operation mere weeks after Sen. Obama publicly announced that he would run for president. He made his intentions known at a high-profile news conference in mid-February, and seven weeks later, we officially opened the doors of our headquarters.

When the first staffers spilled out of the elevator and through the doors, computers were still being ripped from boxes, and our IT team was scrambling to get servers up. Checks from donors were streaming in while our financial team was on a mad dash to open the bank accounts that would receive them. Phones rang at the reception desk, but the small volunteer team fielding those calls didn't know where to send them— after all, we had yet to learn each other's names, and department rosters were being shuffled almost daily. Our walls were noticeably bare, clear evidence that our campaign signage had yet to be delivered. In fact, we'd only recently finalized the design of that now-famous logo with the red and white highway running into the blue sun, and we were in the process of ordering the posters and signs to carry it. Campaign headquarters was quickly exploding into a bustling community, but it was still a blank space with no rules, no norms, no systems, and no institutional or cultural history to guide us.

Building an organization in this kind of chaos is like building an airplane midflight. You put a team in charge of constructing the fuselage, another to secure the wings, others the cockpit or the engines, and so on. You get people into lanes, and each team gets their heads down and works on their individual pieces. The predictable result is the emergence of a series of well-defined silos that form the organizational architecture. It is a familiar design, characterized by having a few people at the top of the system telling everyone else to repeat their specialized skills harmoniously, faster and faster. In our defense, it was perhaps the most efficient way to get control of the chaos that greeted us.

Change on Steroids

If I could characterize the startup phase of the campaign as a time of hope and chaos—a riff off our recognizable theme of "Hope and Change"—the subsequent period, including the hotly contested 56 primary races, could be described as "Change on Steroids." It was during this second stage of our development that I became acquainted with a transformation within the organization that helped me understand the truly radical nature of paradigm change.

Chicago was turning cold, signaling the arrival of the election's primary season, but inside, the temperature was quickly rising. In the early days, we had succeeded in stringing together the silo leaders—we called them department heads—into some kind of communications and organizational system. We met in the mornings in a senior staff meeting where we shared information and planned activities, and then each of us reported back to our individual silos where our focus remained the rest of the day.

This had worked for us at first, but as the initial races grew near, the pace of events began to pick up. After the Iowa caucus in early January, there were three more individual races in four weeks, keeping the intensity steady. Then, heading into February, when there were typically multiple state contests on any given election day—twenty-three on Super Tuesday alone, on February 5—the feeling of rapid change became palpable. The stakes around every race were incredibly high, and the glare of the white-hot media spotlight trained on our campaign only increased the pressure on our staff. When you add in the occasional PR crisis that predictably swamps campaign operations—a bad news story about the candidate that could decisively slow fundraising or a botched exchange in a debate that needed to be addressed by our communications team— headquarters had become a tinder box of emotions.

Our *one-leader-at-a-time* organizational design simply could not keep pace with the myriad challenges constantly coming at us. We had to tear down the silos and allow everyone to step more fully into their own leadership. This change wasn't the result of a senior staff meeting conversation. It wasn't an idea that had been carefully studied by an internal task force. It just seemed to happen, and we almost didn't recognize it in the moment. But it was dramatic, nonetheless. Our organization before and our organization after were quite different animals.

Everyone a Leader

Our transition to a more open system was helped along by the fact that the vertical organization we'd constructed wasn't suited to commanding the forces of change constantly coming at us. It kept our leaders mired in the demands of our respective silos, creating an internal downward pressure that choked off innovation and crosscutting collaboration, which were so badly needed. In my case, I joked that my nickname might as well have been, "Henry, can I...?" It seemed to be how everyone greeted me at the beginning of just about every conversation, whether it was in person, on the phone, or via email: "Henry, can I open an office?" "Henry, can I hire some staff?" "Henry, can I spend this money?"

We needed to break from the traditional system where department heads functioned as silo-protectors whose standing with subordinates was mostly based on keeping morale up by keeping new work out. We also needed to free our talented staff in the lower and middle rungs of the organization, who were hemmed in by these clearly defined departmental boundaries. We learned early that our greatest organizational asset was the spirit of our people, and they were absolutely not suited to silos and hierarchy.

As the silos came down, people at all levels and across the organization were freed to lead, and a different way of working emerged. Folks worked fluidly and often informally across the old, traditional departmental boundaries to solve problems and pursue opportunities. Managers also could change their styles to suit the new environment, acting more as coaches than authoritarians. This was another marker of the transition into what I now describe as an *everyone-leads* system.

Technology was certainly a decisive factor in the democratization of leadership driving this shift. About a year into the campaign, we began experiencing a kind of decentralization that was unusual for political campaign organizations. The importance of the burgeoning Internet community we'd been cultivating on our digital platform, MyBarackObama.com, began to take on new dimensions. With the online tools our campaign staff had developed, any kitchen table could be transformed into a precinct office with just a personal computer, an Internet connection, and a cell phone. Volunteers could call prospective supporters anywhere in the country at any time through an online phone application that put names, phone numbers, and a calling script a click away.

As we powered past the first contests in Iowa and New Hampshire, even as offices in those states closed, our supporters remained seamlessly connected to the campaign and to each other 24/7 for the duration. Those who lived in states with races that were weeks away could call and convince undecided voters in the immediate battlegrounds to back our candidate, or urge family and friends to make a donation through their personalized fundraising page. All this had the effect of distributing leadership throughout our campaign ecosystem. In the past, local and neighborhood activities were built around a dominant figure at the precinct office who handed out walking packets or phone-bank lists to supporters. Just as iTunes and Amazon had rendered the "middlemen" in the physical retail store obsolete, we'd created a way for volunteers to fully engage in traditional campaign activities without having to rely on a precinct organizer at the local campaign office. This collapsed our structure, which had been designed to maintain the system of physical offices and local staff, and it hastened our transition into a borderless campaign, and correspondingly into an *everybody-leads* system.

Rethinking Leadership in the Everyone-Leads System

This organizational shift didn't actually come into sharp focus for me until the last days of the campaign, when I met with an old friend and mentor, David Gergen. We were just weeks away from the election when I received word that the veteran advisor to four US presidents and a frequent political news analyst on CNN was in town and interested in meeting. I still addressed him as Professor Gergen, pinpointing the birth of our association to eight years prior, when I studied under his guidance as a mid-career graduate student at Harvard University's Kennedy School.

For me, his visit was very welcome, though it came at a demanding time. My last meeting of every day in the campaign's final stretch was with Jim Messina, a personable but crafty and politically savvy aide to a US senator from Montana who'd been recently brought in as our new Chief of Staff. We closed out our days with a check-in together to compare notes around 9 p.m. On this particular night, rather than race home after we broke, I sprinted off to meet Professor Gergen for a late drink at a nearby wine bar.

Upon my arrival, the familiar figure stood to greet me. He has about six or seven inches on my six-foot frame, which gives him a considerable presence, even before he speaks to reveal his gruff, commanding, deep voice. His many years in politics have fashioned his wisdom, and his gracious sense of humor is showcased with a loud, joyful laugh.

He was quick in getting to the point. "So, what would you say is the secret of your campaign's success to date?" he asked.

"It's the people," I immediately chimed, without needing time to reflect. I quickly launched into a description of the dominant DNA of our campaign staff: "Innovative mind, service heart, entrepreneurial spirit, and collaborative outlook—that's the common thread from person to person."

On hearing this, my former professor of leadership heartily exclaimed, "You hired leaders!"

Excited by his revelation, I responded that I *only* hired leaders. "If a position was filled with a non-leader, it was a wasted opportunity," I said.

This would have seemed counterintuitive to some—conventional thinking holds that not everyone can be the leader—but it was exactly the right conclusion in our situation. I wasn't talking about everyone being *the* leader, and it wasn't like we'd shifted to a flat management structure, but every action in any given moment had to be an act of leadership. Even stepping back to let the right person step up was an act of leadership. And certainly, when a crisis erupted, like the Reverend Wright controversy centered around sermons by the candidate's pastor, staff knew to step back and managers knew to step up.

The emergence of our *everyone-leads* ecosystem wasn't entirely accidental. The staff's identity grew from the cultural character that we had established in the campaign's earliest days, when we were still forming an organization from scratch. At the time of my meeting with Professor Gergen, in those final weeks, we were well on our way to eclipsing 6,000 staff in our national organization. But in our first days, when our staff was still so small we could literally form into a half-moon around David Plouffe's office door for our all-staff meetings, we received three pieces of guidance from the candidate, which ultimately informed our cultural identity: respect everyone, build it from the bottom up, and no drama—that last rule obviously having gotten the most attention outside of headquarters.

This framework gave us a much-needed cultural compass, but it also contributed to a subtle hiring bias toward the qualities that I'd recounted to Gergen. An innovative mind could proactively solve unsolvable problems; a service heart had the capacity for earnestly understanding the needs of others; an entrepreneurial spirit could courageously step into the tensions inherent in a presidential campaign and see the toughest challenges through to the end; and a collaborative spirit was fundamental in a fluid and interdependent work environment.[1]

The New Rules for the New Game

This transition from *one-leader-at-a-time* to *everyone-leads* was a fascinating process, particularly for the new physics of leadership I'd discovered associated with this paradigm change. These were polar opposite systems. And to my surprise, I uncovered three specific principles that distinguished the two.

The first principle exposed that in the new *everyone-leads* system there was no room for smallness. Everyone had to bring their full game. The old system of *one-leader-at-a-time* is based on one person being big and everyone else being small in any given moment. This was a different game, however, requiring a different outlook. Small people couldn't do big things; that was just simple mathematics. As an organization, we were only as big as the smallest among us.

Working collectively, we'd battled Hillary Clinton's formidable operation, and she was widely considered the favorite to win the party's nomination; we would next come up against an impressive Republican machine fronted by war hero John McCain and his running mate, Sarah Palin. In our hotly contested election, it wasn't enough for people to just show up and do their jobs. Everyone around me needed to see the big picture, advance solutions, and open up useful opportunities. We all needed to resist those forces that continually make us small. I may have been the chief operating officer, but I quickly learned that in this new system, my most important role was chief BIGness officer. It became my personal mission to help everyone around me step into their BIGness.

The second distinguishing principle was that in the new way of working, when walls came down between two or more sides that wouldn't otherwise connect, innovation happened. Observers often sum up our 2008 run as being innovative because of our technological supremacy or our skillful use of social media. But in reality, it wasn't the hottest, newest piece of technology that made our campaign novel. Rather, we unleashed smart, innovative people who knew how to form new teams across those old boundaries to solve problems or create opportunities. Sometimes, technology helped tear down walls and bring people together—like MyBarackObama.com—and other times, a technology solution was the result of a team coming together. Thus, tearing down walls to build new teams became the requisite new leadership skill in this increasingly hybrid system. I liked to say that in the old siloed system, for every challenge, a department. In this new, open system, for every problem or opportunity, a different team.

Now, one might assume that in opening things up, we'd have been able to get control of the forces of change that were constantly pestering us—that we could just wrestle change to the ground. In fact, the opposite happened. Change actually accelerated.

This revealed a third distinguishing principle, and it helped me to realize an important axiom associated with this paradigm change: When everyone leads in every moment, the speed of change accelerates relative to the old *one-leader-at-a-time* way of working. Why? Leaders make change. And if you agree that everything you change changes everything, and everyone is doing it, then you are in a system of explosive, omnidirectional change.

To be clear, this was a very different kind of change. What we experienced wasn't simply linearly faster change, like in the old repetitive system. It was exponentially omnidirectional, firing off in all directions. Change was bouncing off itself.

I became increasingly fascinated with this paradigm shift in leadership as we went from *one-leader-at-a-time* to *everyone-leads* in the course of just 21 months. It was so profound that we were literally forced to reorganize into a system that better accommodated the emergent new way of working.

As an example, we actually changed our office seating arrangements to accommodate the change. In our 1.0 iteration, we all sat in our departments. In our 2.0 version, during the campaign's final months, staff sat in teams—a series of clusters across the headquarters floor—with an operations manager sitting next to a communications staffer, sitting next to an event organizer, sitting next to a budget cruncher, and so on. The clusters were formulated to interact with a similar team in a state or local office. In this way, the teams from each of the sides formed a joint team in a moment that flowed to the various other teams with which they were connected.

Through this process, I became intimately acquainted with a new type of teamwork that was anchoring our system. It wasn't uniquely functionally based, with tasks doled out based on position descriptions or job labels. In this new form of teamwork, individuals were recruited for their *possibilities* more than their responsibilities. Your passions and talents defined you more than your job assignments. While old teamwork was based on static teams organized into functional, repetitive roles to execute specialized tasks, this new teamwork featured fluid, shifting teams organized around dynamic challenges and opportunities. This met the need to command the rapidly changing environment in which we found ourselves.

For every office opened, for every staff member hired, for every purchase made, and for every event organized, combinations of teams formed around each to make decisions and act. Every staffer who left Iowa for another state at the conclusion of that first caucus had a unique team around them, typically with a different set of individuals. The shape of this collaboration often flowed to a team on our side at headquarters, a team on the ground in Iowa, and another in the receiving state—all ensuring the individual's seamless redeployment. It was connected as a sprawling nerve system more than a top-down delivery system. Every detail was considered, from securing transportation and hotels along the way to a new destination, to assembling travel packets with a route map, to making arrangements for temporary housing and a workspace in the staffer's new state. Thousands of people were shuffled across the country courtesy of this unique hybrid system of teamwork.

My experiences at the heart of a fast-paced presidential campaign's HQ taught me the new rules for new leadership. *One-leader-at-a-time* and *everyone-leading-in-every-moment* were completely opposite systems, and the experience challenged me to rethink what leadership actually means. The old game was about having a skill and executing that skill in a walled-off silo to repeat it faster and faster. The new game required the skill of tearing down walls and forming a team that could solve a problem or create opportunities together. The old game was characterized by transaction, the new game by interaction. In the old game, a high premium was placed on expertise, authority, and specific knowledge—communication was represented through an authoritative voice. In the new game, value came from credibility and authenticity, with storytelling and knowledge exchange as the most effective vehicles for successful communication. The old-game manager told *underlings* what to do; the new-game manager helped people see together and work together.

Teamwork took on a wholly different dimension in this new game. Where it was once about doing your job—specialized repetitive skills executed within the silo, harmoniously, faster and faster—the new game was about everyone working together as active contributors, reaching across the old boundaries to solve complex problems.

Meetings changed. If the first meeting of the campaign day had once been a gathering of senior managers to report on their respective silos and collect instructions to send down the respective chains, now it was about curating information upward in real time and seeking new opportunities for collaboration across the organization.

Our infrastructure had to change to accommodate this new way of working. If each silo had created processes and technology platforms to serve their respective unique activities in the early days, we now required systems that would enable open collaboration. With the shift from the old game to the new, we had to design new systems. We couldn't play the new game with old-game technology, processes, and mindsets. We needed platforms that supported teams forming across the organization, not functional tools for the silo. For example, we took our *one-approval-at-a-time* method for hiring and spending from a crude system featuring approval forms, fax machines, and human runners, to an Internet-based platform that enabled any relevant team member anywhere in the country to log in and see where their request was in the process. This was a collaborative tool deployed across the organization that facilitated full transparency and engagement.

The high premium on full transparency that this new game required was further evidence of a mindset shift that was necessary to succeed. The old view held that there should be limited distribution of information doled out on a "need to know" basis; an individual should only have enough information to perform a task or function. The open system demanded open, transparent communication. For a team to act—for anyone on the team to act—everyone had to have unfettered access to the information they needed to lead.

In this new system, obstacles to success were falling everywhere, all the time, no meeting required. I learned firsthand that people acting together on their full agency could generate unimaginable power to advance a common purpose. Conversely, I recognized that deployed carelessly, it could be equally destructive. It was a discovery that was both invigorating and sobering.

Scaling for Change

This understanding led to one final lesson from the last days of the campaign that will be relevant to our later exploration of this important paradigm shift. As we moved into the general election, our operation exploded in size. Over the campaign's first 16 months, we had amassed about 2,000 staff members and were operating with $40 million in monthly revenues. In just the final 16 weeks, I was faced with the prospect that we would grow from 2,000 to 6,000 staff members, and we would eclipse $100 million in revenues per month.

At first, this kind of scaling seemed impossible—almost unimaginable—to me. As the chief organization manager, I didn't see how we could expand to such dimensions so rapidly without breaking apart. With thousands of ambitious new staff members on-boarding, I was worried that we would see unauthorized spending, hiring, and other reckless activity that could compromise the organization and damage the candidate's image.

This was a problem. I struggled to determine my leverage in holding the organization together and maintaining order throughout this process. I could communicate expectations, but a campaign doesn't have the same incentives as a normal business to enforce general good behavior. There are no promises of pay raises or stock options. Even the idea of job security is problematic, as it isn't clear whether your candidate will win. Succeeding at any cost can quickly become a dominant attitude among staff.

In confronting this particular dilemma, I was forced to break with a way of thinking that was very much attached to the old management paradigm predicated on authority and control. For me as a manger, perhaps the most uncomfortable feature of the *everyone-leads* landscape was the shift away from the permission-based organizational model—a notable characteristic of the silo—to a culture that was uniquely trust-based.

This was a natural progression, as I had already discovered that rules could not keep up with the pace of change in our new ecosystem. I felt this acutely since, as the chief operating officer, I was essentially the rule-maker. Placing so much trust in my colleagues, many hundreds of whom I didn't personally know, in offices all over the country, was a big leap of faith for me. I ultimately decided that I should position my leadership to ensure the hiring of well-intentioned people who would do the right thing. I made a deliberate choice that my managers should spend more time investing in the leadership of others across the organization and communicating our expectations for how staff should conduct themselves and less time making or enforcing rules.

This ultimately proved to be the correct choice. To my surprise, I discovered that in the trust-based system, others in the community did not tolerate rogue behavior, producing a self-regulating culture. With full understanding of the norms, one's credibility is based on innovating for good and not harming others in the process. Enabling and ensuring proper conduct was no longer the exclusive domain of management. In a system where everyone was a leader, everyone was a stakeholder and, therefore, everyone was also a steward. This kept the organization on a stable course through those precarious final weeks. Even given our staff's entrepreneurial spirit, we closed out our overall effort without the unruly "rogue" behaviors that typically plague campaigns. No unauthorized contracts. No unplanned offices opened. No unapproved staff hires.

Coming off of my campaign experience, I thought I had discovered a new leadership paradigm that organizational leaders would welcome. I didn't immediately realize that I'd stumbled upon the new rules for the new game that *everyone* needs.

CHAPTER THREE

Everyone a Changemaker

IT IS OFTEN said that the White House is a bubble. In my experience, this is absolutely true. After 21 months spent building our campaign organization from a startup to an operation approaching the size of a Fortune 1000 company, the 18-acre White House complex seemed oddly small. At the White House, I had a big job with big responsibilities. I was at the center of world power, and yet, in my role, which was internally focused, I was also strangely divorced from the outside world.

My personal life had narrowed, as well. I returned to Northern Virginia with my wife, Sine (See-na), in 2009. During the campaign, I had become a new father to Dante, and we welcomed our second child, Zane, soon after I had joined the Obama administration. Long days at work were followed by long nights with our baby boys at home. I moderated fights over toys during the late evening hours and then I did the same thing by day, just using a different voice. I didn't really have many adult conversations outside of work. There was no socializing over lunch or having drinks with friends after work. I was just too busy. These conditions were inherently isolating, and they only hardened the bubble that had formed around me.

Without a doubt, working in the White House and serving a president was the best job I have ever had. I loved it. My office was referred to as "the Mayor's Office" on the White House complex, and it was never the same from one day to the next. My teams led the internal H1N1 (swine flu) pandemic response; coordinated the on-site meetings with Harvard University professor Henry Louis Gates, Jr., Cambridge police officer James Crowley, and their guests as part of the famous "Beer Summit" in the Rose Garden at the invitation of the president and vice president; organized marquee events like the White House Easter Egg Roll—the largest annual public event held on the South Lawn, accommodating tens of thousands of visitors in a day; and we met the daily demands of keeping the White House Office running smoothly. The administration around the president was organizationally sound.

That's why I struggled with the impulse to make a break for the wider world when I was just two years into my tenure. It wasn't so much that I wanted to leave as much as I felt I was being pulled away. The pastures outside the White House gates seemed suddenly greener.

I thought I knew what my next act would be. I was determined to write a book about the leadership lessons I had learned from the campaign. But I would also need a real job, and I had no idea what it would be. What do you do after running a campaign like ours and then working in the White House? A life of running congressional races every two years didn't excite me. Besides, I was never one to just keep doing more of the same. In addition to the book, I did have a particular idea in my head, or perhaps in my heart—I don't know which—but had been too embarrassed to openly share it. It also didn't seem like a moneymaker.

Just as I was planning my exit, David Plouffe, my old friend and colleague from the campaign, was on his way in. Soon after he joined the administration, we ran into each other one morning at the White House Mess as we were both picking up our coffee, and he invited me to his office for a chat.

The office was a big step up from our campaign days, but it still lacked his personal effects, an indicator of how new he was on the scene. We almost seemed like different people in our fancy suits and ties compared to the more casual days inside our Chicago headquarters. Our opposite trajectories added to the strangeness. He was getting his footing in his new environment as I was trying to figure out my next steps outside of it. It made for an awkward reunion.

During our visit, he asked what was next for me, but I didn't really have a good answer. Sensing my struggle, he offered his own suggestion.

"You should put a shingle out—put your sign on the door," he announced. David is truly one of the great political strategists of our time, so I was flattered by the suggestion that I should start a consultancy.

I half-heartedly went along with his counsel, but I now felt compelled to share that idea I'd been mulling over privately. It wasn't at all formed. In fact, I had only just announced it out loud for the first time earlier that morning to my wife. "So, here's the thing, David," I finally offered up sheepishly. "I want to do something around executive leadership based on what I learned from the campaign. I want to change the leadership paradigm."

I watched his smile fade and his eyes drift. This was bad. I'd brought up my share of clumsy ideas and delivered some bad news over the course of our time together, but I had never seen his demeanor change so noticeably. Based on his reaction, I knew I couldn't expand further and talk with him about new leadership physics or the like.

My wife had the same reaction to my announcement, except she wasn't just silent; she was downright explicit about her feelings. Sine is normally my biggest booster, but she was surprisingly clear about not boosting this particular idea. I figured it was a reasonable response, given that she had been out of the workforce to stay home with our kids and that I was talking about leaving the security of the White House to change the leadership paradigm.

I quickly pivoted my conversation with David back to his idea about starting a consulting practice, mostly to protect myself from further embarrassment. He kindly referred me to some people who had experience starting their own similar businesses, then we downshifted to small talk about our families. It wasn't a long visit.

Soon after, I met with Pete Rouse, one of President Obama's closest aides. He'd had a long, distinguished career as a top Capitol Hill aide, including serving as former Senate Democratic leader Tom Daschle's chief of staff, and later in that same role for incoming Senator Obama. His vast knowledge and influence had earned him the enviable moniker in the media as "the 101st US Senator." Pete has the husky frame, round face, and grizzled voice of a hardened political operative, which makes him seem like a bear of a man—though he's actually more of the teddy-bear variety than the grizzly he projects. He's extraordinarily kind and unusually loyal to everyone who has ever worked for him, and he showed the same consideration for me as we sat down to talk about my future.

"Here's the thing, Pete," I said, after settling into his office. "I want to change the leadership paradigm." I was nervous, but I tried sounding more assertive than I had with David. I wanted to communicate my sense of conviction about my discovery in our campaign laboratory. Pete was friendly, offering the names of a few people I could talk to about leadership. But I sensed that he, too, was struggling to understand how he could help.

Journey Out of the Bubble

A few months later, I took the leap back to the life of a private citizen. After completing the many signoffs and debriefs required for my White House departure, and having already transported all of my personal belongings home, I grabbed one remaining item to take with me before I closed my door for the last time. It was Dante's black mesh toy box, which sat in a corner of my office awaiting his weekly Thursday afternoon visits. This made for an awkward conversation piece as I bumped into well-wishers on my way out. It occurred to me then that I was leaving people and work behind that I truly enjoyed in pursuit of a plan to change the leadership paradigm that admittedly felt half-baked.

If I was uncomfortable with the change, our 3½-year-old was quite out-of-sorts over it. Sine and I had tried to explain my pending transition—that I would no longer be working with "Mr. Barack" as he called him—but I don't think it really sank in. When I arrived home, Dante greeted me at the door and looked me over in the entryway before asking, "Dad, what are you doing with my toy box?"

I felt the gravity of this life change immediately. I came off my White House career with the confidence of a champion, but I was also feeling a little out of step. In the White House, I was at the center of activity, but as soon as I left, my phone stopped ringing and the flow of email slowed. I found myself becoming more and more isolated.

I followed up my departure from the White House with a slew of referrals to political types that David, Pete, and other friends had given me. I talked to Democrats and Republicans alike. But when I met with them, they all seemed unimpressed—if not confounded—by my ambition. After a pause, one political icon replied, "That sounds like something you should do in your retirement."

Another was a big man with a friendly smile and a successful track record in Washington politics. His response was even more unsettling: "If I didn't know you and you told me that you'd left your job in front of an important election so you could go out and change the leadership paradigm, I suppose I'd want to know what you did to piss off the First Lady."

That was another short meeting.

Trending Now

I knew that if I wanted to be an author, I would need to raise my public profile. This was painfully clear after I had been introduced by a politico to a small group of D.C. insiders power-lunching at a table near ours as "the most important person in the Obama campaign that nobody knew." That's what led me to my new publicist, Jennifer Pullinger. Jennifer had the distinction of helping put celebrity chef Rachael Ray on the map, and that was enough for me. Jennifer had a warm smile and a friendly Southern demeanor. She could also be frank, which I appreciated, and perhaps needed. Jennifer was being quite frank now.

"You have no online presence, Henry!" she exclaimed, waving her hand, palm-up, at her computer screen. She was pushing back against my reluctance to embrace her ideas. She looked at me sternly and drove home her point. "There's just nothing at all," she said. "You *need* to get a website, a blog, and some content. Get on Twitter and push yourself out there."

"Okay, so explain this Twitter thing to me," I said, with a hint of resignation. Her advice was good, but being a private person, I just wasn't excited about self-promotion. Besides, this whole conversation was a little awkward for me. I was the guy from the Obama campaign. We were supposed to be the cool, social media–savvy ones. I'd overseen a mammoth communications-driven operation, but I felt exposed as some kind of relic.

Of course, I knew what Twitter was. It had been around during the '08 campaign, though we didn't use it much at that point. I was also on LinkedIn back then, but when someone new joined our staff, we didn't go to LinkedIn to get their professional history. We didn't even Google them. That came later. Anyway, the whole online social-media thing really exploded between 2007 and 2012, the same years I was holed up inside my bubble within the Obama campaign and White House.

In my defense, upon my reentry to everyday life, I noticed that the world had moved on in my absence, and it had transformed during those five years I'd spent inside the bubble. The Obama campaign launched in February of 2007, just a few months before Apple released the iPhone. These two launches, the iPhone and our campaign, were both game-changers. The smartphone put more power in our hands, and it transformed the Internet into a virtual iEverything world, putting tools at our fingertips for just about anything we could imagine. The Obama campaign was the visible evidence of how everyday people could engage and direct the tools of our time to drive change in ways never before experienced.

In the wake of the iPhone's launch, Facebook went from 50 million users in 2007 to a billion in 2012;[1] Twitter, which was still in its infancy in 2007, grew from 50,000 active users to more than 100 million;[2] and YouTube went from users uploading six hours' worth of video content every minute to 72 hours,[3] putting more and more everyday people in the content-creation business. During that same five-year period, we went from 11 percent of US adults using social media to 50 percent.[4] Today's numbers dwarf these, but the wave was undeniable. Jennifer was making it clear that it was high time I joined in.

Even for those of us who hadn't immediately hopped aboard the social-media bandwagon, advances in smartphone technology transformed the way we worked. In 2006, I took the call inviting me to work for the campaign on a portable flip phone that lived in my back pocket and functioned much like the large phone sitting on the corner of my desk at work. Dotting that desk were sticky notes with scribbled phone messages and stacks of papers that needed to be sorted and filed in the cabinet behind me. Business cards with the contact information of professional acquaintances were stuffed into a Rolodex. I had two different paper calendar systems and a detailed written to-do list. Paper and writing utensils sat next to my computer keyboard, which was connected by cables to the central processing unit and a large, clunky monitor, with more cables connected to the printer on the desk. Newspapers and magazines were piled up in spots that were supposed to be out of the way, but there were so many piles that they overtook my workspace. A bookshelf held my favorite books. A boom box sat on the table behind me, where I played CDs or cassette tapes to help me get through late-night projects. Any papers I needed to take home were stuffed into a messenger bag that I flung over my shoulder.

By 2012, all of that had been replaced by the new iPhone in my back pocket. The App Store launched in July 2008, cutting us loose from our desktop and laptop computers. Now, I could easily store and find documents on my phone. Because all my work files were so handy, I didn't really need a printer anymore. If I wanted to research something, I just Googled it on my phone, so I didn't need periodicals or reference materials. I could do my banking, make restaurant reservations, take and share photos, play music, and just about anything else I could think of with a few keystrokes or taps on the screen. My desk was now empty, and my office was mobile.

The world was transforming so quickly that in just a few years, when my youngest son, Zane, was about 5, he announced that he recognized a song on the car radio: "Dad! I know that one! Mom has it on her phone."

Zane's idea of a phone and mine when I was 5 were utterly different. He knew it as a multifunctional device that could snap pictures and deliver text messages. Because we didn't have a dedicated landline in our home, I literally took him out to the airport, where I knew there was a pay phone, just so he could place a call using one of those technological dinosaurs. I still recall his wonderment as he put that oversized receiver up to his ear and listened silently, while his mother repeatedly inquired who the caller was on the other end of her phone. He didn't know to speak into a traditional telephone.

We See What We Expect

This may all sound quaint today, but having worked in the relatively isolated environments of the campaign and then the White House during that watershed period, I oddly needed to catch up to the times. This temporary handicap would prove to be my edge in understanding the change I had actually had a role in shaping. It enabled me to appreciate just how much the world had changed in a mere five years. These changes were profound, and they were just the beginning.

The pace of change was accelerating, and it was explosive. For others around me who were surfing along, it mostly went unnoticed. But from my unusual vantage point, I had a strong sense that this explosion of technology was just one part of a larger pattern of accelerating change. I quickly realized that this had to be the effect of the "new game" and the "everyone-leads" paradigm that I'd stumbled upon during the campaign. All around me, I saw rising individual agency, boosted by the tools at our fingertips that were once available to just an elite few. Printing presses, media-distribution channels, personal networks, collaboration platforms, and commerce applications—these were now at our disposal, combined in a single device, and could, in a moment, be applied to any problem or opportunity.

What the world was experiencing now wasn't the familiar pattern of linearly faster change; this was explosive and omnidirectional. But people around me hadn't noticed. They were still seeing the old game, but playing in the new one. We worked seamlessly across old boundaries, even as we still saw our old siloed world.

This became abundantly clear when, around this time, my wife and I learned that children at my sons' school were playing an exclusionary game on the playground, called *Monster*. I'm not quite sure of the rules the kids played by, but it was clear that the child chasing after the others desperately didn't want to be in that role—and it seemed like it was often the same one. While all of the parents would have agreed that the person in charge of the school was the principal, we didn't direct our concerns to her or to any of the teachers to resolve the problem. Instead, the parents took care of it informally, without expert assistance, by emailing each other and counting on one another to speak to our kids. The game ended virtually overnight, and our only formal interaction with the school was to inform the appropriate teachers of our actions so that they could be on alert to the problem they'd missed in the first place. We now lived in a world where we could resolve problems across old boundary lines, but we still saw a world where someone else was in charge inside that boundary.

Everyone in Everyone Else's Business

"You tell Obama! I'll tell Hillary!"

With those words, former President Bill Clinton and I broke our huddle. It ended what felt like a 30-minute riff, though, in truth, it was probably only about five minutes.

That was intense, I thought as I walked away from him and toward the perimeter of people who had stepped well back to give us some space. The former president is a force of nature. I'd heard this, but now I'd experienced it firsthand. The passion he brought to our conversation was made more obvious as he waved his hand perilously near my face.

What exactly had him so fired up? It was the spring of 2012, and we were at an event inside the Newseum building in the heart of Washington, D.C., to raise awareness and money for a memorial at the crash site of Flight 93—the plane that went down on 9/11 near Shanksville, Pennsylvania. Former President Clinton was pitching me an idea that President Obama should make a speech at the site, perhaps not realizing that I was no longer at the White House. But there was something else on his mind that we would continue to talk about.

The evening's main event that had just concluded was powerfully moving and had been a veritable who's who from the worlds of media and politics. President George W. Bush's trademark modesty and sharp-edged humor had started the night out on a good note, but it was Clinton's ensuing speech that particularly grabbed my attention.

"The people on that plane were not victims," Clinton's voice boomed, even as it was tinged with a quiver of emotion. "It is inherent in the human spirit to choose survival. And while we may never know the exact moment when the passengers and crew members came to a conclusion about the intentions for their hijacked plane, we do know that once they did, they made a decision to bring that plane down."

The former president said what should be celebrated was the conscious bravery in what he called the decision to enlist in the nation's defense. Then came the finale: "Those people were not victims, they were heroes."

I've long admired Bill Clinton's ability to flip the frame, meeting the audience where conventional thinking resides and then shifting their perspective to a seemingly opposite view. His ability to reframe our perspective about the passengers on that plane from victim to enlisted to hero was sheer mastery. He'd dazzled the room, but he wasn't done with me personally.

The event had ended and the room was starting to break up into clusters for the ensuing banter. As an introvert, that's normally my cue to leave. But before I could do so, I felt a hand on my shoulder. "Come with me," a voice said from behind me. "The president wants to speak with you."

I followed my escort, a former Clinton administration senior aide I knew, toward the charismatic figure who was forcefully arguing a point to his listener. I had no idea why I was being summoned, and I was uneasy about cutting in front of others who'd been anxiously anticipating their turn with the former president. I didn't have much say in the matter, though. As soon as Clinton was finished with his current conversation, my guide slipped in to say, "Mr. President, this is Henry De Sio."

Clinton looked at me as if he'd been waiting impatiently for me to show up. The others waiting to speak with him forfeited their place in line and stepped back. As our conversation grew more animated, they seemed to slide even farther away until they were out of earshot. The host of the event, who was nearby, took a few pictures on his phone, capturing the scene of us caucusing together—Clinton leaning in decisively, gesturing wildly in my direction for emphasis.

Truthfully, I don't remember the beginning of our conversation, only its intensity. But then, my mind snapped into focus as he launched into a startling refrain. "When I was president, there was a department for everything," Clinton said, citing Education, Health, Defense, and Housing among others. "But your president is leading in a different time." He described the emergence of a new world in which citizens no longer had to wait for a hierarchized federal agency to solve a problem. We all had our own individual agency; we could step into any situation and lead. We could organize around a catastrophe like never before. We could be first responders. And we could enlist in the nation's security—just like the people whom we had just gathered to honor and remember.

He expanded on his point, driving it home with friendly finger jabs directed at my left arm, as if to keep my focus. "This is a highly integrated world today," he said. "It is far more complex, and it calls on so much more from us as citizens."

His presidency, he said, occurred at a time when threats were more predictable and society was more compartmentalized. We could generally count on the traditional institutional apparatuses to keep our citizenry safe and meet our needs. But increasingly, it was everyone's responsibility to actively contribute to the welfare of society on multiple fronts, even in areas that used to be the exclusive domain of government.

I was astonished. Clinton was describing the "new game" and the "everyone-leads" world I had discovered back in my campaign laboratory. He'd skillfully identified and detailed the role of citizen agency in a world where silos were falling and set it against the extraordinary backdrop of the actions by those passengers on Flight 93.

"Our kids must be prepared differently for this new world," he urged. "We have to finish the [fundraising] work, and we have to get that learning center for children built out at the site."

President Clinton concluded our tête-à-tête with a remarkable insight that has stayed with me ever since. We can never know when any of us might be similarly pressed into the nation's service at a moment's notice like the brave people on that flight. That's why he believed that young people needed to know the story of Flight 93. His ultimate point was that we must cultivate in our people from a young age the skills and understanding that will enable them to harness the opportunities and responsibilities of this new form of citizen agency.

"That should be a legacy of the people on that flight," he added.

Whew! I don't remember whether I offered him any snippet of my discovery of the new leadership paradigm, but it hardly mattered. It was clear he was way ahead of me. In fact, he had fast-forwarded my attention outside my campaign laboratory to recognize a larger imperative to equip a rising generation as new citizen leaders to the challenges of this new world.

Innovator for the Public

Around this time, I found another kindred spirit who "got" the new leadership paradigm and was operating on its leading edge. Bill Drayton is widely credited with founding and defining the field of social entrepreneurship, dating back to the 1980s. Social entrepreneurs, in layman's terms, are everyday citizens who put their entrepreneurial capacities to work for the public good, laboring diligently to solve society's most complex issues. Drayton describes such individuals as society's essential corrective force. He's famously said, "Social entrepreneurs are not content to just give a fish or teach how to fish. They will not rest until they have revolutionized the fishing industry."[5]

My acquaintance with Bill came about by chance. Having navigated more than enough meetings filled with awkward silences, I'd stopped pitching my ideas about new leadership. Then, randomly, I ran into my old friend Peter Loge in Dupont Circle. We quickly caught up on each other's lives while awkwardly bobbing in and out of sidewalk traffic, when he casually mentioned that he'd recently had a meeting with an interesting guy named Bill Drayton from Ashoka Innovators for the Public.

"Bill Drayton?!" I exclaimed, immediately recognizing the name. "I've been wanting to meet him since 2000!" I first became familiar with his work back when I was a master's degree student at Harvard's Kennedy School. Peter kindly connected us, and soon after, I was in Bill's office.

My first meeting with Bill took place at Ashoka's global headquarters in the D.C. suburbs. I was expecting a larger-than-life figure to match Bill's outsized reputation, but I encountered a man with a very slender physique and a soft voice. Approaching 70 years of age, his greeting of a slight head bow and a gentle handshake conveyed his true respect and authentic humility.

I took my place across from him at a huge, round wooden table that dominated his office. One of his staff members brought in a green basket of blueberries, which he began eating in rapid-fire succession, one by one, as he listened patiently to my careful explanation of my campaign epiphany.

I viewed Bill as the perfect audience for my story detailing my discovery of the new leadership physics, and in a spectacular display of personal hubris, I embarked on a mission to convince Bill that his conception of the citizen superhero might be a bit passé. "Let me tell you about *everyone a leader*," I began.

Bill was a generous listener, and some 30 minutes later, when I finished, he thanked me with complete sincerity and then respectfully probed some of my ideas. Then, as if knowing he had an idea that I would devour, he took the reins of the conversation with the closed smile of the cat who'd swallowed the canary. "Let me get your thoughts about *everyone a changemaker*," he said.

Everyone a changemaker? I thought. His idea sounded way more interesting than mine. I was a bit fuzzy on what Bill's "changemaker" was exactly, but I could tell that his worldview was quite aligned with mine. Like me, Bill saw something qualitatively different about the time in which we live—a period marked by unusual change, which was palpable to me, but which so many others around me seemed not to notice.

"We are living in a truly historic moment," he said. He spoke softly, but I could feel his enthusiasm rising. "We are moving rapidly into a world defined by change, and this is the opposite of the world of repetition we are leaving behind."

I understood that. *When everyone leads, everyone makes change,* I thought. I also recognized from my discovery in the campaign that the world of a few people telling everyone else what to do and the *everyone-leads* world were polar opposites. The new physics at work in the world, where everybody is contributing to create change, is literally altering the nature of change itself. And it is disrupting our lives in just about every way imaginable. My host described it as "the kaleidoscope of change processes actively bumping up against one another."

"With problems outracing solutions," he said, "everyone in the system must be able to identify and solve problems by putting a team around the need." This, he continued, would require a new organizational model that encouraged everyone to form fluid teams and channel individual capabilities toward a new kind of collaboration to meet complex challenges and open up new opportunities. Bill called this organizational system *team of teams.* He repeated the term by specifically emphasizing each part: "a team" (and then after a pause) "of teams." It was his way of distinguishing his idea from the familiar hierarchical model we know. His is a way of working based on breaking down silos to enable fluid, open, and integrated collaborations directed toward the betterment of all.

He was again speaking to what I had discovered in my campaign laboratory, what I had then called "co-creative teamwork." The only difference was that he was describing our organizational model with more clarity. *"Team of teams" is brilliant,* I thought. As he spoke, I could envision how this concept could be deployed outside the organizational boundaries of the office and in the world more broadly.

He summarized the qualities needed to be a full contributor in this new system, based on patterns that he observed among the world's leading social entrepreneurs. They were all qualities I recognized from my own system. Social entrepreneurs are powered by empathy. They tear down walls and break through barriers. They innovate and renovate outmoded ideas and structures for the good of all. Where there is a complex social problem, they find uniquely inventive ways to bring diverse actors together and leverage their various talents and perspectives to find and implement solutions.

I was hooked. There was something uniquely wonderful about this community that I wanted to understand more deeply. This was the beginning of many hours of meetings over the course of several weeks. Finally, I'd found somebody who didn't think I was crazy, whose outlook was similar to mine, and who could advance my own thinking.

About three months into our exchanges, Bill invited me to work with Ashoka to accelerate and normalize these ideas worldwide, and to use my skills and experience to help Ashoka position its message and organizational construct to align with the new paradigm it had itself illuminated. I would lead our global work through a newly created role we called *framework change*. This, I thought, was the chance of a lifetime. Unbelievably, I had found the professional equivalent of a needle in a haystack—a job that would allow me to work toward changing the leadership paradigm for the good of society.

It promised to be a campaign unlike any other I'd attempted. Helping people all over the world see and play in this new game was an audacious proposition. I would throw myself into the task enthusiastically, logging nearly 500,000 miles around the globe over seven years to learn about and share this new way of living and working together in a world defined by explosive change. My travel was so exhaustive, I would liken it to that of Secretaries of State Condoleezza Rice and Hillary Clinton. I even came to refer to my role as the global ambassador for changemakers.

I worked alongside the world's leading social entrepreneurs, the prototypes for how to play in this new game. I met people in all walks of life—from the Royal Palace in Stockholm, to the Casa Rosada (Pink House) in Buenos Aires, to the streets of Bangalore, to a neighborhood in Harlem—all of whom were learning how to play in this new, complex world defined by dynamic, disruptive change.

It had all come together for me. I could see now that a new kind of leadership was driving a new kind of change, which required a new way of working. This *was* the new game. I was now fully committed to discovering the playbook for thriving in this new game, and I embarked on a journey into a whole new world filled with imaginative innovators to uncover it.

CHAPTER FOUR

Follow the Fool

S HORTLY AFTER SIGNING on with Ashoka, I was sent to São Paulo,
Brazil, to see the work of my new organization there and to become
acquainted with the social entrepreneurs in the region. After my initial
sessions with Bill, I was quite eager to meet these highly effective changemakers I'd been hearing about. I anticipated my visits would be rich with
exposure to their leadership ideas.

I wasn't given a lot of information in advance of this trip, and after
I arrived I found myself shuttled from meeting to meeting over several days. The work being carried out across the region was fascinating.
Karen Worcman had created a system for marginalized individuals in
communities to record their oral histories as a tool to further social
change. Rodrigo Baggio led a movement to make computers and training available to underserved youth in an effort to improve employment
outlooks. Anna Penido taught communications skills to young people as
a pathway for advancing civic engagement.

I was scheduled to meet with Wellington Nogueira, and for this particular visit, I was feeling a bit unsure. I didn't know much about him
except that he was passionate about healthcare and that he cared a lot
about young people. He also was a leadership enthusiast like me. Upon
arriving at his office, Wellington wasn't immediately available to see me,
so I waited in the lobby. The space looked and felt like a regular business office, except it was painted with bright colors, giving it the air of a
hospital pediatric unit. This seemed unusual. There weren't any children

around. The art on the walls depicted clowns and seemed to celebrate the idea of the circus. This also seemed odd. *Maybe it's a Brazilian thing*, I thought.

Continuing to look for clues as to the nature of the work carried out in this curious space, I strolled over to a window. We were on the third floor, and this window overlooked a large garage—or maybe it was a studio—where more than a dozen people in their mid-to-late teens were moving in synchronized patterns. It looked like some sort of yoga class, except there were no mats.

What am I doing here? I wondered. I was starting to feel like this was all a mistake. Perhaps I'd come to the wrong address.

"They are in training," a confident voice boomed from behind me, acknowledging my curiosity about the happenings below. When I turned around, I was surprised to see an unimposing figure whose casual dress and warm smile exuded playfulness. With his goatee and long salt-and-pepper hair swept back, Wellington looked like a magician you might find entertaining young children at a party.

"Training for what?" I asked after we shook hands and exchanged greetings.

"To be clowns," he answered. I honestly didn't know what to say. "It is a career in Brazil," he explained, perceiving my confusion. So it *was* a cultural thing after all. Clowning, he explained, was a trade in which students could find gainful employment. "Some will be clowns," he said, "and others will learn the skills of the clown that they can use in other careers."

Wellington then proudly announced that he, himself, was a clown. Things were beginning to come into focus, but I was still confused. Bill Drayton had promised to introduce me to new leadership thinking. What lessons in leadership could I possibly learn from a clown?

After a quick tour of Wellington's office, we took a cab to a local restaurant, where the clown motif continued. The restaurant was festive and colorful, with images of jesters mixed with folkloric Brazilian décor. We sat in a booth adorned with miniature clown ornaments dangling from the light fixtures by elastic bands, making them seem like they were dancing all around us. My mood immediately lightened.

As Wellington spoke, I found myself drawn into his story. He described his middle-class upbringing in the 1960s and 1970s in Brazil during a time of oppressive authoritarianism and censorship. Despite the stifling effect this had on the arts, Wellington discovered a passion for theater that ultimately brought him to New York City as a young man. He found success there in the late 1980s, landing roles in musicals, off-Broadway plays, and doing voiceover work in commercials. He was following his dream and finding joy. His career seemed set. However, it took a sharp turn when Wellington was invited to spend a day with the Big Apple Circus Clown Care Unit, which had been founded by a clown named Michael Christensen. There, Wellington got to experience first-hand how clowning impacted the lives of terminally ill children, and it changed his life forever.

Soon after, he was called back to Brazil to tend to his dying father. Wellington was deeply affected by what he saw in his country's health-care system. Brazilian hospitals were in disrepair; they were austere, gloomy places. Many were housed in deteriorating old buildings with dull, dingy walls. Wellington connected these two recent discoveries—that clowning could give joy to sick children, and that Brazil's hospitals were joyless places. That was the genesis of his organization, Doctors of Joy. He returned to Brazil permanently to launch a venture to bring clowns into the nation's hospitals.

"For children with extended illness, their life feels out of their own control," Wellington said. "We train people to be clowns to help them regain control of their lives and their bodies."

As he described his ideas about the power of humor and happiness in the healthcare equation, I imagined clowns armed with tambourines and balloons bursting into hospital lobbies and patient rooms.

"We go into the operating room," he said wryly when I shared my mental image.

I laughed in astonishment. "I can't imagine that," I replied. "What doctor would let a clown in the operating room?"

"We are part of the medical team," Wellington said with a look that combined his enjoyment of the idea with that of deadly seriousness.

"So, you are actually a doctor?" I asked.

"No, we are not technically doctors," Wellington answered, "but we are members of the medical team."

Clowns as part of the medical team? How is that possible? The operating room hardly seems like a place for clowns. But I wasn't being snarky in my questioning. I was over my earlier skepticism and was now genuinely curious. Clowns infiltrating medical teams seemed as improbable as clowns squeezing into a space capsule with astronauts before liftoff. It couldn't possibly have been welcomed, right? Did they just barge in?

A clown would never just storm in, Wellington assured me. A clown has to be *invited* in.

When Wellington started Doctors of Joy, he wasn't envisioning leading a parade of clowns into hospital reception spaces or recovery rooms for visits. His goal was for clowns to work as integrated members of the hospital staff alongside surgeons, nurses, and psychologists. He saw "clown doctors" as being integral to the healthcare team. He credits the idea's success to a few very special doctors with the power to open doors, allowing Wellington's clowns into the operating room. "It was a conquest based on trust," he said.

The clowns play a role as part of the child's familial system, and they meet with the family regularly so they can engage with the child and the child's family away from the medical staff. But, to be effective, clowns also need to understand the medical treatment the child is undergoing so that they can coordinate and integrate their work into the young patient's care. They actually attend meetings as members of the medical team. Outside of these structures, clowns also have their own teams connected to Doctors of Joy, which continuously looks for new ways to bring humor and joy into children's lives. Thus, the clown is actually a member of three teams: the familial team, the medical team, and the clown team, all of which work together for the child's well-being.

I instantly recognized that Wellington was describing a *team of teams* system, a fluid, collaborative organizational model not unlike the one that we transitioned into during the Obama campaign. It was the same system Bill Drayton and I had discussed. But how did this work in the operating room?

"The first thing to know is that, for the clown, the child is always in charge," he said. "If the child says jump, the clown jumps."

The clown is likely the only one in the operating room with that mindset. Certainly, a traditional surgeon wouldn't think that way. I was starting to see that the clown could be an empowering advocate for a child in a way that doctors and nurses couldn't. Before anesthesia takes effect, the child knows that at least one person in the operating room is there to do whatever they want. Others in the room may be in charge, but the child hasn't lost control completely. Knowing that the clown is there to do their bidding may ease their fear.

At the same time, the clown has to be mindful of the others on the team, Wellington explained. The doctors, nurses, and others in the room are providing life-saving, life-enriching care, and the clown has to contribute collaboratively, in a way that respects their work.

Both mindsets require one important quality: empathy. The clown in the hospital is the quintessential outsider, yet they must connect with the people they are working with. As a core member of the child's team, they need to have one eye on the child and their wants and needs, and as a collaborative member of the medical team, they need to have the other eye on what doctors and nurses need to avoid disrupting their medical care. The clown must be able to put themselves in the place of the medical professionals, while still accommodating the needs of the child. It's a high-wire act requiring remarkable emotional dexterity and a highly developed capacity for empathy to work with totally different types of people and personalities.

All of this was a lot for me to take in—clowns in the operating room, outsiders on the inside, children in charge, teams of teams, radical empathy. But I was blown away by Wellington's personal story and his work, and I wanted to understand it better.

Back at his studio, where the clowns-in-training had been practicing, I had a million questions, and it was hard to know where to begin. Perhaps I was still a little embarrassed by my own prejudices about clowns earlier that day. I started by asking Wellington how his family reacted to his choice of a clowning career. I recalled the moment in my own youth, when, having graduated from college with a degree in political science, I told my parents that I had decided to pursue a career as a rock-and-roll saxophone player. They certainly didn't discourage me, but they didn't share my level of enthusiasm over this decision. I imagined a similar reaction to his announcement.

Wellington pointed to a charming clown outfit arranged conspicuously on a rack near us. It looked handmade and not overly polished, especially when compared to the other outfits populating other racks in the room. "Do you see that costume there?" he asked. "My mom made it for me. It was my first."

The Fool as Social Entrepreneur

Wellington was quickly becoming one of my favorite people. There were so many different dimensions to his work. He has trained many everyday citizens to be clown-doctors through Doctors of Joy, and they now work in hospitals throughout São Paulo, Rio de Janeiro, and Recife, reaching hundreds of thousands of patients. This has made him a credible voice within the larger medical community, bringing his perspective on Brazil's healthcare system to symposia and policymaking forums. His work influenced the development of policy that led to the creation of the Department of Humanization of Hospital Services, inaugurated by the Brazilian government in 1999.

He also spearheaded outreach programs for disadvantaged and marginalized young people, giving them skills training so they can get clowning jobs and offering what he calls "advanced clown courses in innovation and entrepreneurship." A passionate advocate for the odd-sounding idea that clowning skills build careers, he maintains that the abilities he's honed for his multifaceted career—other-awareness, empathy, and collaborative teamwork—translate into all kinds of professional settings, including leadership positions. In that regard, Wellington is also a fixture in Brazilian board rooms, offering leadership lessons for executives that are drawn from clowning.

If clowns in a hospital operating room seemed pretty dazzling to me at first, clowns penetrating the C-suite sounded even more improbable.

And yet, Wellington offered me leadership lessons from the example of the clown's ancestor, the court jester. "The fool always knew where to position himself to be noticed by the king or the emperor's men," he explained. "He found a place just outside the gate and devised a clever way for being invited in, perhaps with tricks or shows of illusion." Wellington was in full storytelling mode now, and he paused for dramatic effect to drive home his point. "The fool, you see, is always invited in," he added.

"Once inside the palace, the fool uses the host for his objective," Wellington continued, likening him to a kind of parasite or "leech." Since the fool doesn't have a staff, money, or other resources of his own, he leverages the host's resources for his personal agenda. Once he had latched onto the host, the jester could become a voice for the common people in the ruler's ear and get the ruler to act for their benefit. The fool held up a mirror to the ruler (literally—mirrors were often part of their equipment), showing them the truth. But like the clown in the operating room, this was a high-wire act requiring great dexterity to pull off. Speaking truth to power in this way often meant the fool was putting his life on the line. He had to be highly inventive to bring together these two spheres—the court insiders and the outsiders—without going too far.

Then, Wellington pivoted to the modern-day clown and how he migrated from the court to the theater to the circus tent. The Big Top, he explained, was originally for the elephants and other animals. Next, it became the venue for daredevils attempting death-defying feats. "This wasn't the natural home for the clown," he said. "The rise of the repetitive industrial world, fortified by the arrival of the assembly line, couldn't tolerate the inspirational creativity of the clown, and he was pushed into confinement."

This was an interesting point that I wanted to understand better, but Wellington was on a roll, and I didn't want to interrupt his flow. He suggested that the world of repetition had forced the freewheeling clown into a new home where he was again an outsider. This time, it was among an assorted collection of animals and acrobats. But like his ancestor at court, once inside, the clown hijacked the Big Top and quickly became synonymous with it. Today, one couldn't imagine the circus without the clown.

"The image of the elephant was branded on one side of the tent, and the clown was on the other," Wellington said. "But, notice that inside, the clown put the child in charge." I was beginning to see the analogy he was drawing to the clowns in the operating room. Circus clowns were on the child's team; they were also part of the team that contained animal trainers and other entertainers. The clowns were especially focused on children, but they also had to be mindful of the other parts of the show. They had to be nimble and resourceful. "If there was only a pocket handkerchief on hand," Wellington said, "the clown used that to entertain the child."

Wellington was blowing my mind, and I complimented him on his brilliance as a storyteller. He gently chided me, putting his hand on my arm. "I am a clown," he said with pride. Then, after a pause, he added, "I am also a social entrepreneur."

It was through Wellington's story that I came to understand what a social entrepreneur actually was. Like the jester or the clown, social entrepreneurs bring different spheres of society together. To do so, they must be dexterous, skilled, resourceful, and above all, empathetic. They advocate for children and common people and serve the common good. In some ways, they are the quintessential outsiders, gadflies, or observers with a unique perspective or insight, yet they also understand how to get "inside." They are skilled at getting themselves invited into circles of power, and from this unusual vantage point, they are able to speak truth and bring about insights that had been missing. Lacking resources of their own, once inside, they leverage the resources they find there.

These ideas were all new to me, yet I felt them clicking into place. I came to São Paolo looking for perspective on new leadership for the new game. Wellington supplied that, plus a whole lot more. For me, Wellington's work and his view of the clown was a kind of source code for understanding the social entrepreneur—the prototype example of a changemaker.

From Repetition to Change

Back in D.C., I was eager to meet with Bill Drayton to discuss what I had learned from Wellington. From the other side of that large table in his office, I told Bill how skillfully Wellington had laid out the connections between the social entrepreneur and the fool. Bill interjected that, when social entrepreneurs begin their quests, they are often considered fools by those closest to them because of their unique ideas and ambitions. For a brief moment, I recalled the awkward silences that had been the hallmark of my meetings when I was exiting the White House bubble. Wellington had offered me a kind of blueprint for how highly effective changemakers actually make change. I enumerated for Bill the principles he'd illustrated, and I shared how they were informing my view of social entrepreneurship and changemaking. I ticked them off one at a time:

"First, social entrepreneurs have the good of all as a primary motivator," I said. "They work collaboratively, forming unlikely teams, or *teams of teams*, to create positive change." What Wellington shared about collaboration was a prominent feature of the new leadership physics I'd discovered back in my campaign-headquarters laboratory.

"Second, social entrepreneurs position themselves strategically to get noticed and they are invited into influential systems," I said. "Then they influence those who can motivate broad change quickly. They move the biggest movers for the betterment of all." In particular, I recalled Wellington's words: "There are those who are critical of us for not having large, robust organizations. But we don't so much create new organizations as hijack existing systems available for achieving our purpose." That's how social entrepreneurs leverage big changes with few resources and hyper-lean organizations. Like the clown, they use whatever resources are immediately available.

I added the third point that, like the court jester of old, social entrepreneurs hold up a mirror, bringing insights or a unique perspective that others lack. But they don't just point out what is wrong and reject it. Being fundamentally motivated by empathy, they enable others to discover for themselves what they hadn't previously seen, and that added perspective often changes behavior that leads to a better outcome.

Finally—and this was the part that took me by surprise—like the clown under the Big Top or the Doctors of Joy in the operating room, the social entrepreneur puts children in charge. Wellington was adamant about this. "Pay attention," he'd said. "Where there is a changemaker, there is a young person in charge."

Bill nodded approvingly at this condensed list of social entrepreneurial qualities, particularly the last, counterintuitive one. He noted that 90 percent of social entrepreneurs in the Ashoka fellowship put kids in charge in "amazingly diverse ways."

But my list didn't feel complete to me. I openly mulled something odd Wellington had said that I was still trying to understand, about how the industrial age with its assembly lines and rigid hierarchies couldn't tolerate the inspirational creativity of the clown, and he was pushed into the confinement of the Big Top. Bill picked up the thread immediately.

"Think about it, Henry," he said. "We have moved from a world defined by repetition to a world defined by change." While I understood his point, I initially struggled with it. After all, the world has always changed. What's so different about this change now? Still, I wanted to hear Bill out, as both he and Wellington seemed to be similarly tuned in to the same thing.

Bill went on to explain that many of our existing organizational systems had their roots in the first agricultural revolution that occurred 10,000 to 15,000 years ago. This changed the fundamental way of life for many humans, bringing the age of hunting and gathering to an end and ushering in the age of farming and settled communities. During this era, humans began to develop a social structure based on a centralized hierarchy built around the few who understood the system's enabling ideas and who managed everyone else according to those ideas, with the notable exception of a brief interruption when a more open system—democracy—blossomed in classical Greece and in northern India during the sixth century BCE.

From the fall of the Roman Empire until around 1700, Bill noted there was little to no growth in average per capita income in the west. "Then, the rate of change broke out into now more than three centuries of exponential growth," Bill said, "in both the rate of change and the degree and extent of interconnection. Part of this was people moving to the cities, where there was dramatically more interaction and exchange—and change."

Rising commerce coincided with an exponentially rising rate of change. Workers became increasingly specialized, repeating the specific task they had gotten good at over and over again to create value and make a living, whether in a factory or a law office.

"However, as the world became more complicated, we needed more people to be more involved on a whole new scale," Bill said. "Hence, the revolution 150 years ago to require everyone to read and write. Society suddenly needed everyone to be able to read the signs and instruction manuals."

Over time, as the pace and complexity of change grew, more and more people became adept at commanding and contributing to the rapidly changing landscape. "Our institutions were designed to support the old model of a few people managing everyone—it's what we have lived with for some time now," Bill added. "However, in an everything changing and everyone interconnected new reality, this organizational model is unsustainable. It simply cannot accommodate escalating change coming from infinitely more dimensions. Nor can the rules keep up with this kind of change."

Bill's analysis validated my own discovery inside my campaign-headquarters laboratory. As we transitioned away from the one-leader-at-a-time model and more people became more fully engaged, they not only adapted to changing conditions—they also drove up the rate and complexity of change. Traditional top-down organizational structures with their rigid hierarchies, siloed departments, and static rules can't manage such complex omnidirectional change. Of necessity, we had to find a better model, and we evolved into a fluid, open, and integrated team-of-teams system governed not by fixed rules but by situational, empathy-based ethics. It was a system that enabled and even facilitated all players to act as nimble collaborators representing different viewpoints. In it, everyone was valued, and everyone was expected to work for the good of all.

This is the basis for what I, today, call the *changemaker effect* on society: in the new *everyone-leads* system, change accelerates relative to the *one-leader-at-a-time* system of the past because when we all lead, we all make change. And, if everything you change changes everything, and everyone is doing it, you are in an *everyone-a-changemaker* system.

This is not to suggest that everyone *is* a fully contributing changemaker;

rather, it's to say that *everyone a changemaker* is the new game we are in. Therefore, everyone must have the skills and capacities of the change-maker to play skillfully and confidently in this new game. And we all can develop that ability.

Built for Repetition

Our country's organizational system, with its origins in an agrarian past, was built for repetition. The farm system of the middle 1700s was structured around the hierarchical management of individual skills per-formed against a recurring planting and reaping schedule. Individuals were divided into functional skill groups to execute the farm's repetitive tasks, and this sadly included the widespread use of enslaved Black men, women, and children for labor. The farm's leader constantly iterated pro-cesses in a quest to direct all human, financial, and technological capital to achieving greater efficiency in repetition. It was a distinctly one-leader-at-a-time work ecosystem.

As we moved through the 1700s, the United States saw the rise of the local business entrepreneur, a person offering specialized services that were valuable to the community. It was primarily a direct-payment-for-service model, and as demand rose for specific services, mastery of those services became increasingly prized. Whereas farm life was carried out within the boundaries of a specific property, now children were being sent down the street or even to the next village over to apprentice with a local tradesman.

In many ways, Ben Franklin was the ultimate craftsman, creating a new dominant national identity to compete with that of the farmer. George Washington, the first president, brought both together—having been born to a wealthy plantation owner (which he inherited at age 11) and also apprenticing as a surveyor.[1, 2] To emerge into the middle class in Ben Franklin's America, one simply needed to be born into the right circumstance, learn a valuable skill, and then execute that skill again and again, for life. Even with the changing face of national life in America, what we had was the continuance of a clear system of repetition.

In the mid-1800s, another wave of change swept across the nation with the rise of the industrialist. "You get an idea, and we'll copy you and make you rich," Bill Drayton likes to say when characterizing the ethos that grew out of that time. Abraham Lincoln, himself a frontiersman, had an outlook that was very much aligned with the national acceptance of this new breed of entrepreneur. The nation was changing as families began to migrate from villages to sprouting urban centers, and workers moved from farms into factories, but the nature of this change was still a doubling down on the dogged pursuit of efficiency in repetition.

The Age of Repetition reached its zenith when Henry Ford's assembly line came fully online in the early 1900s. It's ironic that Ford's reputation is so firmly attached to the invention of the assembly line, the quintessential example of repetition, because he was also an innovator who waged a lifelong battle against repeating what had already been done. Ford was greatly influenced by Ralph Waldo Emerson, and he adopted Emerson's mantra, "Imitation is suicide."[3]

In addition to his automotive innovations, Ford's professional portfolio included stints as a machinist, a serviceman of steam engines at Westinghouse, and the position of chief engineer at Edison Illuminating Company of Detroit.[4] Bob Casey, retired curator of transportation at the Henry Ford Museum, said that Ford didn't take jobs because he knew how to do them; he took them because he *didn't* know how to do them.[5] Largely self-taught, he also warned against neglecting formal education, saying, "You cannot learn in any school what the world is going to do next year, but you can learn some of the things which the world has tried to do in former years, and where it failed and where it succeeded."[6]

A complex figure, Ford embodied the tensions of the time. He believed that machines would improve people's lives, and in particular, he wanted automobiles to be affordable and accessible to the masses. But as machines were increasingly deployed in production, wages fell. There was more and more of a push for labor to organize. Ford bristled at this, largely because he likened it to a socialist path to mediocrity that wouldn't serve the common good.[7]

Ford ultimately concluded that people preferred to have jobs that didn't require them to think, and he set out to create employment for the multitudes in which they would mass-produce the ideas of the exceptional few.[8] Faithful to his mother's teachings that serving others was the highest duty,[9] and seeking to improve the lives of everyday people, he succeeded in two of his greatest aspirations. By refining the assembly-line model of work, he cut the cost of automobiles and made them accessible to the masses. People could now go farther from where they were, faster. In addition, as this mode of production was adopted across industries, it elevated the social standing of millions of people, and the American economy took off.[10]

Henry Ford is frequently remembered for saying, "To resent efficiency is a mark of inefficiency."[11] That remark epitomized the era he helped to create.

After mass production, the next phase of industrial organization was the elevation of the specialized consulting firm in the 1950s and 1960s—the era depicted in the TV show *Mad Men*. As the business-entrepreneur class grew, so did competition within it, and a new professional class arose to help white-collar management compete and develop ever-more-advanced and specialized systems of repetition. Universities produced a new type of worker who could further refine the system: a professional cadre of lawyers, advertising specialists, and management consultants. John F. Kennedy represented the ascendancy of this type, rising as meteorically in politics as ad man Don Draper did in the fictional television show. As this class established itself, it seemed as though the system of repetition, like the US economy itself, would be endlessly refined and expanded. But in reality, humankind was beginning to squeeze the last drops from the repetition sponge.

The top-down, siloed social structure of repetition was based on the few telling the many how to repeat their specialized skills, faster and faster, inside four walls, for life. Those at the top of the system got rich as their ideas were implemented and endlessly copied. Those in white-collar jobs were either silo leaders, such as the department head, or consultants to silo leaders. They were paid handsomely to advance and improve the system of repetition. Everyone else was placed on a lifelong track in which they would endlessly repeat their specialized skills. There was an implicit understanding—a social contract—that if you took your place on one of these defined paths and played by the rules, you would be a candidate for some iteration of the American dream. You could have a steady job, be a productive member of society, own a home, finance your children's education, and retire with some kind of a safety net.

At some point, though, these rules stopped working. The social contract frayed, and this is largely because we have begun to leave the old world of repetition behind. Social movements are tearing down the walls of hierarchical society. Individual agency, as Bill Clinton pointed out to me, is rising. Technology is putting the tools of social change in the hands of everyday citizens, and this has democratized leadership. Naturally, there is a lag between these changes and our conscious perception of them. But Americans often tap seminal political leaders who mirror the emerging national identity of their time, and this is true even as we are leaving the era of one-leader-at-a-time in favor of a new everyone-leads world. The election of Ronald Reagan in 1980 may be the first such example coinciding with this historic shift.

When I graduated from college in the mid-1980s, planning a career meant obtaining a specialized skill, landing a job, and holding it for life, much like our parents had. The more ambitious among us believed that we could retire at age 50, likely from the same job we took upon entering the workforce. We were still working from the playbook handed down to us from previous generations.

But the Reagan era signaled the beginning of a departure from that playbook. He pointed out that young people might have five different kinds of jobs in their lifetime and made the argument that we would need to have a portable retirement fund that would follow us wherever we went. This was the genesis of the 401(k). It was controversial. Some thought Reagan was undoing the social contract that working families had kept for generations. Others thought he had a practical policy idea. Personally, I felt disrupted and even disturbed by the notion that I'd have such an uneven career trajectory. That wasn't the world I had been preparing for. My father seemed caught off-guard as well, and had little advice to offer beyond insisting that I get a job that would offer health insurance.

In hindsight, I can see that something big was going on. Reagan's election was a recognition of a dominant national aspiration—or perhaps an emerging reality—of an increasingly empowered citizenry. In effect, he was saying, "Yes, you can," a generation before Barack Obama's "Yes, we can." He was speaking to *The Startup of You* decades before Reid Hoffman's book of the same title. In a way, he was anticipating Daniel Pink's *Free Agent Nation*.

Public awareness of this shift took a while to catch up to the new reality. Workers in the 1980s still branded themselves with their union jackets or company logos. Identifying with an organization was still the primary means of self-identification. But since then, individuals have increasingly become our own brand that we marry to our employers' brand. Aligning our career choices with our personal values has become the norm.

When asked about the secret behind the Obama campaign's success, my answer is simple. In 2008, we tapped into something that already existed in the electorate and was increasingly valued by society: an innovative mind, a service heart, an entrepreneurial spirit, and a collaborative outlook. This was the new national DNA. It's not exclusively Democrat or Republican, Right or Left—it's not even exclusively American. Ronald Reagan intuited what was already happening as more and more Americans were rejecting the role of a cog in a large, repetitive machine in favor of stepping up to contribute more fully at work and in society. Twenty years after Reagan's presidency, the hierarchical, repetition-based world was declining rapidly, and the pace of change was accelerating. Obama recognized that successfully navigating a world of rapid, accelerating change requires an empowered citizenry working together, saying, "Yes, we can." In retrospect, this was an acknowledgment of our new *team of teams* world.

These epoch-making changes were definitely amplified by the computers most of us now have at our fingertips. Some might even say that they are responsible for these changes. But in fact, it's the other way around. Smartphones emerged because they were needed to help us handle and engage with the uniquely different changes that were already underway. We needed new technology to accommodate our new societal DNA. And as we are able to see the new game more clearly and collaborate more fully to command it, we will need yet more sophisticated tools and systems.

Our society, built for repetition, will become increasingly challenged as we transition to an *everyone a changemaker* world. Jobs that are based on repetitively cranking out the same product over and over again are being automated. As change accelerates and pervades our lives more and more, the way human beings work and engage socially becomes ever more complex. It takes the traits of a changemaker and a fluid, collaborative team of teams to navigate it. Or, as Wellington might say, it takes the resourcefulness, dexterity, radical empathy, and inspirational creativity of the fool. We can't use the same playbook that has been handed down for generations. It's now a game of changemakers, played by a team of teams, and requiring a whole new playbook.

So, now that we can clearly see and understand the new game, it's time to play.

What You Need to Know to Play

CHAPTER FIVE

Empathy Is the Driver

I N HIS 2015 commencement address at North Carolina Central University, then–Secretary of Education Arne Duncan made a remarkable pronouncement: "The key factor of success for any society going forward is what percentage of its people are changemakers. It's the new literacy, and empathy is the foundation of that new way of being."[1] He was actually quoting Bill Drayton, but it is significant that the nation's educator-in-chief used such an occasion to present this rather unconventional idea.

Secretary Duncan continued by reasoning, "The most valuable attribute in the world you are about to enter is not critical thinking, or fluency in another language, or an amazing understanding of US history, or chemistry, or math—as important as every single one of those skills are. It's not about learning how to play the game or even primarily about what or who you know. It's about whether you are capable of truly seeing the world through another's eyes or are willing to walk a mile in their shoes."[2] This was striking. The Education Secretary was saying point-blank that empathy was as important as reading or math—perhaps even more.

Four months later, on the anniversary of the 9/11 attack, the entertainment community put on a celebrity-studded Hollywood production called *Think It Up* about reimagining education in a dynamically changing world. It was broadcast on all four TV networks on Friday evening during primetime. Actress Gwyneth Paltrow introduced Tucson, Arizona's Changemaker High School, paying tribute to how its teachers and students modeled teamwork, strong leadership, and real-world problem-solving, all of which are needed for a world of dynamic change and complexity. "Here, empathy is a key ingredient, and success is determined whether students graduate with a sense of purpose and the courage to innovate to challenge the status quo and to improve the society they live in," she said.[3]

Matthew McConaughey narrated a video in which Changemaker High School students talked about individual initiative, co-creative teamwork, and commitment to community both inside and outside school. "We're not trying to be the best school in the world," said the school's chief academic officer, Luis A. Perales. "We're trying to be that best school for the world."[4]

Something was clearly going on. Empathy was being lauded by both cultural and government leaders as a key driver of success. Yet prior to this 2015 event, empathy had rarely ever been mentioned on the list of attributes needed to succeed. In fact, in 2009, President Obama came under fire for saying that empathy was a key quality that he would want to see in a Supreme Court nominee.[5] At that time, the relative importance of empathy hadn't even registered on the public's radar enough to seriously poll. In the weeks following his comments, the Pew Research Center published the data it had on related qualities, like compassion, to show that most Americans thought women were more likely to be empathetic than men. But the actual poll never used the word *empathy*—the pollsters just surmised women had more of it.[6]

In 2012, getting the public to seriously value empathy seemed like a nonstarter when Bill Drayton asked if I could play a role in advancing Ashoka's national and global initiative to make empathy a higher priority in the growing-up experience. I was wary. I wasn't far removed from my political-campaign past, and I was unsure of how the message that kids must have empathy to succeed in the world would be received. For some, the word connotated softness or weakness—the antithesis of the ideal of rugged individualism that was still a dominant value in American culture. Plus, I wasn't sure what I could personally contribute that would elevate empathy as a social ideal. Christ, Buddha, Gandhi, Mother Teresa, and Martin Luther King, Jr., were among those who had taken up this cause. It felt like the wrong job for me.

As I grappled with Bill's request, I shared my dilemma with a friend during a casual conversation. Given her liberal worldview and being quite a few years my junior, I expected she might ignite my zeal for the idea. She was also quite knowledgeable about and supportive of Ashoka's work.

"So, what do you think about our Start Empathy project?" I asked.

"Where I'm from, we wouldn't be for it," she said decisively.

Her answer truly surprised me. I asked why she felt that way. "We don't want our kids to grow up to be doormats!"

As the father of two small boys, I could completely relate to her response. I wanted the best for my kids, but like the generations of fathers before me, I thought my children should learn the skills they needed for the jobs they wanted. Only then could they climb the ladder of success in their respective fields. And in my experience, it was the not-so-empathetic among us who seemed to get to the top. I wanted my boys to be good people but definitely not doormats.

I wrestled with this question for days. Why empathy, and why now? If I couldn't answer it for myself and my kids, there was no way I could make the argument to the wider world. I'd just be one more ignorable voice pleading for a nicer, kinder, better evolved world.

My mind went back to my campaign-headquarters laboratory to assess the role of empathy in the two opposing structures we had at different times—the siloed one-leader-at-a-time hierarchy versus the everyone leading in the fluid, open team-of-teams model. Empathy didn't have much of a place in the old-game structure. Decision-making in that system was relatively simple. Initiatives were hatched at the top and dictated downward in a hierarchy controlled by a few, just as disputes or problems were resolved by the boss with a simple "yes" or "no."

In the old game, a premium was placed on giving and taking orders. You only needed to be skilled at your job and have just enough empathy to get along with others superficially. You didn't really need to understand or empathize with them. In fact, in the old system, those who were the most forceful, the most self-insistent, and the least collaborative had the edge. The sharpest elbows cleared the path to the top.

In the team-of-teams system, new opportunities are unlocked by individuals responsibly taking initiative and working collaboratively with diverse, empowered teams. Getting to "yes" requires dozens of interactions with people across the organization not just a thumbs-up from the top.

In this sense, leadership is no longer a matter of a linear relationship between boss and employee. The old-game leader needed 20/20 vision to see the end goal and the authority to point the way and get others in the chain of command to line up behind them. In the new game, all the players on the team need 360-degree vision to survey the complex landscape all around them. Each has to see how the changes they make affect others across the system, just as they must understand the motivation for the changes initiated by others that are coming their way and affecting them.

Your ability to see and empathize with another's experience is the way you identify challenges and opportunities requiring a solution or a plan. It is also how you maintain trust and credibility, and what allows you to engage in the system. The new game requires the quality that Secretary Duncan talked about—the ability to see through someone else's eyes.

As our campaign organization transitioned to the new game, those who were used to relying on a high degree of structure and wielding personal authority struggled. Some fell away. Passivity and authoritarianism were both viewed dimly in the new system. If conscious empathy was considered a "soft skill" in the old game—a nice-to-have quality, but not necessary—in the new game, it was a requisite "hard" skill. In fact, it was the foundational skill for working in a team of teams. More than that, it was fundamental to individual and organizational success. Everyone needed to understand that every action and inaction had effects and consequences across the system, and we had to be able to imagine and relate to how others experienced them.

What was true in my campaign laboratory is increasingly true in the larger world, which is undergoing the very same transition. And that was how I realized that conscious empathy was a skill that my children needed to have. It wasn't a doormat-maker. It was a door-opener.

This was a breakthrough in my own thinking. I had found the lens through which to understand empathy, not just as a nice quality but as a critical skill. Still, I knew that selling this idea to the rest of the world would be difficult. After hearing my riff on the importance of empathy in a world where silos were fading into an interconnected landscape, a neighborhood dad deadpanned, "I think I'll keep my silo." And then there was my younger friend I had spoken to earlier—the one who said that where she was from they didn't want their kids to become doormats. She was Scandinavian; where could this idea get real traction, if not *there*? This was a puzzle that I knew I couldn't solve alone, so I turned again to my new community of leading changemakers for clues as to how to authentically understand and show empathy's central importance in today's world.

Empathy for the Driver

Katherine Freund is a petite woman with a big presence. When I first met her in 2012, she was seven years into her tenure as CEO of the Independent Transportation Network of America (ITNAmerica), the organization she founded in Portland, Maine, which had affiliates in 20 cities at the time. Her organization offers seniors the option to hand over ownership of their vehicles in exchange for ride credits that can be used to access a driver at any time, for any reason. ITN provides a way for older drivers to give up their car when the time is right, but it also serves as a platform for raising broader social awareness about the mobility challenges seniors and their families face.

I listened as Katherine described the high stakes accompanying that momentous decision to hand over one's car keys. For many, a car represents independence, and I immediately understood the stress of suddenly having to rely upon others to access life's needs and pleasures. I could also imagine the pressure that this transition would put on family and friends. What struck me the most was her characterization of this issue as an unseen problem that was troubling American households.

Katherine believes that every family should have a plan well in advance for addressing the needs and desires of aging drivers. This makes sense to me. When my father was approaching this difficult moment in his life, in the years just before I met Katherine, I really didn't know how to talk to him about it. I didn't have the tools to constructively discuss it with either of my parents. My mom, who was nine years younger than my dad (he has since passed), was balancing professional responsibilities just as he was requiring more frequent access to his doctors. My brother and I lived far away, so we couldn't be much help.

It wasn't a conversation we had ever anticipated as a family, and there were no good alternatives for him. Retiring along California's more sparsely populated central coast, his car gave him the freedom to socialize and get to the places he enjoyed. Public transportation wasn't readily available, and I don't think he would have used it anyway, so his automobile was his connection to the wider world. These were issues that had to be on his mind, too, because he occasionally expressed a wish that he could have a driver to chauffeur him around and cater to his needs as an alternative to driving himself.

Katherine understood this dilemma well. "In areas with smaller populations, like your dad's, a car is viewed as key to survival and for meeting basic needs," she said. "In urban centers, there is a different kind of loss that goes with stepping onto a dirty bus to get where you want to go."

Katherine saw that this script could be flipped. Her view was that when we came to a point in our lives we could no longer capably drive, we should have earned the right to rides with dignity—to be driven in a clean automobile by a caring attendant—and to remain engaged as full contributors in society.

That's what the Independent Transportation Network offers. No more unplanned automobile maintenance costs, no more driving in stressful conditions, and no more worries about burdening friends and family if one doesn't drive their own car. When seniors become members of the ITN and set up a Personal Transportation Account, they can trade in their cars for funds applied to their accounts toward future rides, while also helping ITN build a fleet. Trading a car for rides is not a requirement, however, as many ITN members or their adult children simply pay for their rides. ITN has a cadre of citizen-volunteers and part-time paid drivers who are available to meet the transportation needs of riders 24/7. As an incentive, volunteer drivers earn ride credits that they can either save for their own future needs or donate to help support lower-income seniors.

"Our drivers walk right up to the door and even offer to help," Katherine told me, emphasizing her focus on the rider's dignity.

Her account of the organization she had built was impressive, especially since her degree was in public policy, not business. But I struggled to focus on it, as I was concentrated on Katherine's personal story, which had led her to this idea. In 1988, Katherine's 3-year-old son suffered a traumatic brain injury after running into the street and being struck by a driver in his mid-80s. The car continued on past the scene without stopping. Even more troubling, this tragedy had occurred not long after Katherine's husband passed away in a propane accident.

"Can I ask you something?" I interjected, feeling a bit impolite. "I just can't imagine how in the world you found it within yourself to do this?"

Katherine paused for a moment before answering my question. I watched as her eyes broke from mine to settle on a spot across the room, as if she hadn't expected my question. Then she returned her gaze. "I guess I just had empathy for the driver," she said matter-of-factly. "I don't think I could have ever gotten out of bed," I said after a pause, amazed at her answer and fully absorbed in my own feelings as I imagined myself in her situation. It was a display of total selfishness that was quite the sharp contrast to her obvious capacity for empathy.

She admitted it took some time. "I mean, I do remember hearing the driver say his failure to stop was because he thought he had run over a dog, but he wasn't sure," she offered. Ultimately though, Katherine realized that she had to be strong for her son, who was recovering, and for her 4-year-old daughter, who had also been at the scene.

She recalled her chance meeting with the driver, whom she came upon again later at the accident site. She was returning home from the hospital, where her son was in the intensive care unit, and intending to have dinner with her daughter. "I hugged him," she said.

Sensing my amazement, Katherine elaborated, "I can recall with perfect clarity the feelings I had at the time and my mental reasoning. I thought, 'How would I feel if I were this older driver and I realized I had run over a child?' It is too horrible to imagine—and yet, it happened."

In their conversation, the elderly gentleman expressed that he felt himself to be innocent. The accident was not his fault, he said, because he did not do it on purpose. This must have been difficult to hear, but Katherine said that as he spoke, an image formed in her mind, and it influenced her perspective. "I saw a black hole, black like the complete absence of light," she recalled. "I saw my son fall into it, but I also saw the man who ran over him fall into it. That's how I knew they were both victims."

After a pause, she added, "Grandfathers are not supposed to run over the grandchildren."

Katherine later learned that the older driver who struck her son had dementia, and she realized that he was incapable of understanding that he should not have been behind the wheel. "The inability to self-evaluate is a characteristic of dementia," she explained.

Katherine became involved in senior mobility issues, and she began to research the data. She learned that the question of giving up one's car was a quiet and unnoticed one that affects families and communities everywhere. Whereas others viewed this simply as a question of whether an older person is safe to drive—they measured the person against the needs of the transportation system—Katherine concluded that the existing transportation system was not serving the needs of normally aging people. "Seniors begin to limit their driving and mobility for many years before they stop," Katherine said. "They stop driving in the snow, and they avoid unfamiliar neighborhoods, interstate highways, rush hour, and parking garages. Some people consider these normal adjustments. I say it is like managing air pollution by breathing less. People need mobility, at any age."

She also recognized that the system completely failed us as soon as we stopped driving. And because women outlive their decision to stop driving by an average of 11 years and men by 6 years, these older Americans are vulnerable to being stranded, isolated, and feeling inadequate because they cannot safely operate their own vehicles.

Katherine believed that the solution to this problem needed to serve the aging population at the point where the system had previously failed, so that people could live full and meaningful lives throughout their entire lifespan. It was through her ability to understand the problem that Katherine found herself able to take action. It was the alternative to harboring anger.

But there was something else. Katherine had money from her husband's modest life-insurance policy that she could put behind her idea.

She used some of these finances to get an advanced university degree and set herself up to provide for her family, but she also recognized that she had been put in a position where she could make an initial investment in her idea. "I never had money," she said. "I worked from a young age, and growing up, we were never really affluent."

Katherine saw the chance to solve a problem and also honor her husband's life and legacy. "I thought: *How could I not?* I had the ability to do this."

Katherine thinks of herself as a mobility advocate more than the founding CEO of a transportation service. At 70, she remains dedicated to driving this conversation from kitchen tables into the public discourse. She sees a looming, complex problem ahead for our nation, as 10,000 Americans will turn 65 every day until the end of the decade. By 2030, more than 70 million Americans will be 65 or older.[7]

There are so many ways in which Katherine could have channeled her energy after tragedy shook her life. She used her capacity for empathy to spot a solution, and then she successfully brought a community around it so that older Americans could have the dignity of remaining mobile and in their homes. Thankfully, Katherine's son did recover from his accident. Her energy is noticeably elevated when describing him—a lovely man whom she characterizes as "kind and aware."

Kind and aware—in her portrayal of her son, Katherine has offered a clue to the key attributes that changemakers value.

Close the Empathy Gap

Empathy is fundamental to the changemaker's operating system. We often think of kindness and awareness as individual traits, but in order for everyone to fully play in the new game, we have to aggregate those qualities and close a broader societal empathy gap.

Shelby Coffey III agrees. Shelby had a distinguished career in journalism. He served as the president of CNN Business News and CNNfn, and was the executive vice president at ABC News in New York following his tenure as the editor and executive vice president of *The Los Angeles*

Times from 1989 to 1997. He was at the helm of the *Times* during a time of heightened racial tension marked by the 1992 LA riots, the violence against Rodney King and Reginald Denny, and the O.J. Simpson trial.

I met Shelby after he'd become the vice chair of the Newseum in Washington, D.C., a museum dedicated to the history of the news media. As he showed me around, he offered a perspective on the news that I hadn't previously considered. "Good journalism tells the story of empathy or its absence," the seasoned newsman said. By Shelby's measure, newspapers are the world's official record of empathy in action, as well as the historical archive of mankind's empathy deficits.

A key piece of guidance that he gave to his news staff was to always cover events with an empathetic lens. "Write as if the mother of the person about whom you are writing will be reading." He didn't mean that the facts should be altered or soft-pedaled; he simply meant that journalists should be mindful that in and around every news story were real people with feelings.

As we discussed the skills and attributes needed for the new emerging world, Shelby listened intently to my pitch about the need for us as a society to place a higher premium on empathy. This seemed to resonate with him, and he volunteered a story to support my point.

A young man who had been entangled in the gang culture of Los Angeles in the 1990s made the decision to get out. As Shelby told it, this young man straightened his life out and was on a path to success. Graduating from high school was an exciting milestone and something that would have been unimaginable in his old life.

This is the moment when Shelby's wife, Mary Lee, an emergency room physician in Pasadena, entered the story. On the evening of his high school graduation, the youth came into the ER with serious gunshot wounds. A gang member from his old neighborhood couldn't stand the idea of his rival's success, so he gathered his guns, drove to find him, and shot him. In the ER, Mary Lee assured her patient that he would recover, and he did.

Shelby ended his story with a question: "How much more empathy would the young man's rival have needed to not make that decision?"

Discovering the Empathy Effect

If empathy is foundational for playing in the new game, we must not only cultivate it in ourselves. We must also actively work to cultivate it in others and close the empathy gap in society at large. But how do we do that?

That's the question I brought to my meeting with Roman Krznaric, the author of *Empathy*, *The Wonderbox*, and other books. He is also the founder of the world's first Empathy Museum and digital Empathy Library. Born in Sydney, Australia, he now lives near Oxford University, in England, which is where I caught up with him. Roman holds a PhD in political sociology and taught at Cambridge University, which I might have found intimidating, but Roman is quite easy to relate to. He told me that he had once been a gardener at an Oxford college, and I could picture him busily tending to the grounds as easily as I could envision him delivering a compelling classroom lecture.

We agreed to meet at a coffee shop near the university. Roman, whom I had not previously met, was waiting for me at a table when I arrived, and we left our coats and umbrellas to hold our places while we went to the counter and ordered. When we returned, our stuff had been pushed aside into a small pile, and two men had intentionally taken our seats. I was ready to walk away and find another spot in the crowded space, but to my surprise, Roman, the empathy champion, directly confronted the two men about it.

What Roman did made me secretly happy. He was no doormat. He was assertive but also respectful. And when the men ignored his protest, and after we'd turned away to find new seats, Roman didn't murmur something about needing to understand them better, nor did he grumble angrily about them. While I needed a couple of minutes to collect myself and get past the incident, he was over it right away, quickly switching his full attention to our conversation.

"First things first," I said once we had gotten resituated. "What is empathy?"

Roman answered by first telling me what empathy *wasn't*. "It's not having pity for someone's situation," he explained. "That's sympathy. Empathy is really just stepping imaginatively into someone else's shoes and getting in touch with how they see the world and how they feel—you can then use that understanding to guide your own actions."

That seemed simple enough, but Roman searched for a relatable example. He pivoted the conversation to my children, asking how they got along.

I said that they were typical kids for ages 5 and 4. They got along fine but had their squabbles. Roman continued to probe. He wanted to know how each boy responded when the other was upset.

"Dante usually offers words of understanding for Zane," I said. "In Zane's case, he's an action man. When Dante is upset, he is always quick to find something comforting to give him."

"Is it something he likes himself, such as a favorite toy, or something his brother would like?" Roman asked.

I answered that Zane typically offered something he cherished himself, which I found sweet.

Roman said that Zane was well on his way to building his capacity for empathy, but that there was a clear marker to watch for next. "His response is to act in a way that is soothing to his own feelings," Roman said. "When Zane responds in a way that indicates he understands what might make Dante feel better, he will have achieved a milestone in his empathy development."

Listening to Roman, I suddenly realized that there had been a recent change in Zane's response to his brother being upset that I might not have otherwise noticed. In the past, he had always been quick to bring a stuffed animal to his older brother on those occasions, but Dante had never really been a stuffed-animal man the way Zane was. Recently, however, Zane had begun to deliver Dante's "blue"—his favorite blanket—when he wanted to cheer his brother up. According to Roman's definition, Zane was making the shift from being compassionate to being empathetic.

I appreciated how clearly Roman spoke of empathy and how he had couched it in a way that I could easily understand and relate to. There's a body of neuropsychological research on empathy that can make my eyes gloss over, but Roman's view of it seemed accessible and user-friendly. It helped me see that when you unpack the amazing work of highly effective changemakers like Katherine and Wellington, their underlying driver is really quite simple. They lead with their well-honed ability to understand what others need and then act on that understanding.

I told Roman of my concern that it would be challenging to make empathy more prominent in our daily lives, since today's society places a high value on individualism and self-reliance. The empathy deficit seems to be at crisis levels. Roman acknowledged that human history has been marred with obvious empathy deficits, but he suggested taking a different tack.

"Rather than imagining a world with more empathy, perhaps you should first help people see all the empathy that already exists in our world as it is," he said. "If society lacked basic empathy, we'd have crying babies left unattended and charities being shuttered because no one would care." Roman suggested observing the many things that we take for granted in a world where empathy is already quite present.

"The work might be as simple as first helping others to truly recognize and viscerally experience the prevalence of empathy," he continued. "Then we might be better able to appreciate that the possibilities for us individually and for humanity are as great as our capacity for empathy."

Roman wasn't finished. "There's one other secret for tackling the empathy deficit in society," he said, "and that's to nurture your curiosity about strangers. One of the best ways to flex your empathy muscles is to have a conversation with a stranger at least once a week—someone from a different background than yours, like the person who cleans the office where you work or the quiet librarian living across the street."

And he wasn't suggesting some cursory, superficial exchange. Roman said that we should talk about the stuff that really matters, like love, death, happiness, and the future. He acknowledged that this might take some courage, but it's one of the best ways to challenge stereotypes and assumptions about others. "Making this kind of effort to really understand how another person sees the world is what can really make empathy such a revolutionary force," he said, "and help overcome the divides that are tearing our societies apart."

The Art of Kindness

I met Stefan Einhorn during a visit to Sweden. A medical doctor, professor at the Karolinska Institute, and author, he has written several books, including *The Art of Being Kind*. I put the same questions to him that I had to Roman. I was particularly interested in whether he thought empathy was undervalued in today's world.

"Certainly, kindness and empathy get little respect as named human qualities," Stefan observed, his strong command of English coming through his thick Swedish accent. "However, when I offer audiences the choice to pick just one prominent characteristic—having Nobel-prize-like intelligence, being a rock star at work, possessing a knee-slapping sense of humor, having disgusting wealth, or being a good person—90 percent choose the latter quality," he said.

Stefan believes that this is a quality we most want for ourselves. By simply acknowledging this fact, he said, empathy can be elevated and more highly valued as a societal attribute. "When that happens, a world of possibilities for developing it will open up," he said. "Every interaction with another offers a new training opportunity. And our days consist of many such training opportunities."

Stefan laid out two simple steps for cultivating empathy. The first step is to simply sharpen our empathy awareness by making the conscious decision to try to understand another person. Second, once we've made that choice, we must hone our curiosity as a way to foster dialogue and discovery. "The act of attempting to understand what someone is thinking exercises our empathic ability," he said.

Stefan added that as we develop that empathic understanding, we get the insights we need to respond as the other person would want. "I tell my medical students, we shouldn't simply treat people as we would like to be treated," Stefan said. "We should treat them as they are in need to be treated—it is important to meet them where they are."

Stefan stressed that widespread adoption of these simple principles into our collective consciousness could be transformative for society. "Conflict is most often the result of one party not feeling seen by the other," he said. "When we feel unseen, we distrust that we will be understood."

The advice I had received from both Roman and Stefan seemed easy to put into action, and I quickly began putting it to work in my parenting. On one occasion, Dante, my eldest, decided that he wanted to wear Zane's abandoned snorkeling gear in the pool. This was an attention-getting moment, as I'd rarely seen Dante show any interest in it before. He knew to ask his brother first, who immediately vetoed the idea.

I saw Dante's shoulders slump as he walked away, so I brought the boys together to revisit the issue. I had Dante share what Zane's answer had made him feel. Then I asked Zane to describe his own feelings when he was asked to share his gear. It came to light that Zane's feelings had their roots in an earlier conflict. After talking things through, I asked Zane, "Do you think you can think again about Dante's request and answer with kindness in your heart for your brother?"

I didn't tell him to change his answer. I only asked him if he could shift his perspective and consider things from Dante's point of view. Zane quickly decided that Dante could use his snorkeling gear now, but he also said, kindly, that he would like to have it back to use later. Dante agreed. End of conflict.

Later, I told Zane how proud I was of him for his decision, and I asked him how he thought his brother had felt when he first turned him down.

"I think he felt bad," Zane admitted.

"And how did you feel?" I asked.

"Greedy," he replied.

Then I asked how he felt after he let Dante use his gear.

"Good," Zane said, "because I could see Dante liked using it."

It's a simple example, but bringing these ideas to life in my parenting helped me see that developing one's capacity for empathy can lead to extraordinary things, as Katherine, Wellington, and other changemakers I would meet during the course of my journey demonstrate.

Elevating Empathy

Empathy is a key attribute of changemakers, and developing and mastering it is instrumental to thriving in the new game. It's the foundational skill for the new way of working and living together in the new team-of-teams world of rapidly accelerating, omnidirectional change. Each team member must be empowered and valued—heard and understood—so they can make their contribution to advancing solutions. We must all play fully, and no one can be passive. That requires empathy first and foremost.

This is not an aspirational model or some kind of utopian construct. It literally is the new reality. To succeed in the world that's emerging now, everyone needs to understand the nature of how the world is changing and the skills needed to navigate and lead these changes. The pace of change in every sector and in every individual's life will accelerate. We'll need to rely on open collaboration through high-quality interaction to get ahead of it.

As complexity mounts and we get deeper into uncharted territory, the old, static rulebooks will no longer apply, and there will be a new premium on personal integrity, working for the good of all, and empathy-based ethics rooted in compassion and care for others as wise, flexible guides to action in new situations. Conscious empathy is the prerequisite for all these new ways of working, and the stakes for everyone mastering it have never been higher.

CHAPTER SIX

Define Thyself

M Y GOLDEN RULE on the campaign trail was *define thyself lest you be defined*. Show me a candidate who doesn't understand this, and I'll show you a candidate who will lose. It is the job of the campaign to define the candidate—yours and theirs—hence the endless messaging battles that play out in the media, on the stump, and in debates.

I remember the day when I discovered that this principle also applied to all of us *off* the campaign trail, as well. We had hit an important milestone in the Obama campaign—Hillary Clinton had exited the race. As we pivoted to the general election, I noticed something that surprised me. Our success to date, unimaginable when we started, was gigantic, earth-shaking, and even change-making. Yet, somehow, my coworkers had lost themselves in minutiae. We were suffering an unusual outbreak of *smallness* inside head-quarters. To be clear, our success was the result of our innovations, but the campaign also benefited from the masterful execution of those unnoticed particulars carried out by our staff. I discovered that people had become as small as the details of their work. So I went on a mission to help everyone on the teams I oversaw to fully own our success and see themselves as the actual leaders of something huge. I needed to help everyone step into their BIGness. I held some 15 meetings over three weeks with different units, per-sonalizing examples of the unique contributions each had made.

The key was for everyone to recognize that they were more than merely what their coworkers saw based on everyday tasks and transac-tions. Many of us do more than what our colleagues see, and we aren't

83

always recognized for our big-picture responsibilities. One of the units I met with during this quest was an innovative group of four young staffers who managed transportation logistics—for example, facilitating staff air travel or arranging car rentals to support our massive get-out-the-vote efforts across the country. They secured, managed, and ensured the return of every single one of the many hundreds of leased cars and vans commissioned during the life of the campaign, all with many drivers and keys that passed among different hands. This was a remarkable feat for a campaign of our size and scale. Not one car was lost.

Yet they were known for something quite different. The rest of the staff just called them "the travel bookers," and not always with affection. The way our system worked, if you needed to travel, you booked your trip online and then waited for a call from one of them prior to approval. Their job was to ensure that travel needs were met cost-effectively, and that meant they often encouraged cheaper options. To save money, they had to find and propose different times or routes to their coworkers and bosses. They didn't impose rules; they merely educated their colleagues about other options. They unquestionably contributed to our frugal culture. Still, those calls could get tense, as staff just wanted their requests to be automatically approved.

When I met this team, I reminded them that they were more than mere "travel bookers." They were leaders who could step into the tension of leadership, encourage financial discipline, and come up with alternatives that worked. Every week, on their own initiative, they handed me a report detailing how their interventions had saved the campaign money. It didn't include a running total, and in our meeting, I showed them the cumulative calculation that revealed they had single-handedly logged enough savings during the campaign's first 15 months to fund operations in a small state during the final months. This was something we might not have otherwise been able to afford. It was a big contribution to the ultimate success of the campaign that other workers who saw them as some sort of in-house travel agents knew nothing about. This team wasn't merely "travel bookers." That definition understated the huge responsibility they carried managing a multimillion-dollar line in the campaign budget, the third largest area of spending. If we lost control of that line item in the final weeks, it would throw the whole campaign into a crisis. I urged them to view themselves not as others had defined them but as what they really were—assistant chief financial officers.

This was just one of many groups that was making a much bigger contribution than their label implied. They needed to be bigger than their job titles or routine tasks. They had to see themselves as leaders, I told them. Once, a staffer challenged me, arguing that it was impossible for everyone to be leaders. I understood what she meant. We all played a position. Not every person could lead in the way that our candidate, campaign manager, or the department heads did. That would result in chaos. But, as I explained to that staffer, there was no excuse for any position in the campaign to be occupied by a non-leader. Every person in the organization mattered, and we were missing an opportunity if we put someone in a role who wasn't prepared to use it to assert their leadership.

Just like on the campaign, in the new game, where old hierarchies and silos are giving way to fluid, open, integrated teams of teams, everyone must be a full contributor; no one can be passive. In fact, to be able to play at all, everyone in the game needs to see themselves as a leader and a changemaker. They must give themselves that permission and they must define themselves as such.

Breaking the Box

Changemakers step into their BIGness. They overcome forces that might otherwise keep us small. That's what North Carolina mom Molly Barker did in 1996, when she took 13 preteen girls for a run. Concerned about the unhealthy messages and stereotypes young women are continually subjected to, Molly made it her personal mission to empower them to resist what she called *the girl box*. It's a phrase she coined to describe an imaginary place many girls go around middle school, where they begin to conform to a series of predefined cultural and social stereotypes that limit their life choices and opportunities. An optimist with an energetic persona, *the girl box* is one of the few things Molly speaks about with real disdain. In fact, she often just calls it *that box*.

Molly told me that she had battled those same oppressive forces of insecurity and self-doubt when she was a teenager. She knew all too well how debilitating it felt to get stuffed into that box. Running had helped her, and that was the seed of Molly's idea for a program to support the emotional and physical health of young women. She would help them train for a 5k run as a way to build confidence, while also offering interactive lessons that would promote camaraderie and reflection.

She called it Girls on the Run, and the idea quickly took off. She started with 13 girls in 1996, with registration doubling the following year, then tripling to 75 the next. In 2000, Girls on the Run was formally launched as an organization. When I met Molly in 2012, Girls on the Run had already served a quarter-million girls between the ages of 8 and 13 in all 50 states, the District of Columbia, and Canada.

I got to know Molly because one of my new Ashoka colleagues, Lennon Flowers, had invited me to join the two of them for a road trip across California to showcase the work of other social entrepreneurs. Lennon, like Molly, was also from North Carolina, but had recently relocated to Los Angeles. For me, the trip doubled as a homecoming, since I had been born and spent part of my childhood in Southern California.

We were an unlikely trio, zipping around California in search of changemakers. Molly was an uber-fit triathlon athlete with an outgoing personality, punctuated by her obvious North Carolinian accent. She had a laid-back manner that made her easy to engage. She was about my age, but we were very different. She had grown children, while I was still in the sleep-deprivation stage with my little ones. She had grown up on the other side of the country from me, and I may have made it all the way through college without having ever before met anyone from North Carolina. It seemed like she'd grown up in another world from mine.

Lennon, our host and driver, was an energetic Millennial with a brilliant smile and an incredibly fast mind. This made her an excellent conversationalist, and she did everything at a lightning pace. She and Molly got along so famously that I wondered if they had met before.

From my introvert's perch in the backseat, I listened to Molly and Lennon's conversation. But as extroverts, they couldn't just let me listen; they insisted on drawing me in. Molly came from a political family, so she was constantly asking about my Obama history. As she drew me out, I started to ask as many questions about her journey as a social entrepreneur, and the story behind her having successfully built and scaled her organization. For Molly, it began with her first pair of running shoes.

"Those shoes represented freedom—your hair blowing in the wind and time to be alone with who you really were, that the world seemed to try to steal," she said. "There is just nothing more soul-crushing than not being who you are, because you can't be the force you are meant to be in the world." I could feel her indignation and the loss she was describing. "It really is just soul-crushing," she added.

She spoke of her mother, a proper Southern woman who had lived according to the expectations for women in the South in the 1970s. Then, at about age 50, she suddenly transformed into the woman Molly said she was meant to be. "My mom took up running and began doing yoga and all these crazy things."

But there was a backstory to this change. "Mom was a blackout drunk," Molly said in her always-energetic way. Molly's mother had been deep in the throes of alcoholism when Molly was in third and fourth grade. She would often drop Molly off for activities and then forget all about her. "One time, I had to wait in the choir room at church after choir practice until my dad picked me up hours later."

Molly's dad was a prominent politician, and things came to a head when her mother failed to show up for a very public 50th birthday party she herself had planned for him. "True story," Molly informed me. "And it was the last straw."

With her mother passed out upstairs, 9-year-old Molly was thrust into the role of hostess. She still remembers the fear she felt that night. As the only child still living at home, she had always been regarded as the perfect kid from the perfect family. Now, the lid was certain to be blown off of that charade, and Molly was terrified of the fallout. "There was no hiding it anymore," she said.

Her mother recovered, and the transformation was remarkable. "My mom completely turned her life around and it was truly an inspiration to witness," Molly said. "She completely redefined herself. Totally anew—or maybe it was more like she had revealed what she was all along."

Molly laughed as she described her mom going for a jog in her apron. "She was five-foot-eight, but her hair made her look six-foot-three."

In the 1970s in North Carolina, a 50-year-old woman going for a run would have been viewed as odd, but that didn't stop her. "She would go out in the early morning hours for her runs to avoid being spotted by any neighbors," Molly recalled. "She returned so clearly happy with who she was, while here I was, weighed down with all the stuff that seemed to come with being a young teenage woman."

Molly became so enamored with this new version of her mom that she wanted her friends in seventh grade to hang out with her. "She was the best and coolest mom of them all."

It was a lovely story, but as I got to know Molly better, I learned that there was more to it. Four years into her mother's sobriety, when Molly was a teenager, she started drinking herself. She said that being from a middle-class family and going to a private school, where alcohol was a big part of the culture, she felt the weight of who the world wanted her to be, and she just didn't conform to its expectations.

"First, I had my DNA working against me, and at that same time, I was preoccupied with trying to fit in with my wealthier peers," she explained. "When I drank, instead of being true to who I was, I could be the pretty, popular girl—the precocious, sexy girl."

Nearly two decades later, at age 32, Molly called her sister. It was a cry for help. She was in danger of losing herself to addiction and had fallen into despair. Her sister helped her through that pivotal moment, and then two things ultimately helped her get her life back. First, she followed the path set by her mother, who had taken her on her first run when she was 14 years old. Second, she found joy three years after her recovery when she helped those 13 young women realize their power and build up their self-confidence.

Molly believes that the bond she re-forged with her mother when she was in middle school ultimately saved her life. Offering young girls a chance to form a positive bond with an adult woman who knew something about breaking out of *that box* became the impetus for Molly's program.

"So, what do these girls do when they join your program?" I asked, thinking she'd talk about setting training goals and hitting running milestones.

"We talk. We share. We commune together and discover our feelings together," Molly answered. She explained how the program devised games and activities to help the girls open up about their feelings. During each run, the girls reflect on a topic, and then, afterward, they form a circle and share their insights. "Empathy, teamwork, friendship, inclusion... *exclusion*," she said, with extra emphasis on that last word. "These are some of the things we reflect on."

It started as a program for third- and fourth-grade girls. Molly believed that was the right time because it was just before middle school, when girls are prone to breaking up with *who they are* to become *who society says they should be*. She suspected that having an adult champion at a time when girls are moving from concrete thinking to abstract thinking could go a long way toward helping them develop the self-esteem, resilience, and decision-making skills they needed in life.

I asked how she had selected the first cohort of girls. "They picked me," she confessed. She put up a flyer aimed at her target audience at a local school and added a separate message for parents on the back. "There was nothing like this out there where you had a sports program woven into a curriculum—or maybe it was the other way around," she said.

I thought her idea for delivering a separate message to parents was clever, and I asked her if there had been resistance to a stranger outside the school system offering girls a mentoring program like this. "I definitely stirred curiosity," Molly answered. "Parents were calling me and wanting to know what this Girls-on-the-Run thing was all about." She still recalls one mother's objection: "It sounds like you get in my daughter's brain—her thinking."

"No, I'm actually just creating the space for *her* to do that," Molly replied.

Thirteen girls signed up at first, and every meeting was uplifting and inspirational. "I realized that I fell in love with them as much as they fell in love with me," she said.

As the program grew, Molly knew she needed help. "So, as all things with a pure intent," she said, "the perfectly right women began to show up."

With the benefit of hindsight, Molly can now see that while she set out to make a meaningful impact on those girls, they also made a meaningful impact on her. "I'd missed my third and fourth grades, and this was my chance for a redo," she said. Her mother's blackout years had been so traumatic that Molly had actually blocked them out herself. "It didn't click for me until later that the right age group for this program included the same years of my own life that I needed to redo."

So they all ran together. They learned and shared. Molly said that they ran at the same school and on the same track that she had run on as a girl. "Isn't that crazy?" she exclaimed.

When Molly reflects on what motivated her mother's transformation, or what re-forged their mother-daughter relationship, or what enabled the breakthroughs that occurred between her and the girls she's coached, self-definition is at the heart. She sees the commitment each made to be their most authentic, best selves. She also sees the opportunity that was offered to others to share their own vulnerability and contribute to each other's journeys.

"When women can avoid the trap of *that box*," Molly added, "when we can tune out the noise and truly own and embrace our own unique narratives—then we can genuinely appreciate who we really are and bring ourselves more fully into the world. And believe me, that is a great thing for the world." Her Southern accent got a little thicker as she spoke, and she ended with a giggle.

A negative frame like "the girl box" can box you in, or it can set you free to do powerful, wonderful things. Our deepest desire is to belong, Molly says, and her program aims to give young women the tools they need to step into the world authentically, despite the way others may define them. "It is both exhilarating and terrifying," she says, "like that first 5k run."

That first run with those 13 girls has since grown into a national movement giving young women the chance to find their own footing in life, equipping them to challenge societal frames that try to tell them who they can and can't be. Through this program, today, two million women have defined themselves, as Molly says, outside the girl box, committed to living happily and in harmony with themselves.

Girls on the Run is also the story of how changemaking works. One mother's example, one woman's initiative, 13 brave girls making a bet on themselves, and a small community of adults combining to spark a generational shift toward positive self-definition.

"It's never been about what I was running from," Molly said. "It was always about what we were running to."

Claim Your Frame

"To define a person by their challenge is the definition of stigmatizing them," Trabian Shorters says. "When you view people through the dirty lenses of stigma, you are subconsciously primed to avoid them, control them, or even kill them."

Trabian is the founder of BMe Community, an organization of over 400 Black leaders serving over 2 million families and teaching several thousand philanthropic and communications professionals who seek to define people by their aspirations and contributions, rather than by their challenges. Just as Molly set out to help young women resist the crushing forces pushing them into society's girl box, Trabian wanted to offer a much more accurate narrative of African American men than the antebellum characterizations and stereotypes that we still cling to today.

BMe started out by selecting African American men who were models in their communities and funding initiatives they were passionate about. Those very passions often punctured embedded negative stereotypes because they showed Black men valued the same things as other people: youth development, education, economic opportunity, public safety, and the environment.

But to see that truth, we have to be able to see through the stories we carry in our hearts and minds. More than any other demographic group in the United States, Trabian says, Black men are defined negatively. They are viewed through the negative lens of their imagined deficits, rather than what is known about their aspirations and contributions. It can be a deeply unconscious bias, even in those of us who consciously condemn racism.

As Trabian's organization matured, it extended its focus to tell the story of the Black community broadly. "It's time for a new true story about Black people in this country," he said. "Black people have *always* been assets to this nation. We literally arrived here as assets. We are the foundation of the nation's immeasurable wealth over centuries and have championed liberty and justice *for all* even more than the founding fathers. That's the bold truth that the nation must reconcile."

I first met Trabian around 2015, and I later became more directly acquainted with his work when I attended a workshop he conducted for a predominantly white audience. "Raise your hand if you have heard the story that in some cities, the dropout rate for Black kids hits 50 percent?" The hands shot up. "How about if you have heard Black poverty is higher than the national average? Now, how about if you have heard that Black unemployment is higher than the national average?" Again and again, virtually all hands went up in the air.

Then, he asked who among us knew how many Black males have college degrees or created businesses or are millionaires. No hands were raised.

"How can you tell our story if you don't know it?" Trabian asked. "Who do you really think that we are, when you can only tell the story of our deficits and not our assets? When you can only seek to fix us, rather than build with us?" This is a point he makes with predominantly Black audiences, as well.

Next, Trabian asked us to pair off and shift our chairs around so that we could look directly at one another with nothing between us. "I want you to take 10 seconds right now to try to notice everything you can about what is wrong about that person in front of you." That prompted nervous laughter. Murmurs rolled across the room. "No, no, don't *tell* them your answer!" he joked.

With this exercise, Trabian was pointing to the great difficulty and discomfort of trying to define your truth when others have already defined you negatively. "Human beings are actually hardwired to see what we look for," he said, adding that cognitive psychologists have proven that this is a universal condition. "The narratives we carry with us—the stereotypes—tell us what to look for."

Trabian has the numbers on his side when it comes to telling a new true story about Black people in America. When I met him, 17 percent of African Americans were enlisted in the military, higher than their share of the US population (13 percent).[1] The most recent census would show 2.58 million Black-owned business generating $150 billion annually and employing 3.56 million people.[2] From 2002–2007, Black-owned businesses increased by 60 percent to 1.9 million, more than triple the national growth rate,[3] and African Americans also comprised eight percent of all millionaires.[4]

Current data is also telling. The number of Black-women-owned firms has risen by 164 percent since 2007, making this the fastest-growing block of entrepreneurs of any racial group.[5] When it comes to charitable giving, Black families have contributed the largest proportion of their wealth relative to all racial or ethnic groups since 2010,[6] with nearly two-thirds of Black households giving to charitable causes and organizations totaling $11 billion annually.[7] And when discussing fatherhood, Trabian points to CDC data that show African American dads are the most likely ethnic cohort to engage in such activities as eating, bathing, diapering, and playing with their children.[8]

African Americans are patriotic, enterprising, generous, and family-minded—that *is* the true story.

Trabian's insights, which were gained from his early work with African American men, led him to pioneer "asset-framing" as a fundamental way to overcome negative stigmas and the litany of heinous consequences that arise from them. He based his technique on the discoveries of numerous cognitive and social psychologists, including Nobel Laureate Daniel Kahneman—and any of us can use his technique to reframe and overcome negative definitions.

First, Trabian says, we can begin by defining ourselves (and others) by our aspirations and contributions, not our deficits. You don't need to hide your negative traits, and in fact, you shouldn't. Neither should you let people define you by your challenges.

Next, notice and gather the evidence that supports your new asset-framing narrative. Trabian has three or four go-to statistics that he religiously points to as a way to reinforce Black people as assets to our communities. Since the data he quotes comes from credible sources, people take it more seriously than data cherry-picked from a biased source.

Third, find allies and champions who agree with your new narrative, and who can help fortify it—those who can testify to your abilities and corroborate what you can do. Seek out people who *want* to see the good in others as a starting point for supporting our own self-definitions. And as with any kind of change, Trabian suggests that your likelihood of actually making a change will dramatically increase when you are part of a community of people who reinforce it. That's what BMe is.

We can all define ourselves anew by being truly conscious of how others want to be known and treated. That includes seeing and appreciating each other for our differences. Understanding how we complement and add value to each other should be part of how we define ourselves.

"Here's the thing, Henry," he said, "when you are color blind, for example, you don't see differences. People want to be seen. We all want to be seen for who we are. And if you can't see Black people—if you can't see our differences—then you see the world through a lens of all things as an extension of you, which means you relate all experiences to who *you* are. Then, when someone speaks out about police brutality, your response is, 'That hasn't been my experience.' So, you deny another person's reality just because you are blind to all things that are not you."

"It's not enough to be color blind," Trabian added. "Being blind is not the solution to seeing better. We all need to see and value each other. When you live blind, you can't see the race-conscious reality."

Trabian underscores this last point by highlighting a largely overlooked contribution by Black people that has surfaced during the coronavirus pandemic. "We see that Black people's jobs are disproportionately deemed as 'essential,' which means they had to keep working while others 'sheltered in place,'" Trabian told me. "It also means that the reason that most Americans were *able* to shelter in place is *because* Black people, among others of course, made that possible by providing those essential services."

Trabian sees a way for each of us to define ourselves uniquely, and for all of us to come together around a powerful shared narrative. "In democracies, the people are taught to aspire toward freedom, fairness, and equality," he said. "Since that is the common thread in our individual identities, a constructive pathway opens up when we're reminded that's a vital part of our identity and that *all* members of the society want these things and are willing to work for them. But some are being denied them."

In January 2020, months before global protests erupted over police violence against Black people in America, BMe Community launched their "Live. Own. Vote. Excel. (L.O.V.E.)" campaign, naming Black peoples' core aspirations as identified by hundreds of Black leaders around the country. The campaign is based on the idea that if you believe Black people should be free to live, own, vote and excel, this is the moment in history to make clear where you stand on this question of democracy. "By revealing that this agenda for Black L.O.V.E. clearly arises from our democratic identity," Trabian said, "the campaign lets us recognize that choosing to be pro-Black is choosing to be pro-democracy."

Trabian says that when it comes to reframing harmful narratives, it's more important to connect than to convince. That's why BMe actively works with people in other demographics who need asset-framing for themselves. BMe Community has advised the Anti-Defamation League in the creation of their Civil Society Fellowship, the Aspen Institute in the creation of their Weave the Social Fabric Project, and Encore Public Voices Fellowship in the creation of its fellowship. Once someone sees the value in asset-framing themselves, Trabian's experience is they are then more capable of breaking out of similar stereotypes about others—and in his work, that's African Americans.

To one degree or another, whether we are Black or white, male or female, we all face headwinds. We all encounter forces that would define us unfairly and make us feel small or irrelevant. These forces can undermine our ability to embrace our authentic selves, cause us great internal conflict, and limit what we do in the world. But as Trabian and Molly demonstrate, we can fight those forces and overcome them. We can change the narrative for ourselves and for others.

"We must tell whole stories of people, *beginning* with appreciating them and their contributions," Trabian says, "and ending with removing the injustices that depreciate them."

Maternity as a Master's

Riccarda Zezza remembers the defining moment. "He dismissed the leadership team from our meeting and said he wanted a word with me," said the former Italian executive, recalling the day her CEO shamed her openly for her upcoming maternity leave. "Then, when the room was cleared, he began his temper tantrum. He literally took a pencil and threw it full-force against the wall."

Motherhood is a universally positive narrative—except when it isn't. It's unfairly perceived as a liability in the workplace, and those perceptions pushed Riccarda's career noticeably off track. She had a successful tenure in several major companies. She also twice experienced discrimination for taking maternity leave. The first time she was a rising star in her company, only to return from her legally ensured leave to a demotion. Soon after, she was transferred to another department. She left that company only to relive the experience at her job as an executive three years later, after the birth of her second child.

In response, Riccarda did what changemakers do. She reframed the narrative and used it to inspire far-reaching change. Riccarda started an organization called MAAM, short for "Maternity as a Master's," which reframes the business world's blinkered view of maternity, defining it instead as a time of valuable personal and professional development.

I met Riccarda in her hometown of Milan, Italy, where we worked together to engage companies in the region. She told me that the birth of a child poses a terrible dilemma for a woman's career. She saw firsthand how women were discouraged from taking time off from work for maternity leave. Those who did were viewed negatively, as less committed and more prone to distraction. When (and if) they returned to work, they were marginalized, given less responsibility, and passed over for promotion. That's baseless and unfair, and it's also a blatant double standard, since employees in Italy are often encouraged to take time off to pursue master's degrees and other professional development. When they return, it is often to a promotion.

To change that, Riccarda did something similar to Trabian's asset-framing. She considered how the experience of motherhood could be an asset in business. She understood the true story—that devotion to one's children need not be in conflict with one's career. In fact, it could actually make women better employees and executives. With that insight, Riccarda built Maternity as a Master's, to help women frame their maternity leave as a form of professional development and to encourage companies to credit them for completing it. It structures the maternity leave experience as a seven-part master's degree program focusing on such elements as: empathy, complexity management, and relationship development. Riccarda also founded *Piano* C (or "Plan C" in English), a network of co-working spaces where women could bring their children and work together to create new projects.

Riccarda's discoveries helped her hone a methodology for learning from life's various circumstances, and that now serves as the foundation for her new learning method, called Life-Based Learning. This has allowed her to expand her program offerings to fathers and other caregivers, and her programs are now utilized by 70 firms with users in 23 countries. Riccarda will soon be providing life-based professional education products that extend beyond learning from child-rearing.

The timing of my meeting with Riccarda was fortuitous, as my wife, Sine, was just returning to the workforce after nearly a decade away. Sine had been very intentional about embracing the opportunities of motherhood, and she chose to stay home until our second child had turned eight. It was the right decision for us, but it had long-lasting implications for our household finances. Attitudes in the US workplace toward that kind of extended family leave were not in her favor. Now that she was ready to go back to work, she faced headwinds of her own. Sine had left her last job in 2007, and her field of communications had transitioned from print to digital in the interim. She had to overcome the inevitable perception that sitting out those years at home, she was now out of touch in a new work environment.

From a busy *Piano* C space, Riccarda offered me ideas on how to reframe the narrative so that it worked in Sine's favor. "Let's start with her story," she said. "People see her as a woman spending recreational time at home with her children, but I see a woman who understands risk management. She's had to keep her kids from running into the street or from burning their hands on the stove. Your wife has had to learn how to explain complicated things in a way that young children can understand. I see a woman who knows how to handle an emergency—a crisis—and how to creatively engage temperamental clients." Riccarda was redefining Sine's experience in a way that was powerful, rather than a deficit. "Your wife brings authenticity and a sense of perspective to the workplace that she can own, and she can make it her advantage in any interview."

I shared Riccarda's take with Sine over dinner, since she was preparing for a second interview at a local university for a communications director position. We'd also engaged our boys in the conversation, and 9-year-old Dante chimed in, "Just be fun, Mom. Grown-ups are boring." He had apparently listened in on too many of my work calls.

Sine brought Dante's and Riccarda's advice to her interview. When asked what she knew about working with new technology and social media, she offered evidence of a video short she had co-created with the kids on her phone. Dante and Zane had acted out a comedy sketch of a day in the life of characters from the Transformers movies. Throughout the interview, Sine framed her parenting experience as a workplace advantage. Her odds of beating the competition and landing the job when she had no inside track and a notable experience gap were long. But she got it anyway. "We thought you'd be fun to work with," one of her new colleagues later told her.

With Self-Definition Comes Self-Permission

Define thyself lest you be defined is still my favorite leadership principle. It was my golden rule on the campaign trail, it's the true north on the new leadership compass, and it's essential for the emerging everyone-a-changemaker world, where not just bosses, not just social entrepreneurs, but all of us must learn to see ourselves as leaders. Whether you are running for office or are one of Molly's Girls on the Run, claiming your frame is the first step to stepping into your BIGness.

This flies in the face of what we have historically been taught. Most of us have been groomed to stay small and narrowly defined—to hone a skill, get into a lane, and wait for direction. That's the playbook that has been handed down for generations. But it no longer applies. Defining—and redefining—oneself is a basic part of the mindset of highly effective changemakers. With self-definition comes self-permission to break with precedent, to break out of boxes and make changes. Engaging the complex problems and opportunities that define today's world will require tearing down old walls, breaking old silos, and bringing people together in new forms of collaboration. These are gutsy things to do, and we all need to give ourselves permission to do them.

CHAPTER SEVEN

Tear Down Walls

SILO-BUSTING AND WALL-BREAKING are requisite leadership skills in the new game. When barriers fall between two or more sides that wouldn't otherwise connect, true innovation happens.

In the old game, teamwork was about recruiting like-minded people with specific skillsets. That left many shut out and sidelined, with no way to join and contribute. The old way of working was designed for the convenience of those lucky few who found their place in the linear hierarchy. The goal was maximizing efficiency through specialization, and the culture was about staying within one's comfort zone by working on a homogenous team with people who shared the same basic pedigree and biography—going to a good school, getting a special skill, and applying it repeatedly alongside others doing similar things for their whole career.

If the old game was one of exclusion, the new game is one of radical inclusion. It's now about getting out of one's comfort zone, working in new ways with people who are quite different, and welcoming the tensions, innovations, and disruptions that come with radical inclusion. The new way of working values and leverages the contributions of everyone in a wide, inclusive circle. As change accelerates omnidirectionally, without radical inclusion and the challenges that come with it, no enterprise can succeed for long.

Changemakers know this. We are naturally inclusive, and natural enemies of walls and silos. When Bobby Kennedy famously said (quoting George Bernard Shaw), "Some men see things as they are, and ask why? I dream of things that never were, and ask why not?" he was arguing for breaking down social barriers and practicing radical inclusion. For change-makers, the main barrier that needs knocking down is the one between what is and what can be. Often, the barriers are our own. Bill Drayton likes to say the first walls we must tear down are the ones in our own heads.

Nelson Del Rio, a distinguished attorney and serial entrepreneur who has been highly effective at silo-busting and systems change across sectors, offered his own twist on that idea. In a conversation we had about the new leadership skills needed for today's world, I mentioned to him that changemakers are trained at seeing walls—whether physical or in our minds—and then actively working to tear down those walls. His eyes caught fire as he shot back, "I see all the walls you put around you. There are none around me."

Walls No More

There are no walls around Ana Bella Estevez—not anymore. She has a sunny disposition, a warm heart, and an enterprising mind. She also knows what it's like to be hemmed in by walls and what it is like to break out of them. When I met her, she freely shared her story of escaping from her abuser in her home in Spain and then going on to build a global movement to enable other abused women to break out of their confine-ment and into freedom.

For Ana Bella, the first walls she had to break down were inside her own head. She had to unlearn the norms she had internalized that per-petuated abuse. She also had to overcome the fear she harbored of liv-ing on her own and of providing for herself and her children. Despite having been abused by her husband for many years, she had difficulty recognizing this fact because she had lived with some form of abuse since childhood. Her personal account paints a stark picture of living under the shadow of domestic violence.

Ana Bella grew up in Spain, and she recalls watching her father apply makeup to hide the visible injuries that her mother had left on his face following violent episodes. She remembers late nights when her father would stare out the front window after her mother left to spend long hours out on the town. As a girl, she sometimes ventured out to the bars where her mother drank in an effort to bring her back home. When she was 11, her father finally left. Later, Ana Bella's mother tied her and her sister to their beds during the night to prevent them from going in search of her when she went out drinking.

Like most abused children, Ana Bella thought this was normal. She only realized how unnatural it was after she left her own husband. She was 29 years old, 11 years into her marriage, and raising four kids when she made that brave decision.

Ana Bella recounted the night her husband brought her a document that he wanted her to sign, promising she would never divorce him. His request was made while using force against her. Ana Bella said she would not agree as long as he continued hitting her. "He told me, there is no way you will ever get divorced from me, our marriage is love or death," and the abuse continued. "I was on my knees praying to the Good Father because I thought he will kill me," she said. As she prayed, her husband threatened: "Pray, pray, you will need to pray because this argument is going to be won by the one who stays alive."

That night, Ana Bella succumbed to his demands, signed the paper, and suffered more abuse. She did get the strength to eventually leave him, however, from her youngest child, a 9-month-old, who had been crying in the next room the whole time.

Later, she called a domestic abuse hotline to inquire if she could still get a divorce after having signed the paper her husband had brought. She was referred to an organization that she could visit in person for further support, but Ana Bella felt that she could not go in person.

"Do you have the key to your house?" the hotline worker asked. Ana Bella said that she did. "Do you have a car?" Yes, she had a car. "Then why can't you go?"

Ana Bella replied that she couldn't go somewhere alone without her husband or without at least telling him where she was going. "Twenty-nine years old, and that was my answer," she said. "So my jail was a mental jail. I had the keys to my house, but I knew I couldn't get out without his permission."

Eventually—though not immediately—Ana Bella did follow the

referral she had gotten from the abuse hotline and showed up without an appointment. When asked if she was subjected to abuse, she said no. Then she was asked a series of questions—whether she could use her own money without her husband's permission, whether she was hit or had things thrown at her, whether she was subjected to forced sex and insults. She said yes to all of them. The worker hugged her. It was the first time that she had been embraced by an adult in a caring way in a very long time.

That night, she picked up her four kids and went to the police. She avoided going to the station in her small town because her husband was well known and respected in the community, and he was friendly with local law enforcement there. She felt certain she wouldn't be believed or supported, and instead drove to Seville. At the station, Ana Bella was given a piece of paper and told to write down everything that had happened to her in the course of her 11-year marriage. "They gave me a piece of paper, and at the end, I wrote five hundred papers, because in 11 years, it was many, many things," she said.

Having broken out of the walls of her home, Ana Bella quickly encountered more walls that were put up by society. In her small Spanish community—and in many places around the world—it was a daunting prospect for a woman to live on her own after leaving her husband because it is common to attach the stigma of domestic abuse to the victim, not the perpetrator. This problem is not unique to Spain. For example, forty percent of Mexican women who leave an abusive relationship end up returning to the home of their abuser, she says. And in the US, where one in three women have been physically harmed by an intimate partner, only half of women in abusive relationships leave.[1] This stigma creates barriers to finding work and housing and meeting other basic needs.

Through her marriage, Ana Bella had risen from poverty to owning an art gallery with her husband, and they found financial success. They sold artwork to wealthy clients and celebrities, such as musicians Prince and Rod Stewart. "I had Porsches and Rolls-Royces," she said. They earned a lot of money, but Ana Bella's husband controlled it all. When she escaped, she had nothing. "Just my 29 years of abuses and four kids," she said. She had always worked with him, so she didn't have any career experience of her own. Ana Bella had no university degree, because he refused to let her pursue one.

She was penniless and lived in a shelter. She didn't have a car. She could have gone to live with her mother, but she was an alcoholic and lived in a bad neighborhood. Ana Bella worried that moving in with her mother would undermine her case in her child custody battle against her husband, who was still well-off financially.

Ana Bella was able to qualify for a certificate attesting that she was a victim of domestic violence. It entitled her to a government subsidy of €300 a month (this was in 2002; today, the subsidy is worth €426 a month, which is the equivalent of $507). It was nowhere near enough to support herself and four kids. As she stared at the certificate, remembering everything that had happened to her—the beatings, the insults, the nights without sleep, the suffering, and the rapes—it sank in that her 29 years amounted to victimhood. That's what the certificate officially declared.

In her head, a wall came crashing down. "I was crying, and I discovered that if I passed through all of this, I was not a victim, like this paper says," she said. "I was a survivor."

Ana Bella refused the subsidy and enrolled in a different government program for victims of domestic violence. "It was a workshop to learn how to clean," she explained, "how to become a cleaning lady." She lasted one day in that program. She wouldn't accept that her choices were limited to poverty or cleaning houses and hotels. She wanted to learn business or languages.

Ana Bella eventually got a job selling cars. Then, she sold cell phones. She continued to refuse to accept the "victim" label, and she even came to recognize how her experience gave her some tools for success.

"If we overcome abuse, it is because we are very strong women," she told me. "Abused women can deal with frustration. We can work under pressure. We reinvent ourselves every day to go on. And we are very perseverant. We are success-oriented because we want our marriage to work, so we never give up. We know how to deal with the different tempers of our bosses and clients. We are very tolerant, and we overcome failures very fast. These are keys that we use to resist and overcome abuse."

As harrowing as her experience was, Ana Bella was able to see that the qualities that arose from it could be brought forward proudly in the workplace. "I love a challenge, Henry," she said, in her thick Spanish accent. "I know I can succeed."

That positive self-definition wrested from a dehumanizing experience was the launching point of the Fundación Ana Bella, the organization she founded to help abused women regain their self-confidence so that they could begin the process of separating from their abusers. She started by telling her story in the media. Her first few appearances generated over a thousand calls, and she spent a year answering them all. The women who reached out to her included doctors, a television journalist, and other "very important women." There was a policewoman, abused at home even as she was working to fight crime on the street, and a psychologist from Cuba. Ana Bella had been shocked that a psychologist even *could* be abused.

The psychologist became the first woman the foundation helped. She had refused to go to the police, which meant that she couldn't take refuge in a government shelter. So Ana Bella invited her into her home for safety.

Together, they began a program to set up housing for women who were afraid to go to the police. They enlisted the help of diverse stakeholders across the community and built a team of teams that could make their ambition a reality. Ana Bella was becoming skilled at tearing down all kinds of walls and bringing together people who were on the other side of those walls. They tore down the walls that separated them from capital, working with bankers and negotiating agreements to turn foreclosed homes into shelters for women transitioning out of abuse. They worked with financial institutions to acquire land. They tore down the walls that closed them off from society, enlisting members of the community to work together to build additional housing for survivors of domestic violence. Wherever Ana Bella tore down a wall, there were new teams on the other side of it to join her effort.

Breaking Out of the Shadows and into the Light

Just as the foundation's first housing for survivors of domestic violence became available, Ana Bella learned from a teacher at her child's school that a woman from Poland was being held in a basement without water, a toilet, or electricity by her domestic partner, despite being five months pregnant. Elsa (whose name has been changed to protect her privacy) was a foreigner in Spain. She had no friends or support, and being pregnant compounded the problems of leaving her abuser, finding work, and supporting herself and her baby. The two women rescued Elsa and placed her in the first house in their new system. It was Ana Bella's deep desire to give Elsa the tools and resources to be a survivor and not a victim.

"I was invited to an event where a foundation was giving out monetary awards," she told me. "Big NGOs were there for causes like cancer."

With all the responsibilities she was juggling at the time, Ana Bella didn't plan to go, but she was finally cajoled into it by one of the organizers. As the awards were being announced, she casually said to a volunteer sitting next to her that if she ever won such an award, she would use it to start a business and offer a job to Elsa. "I was saying that, and suddenly, there is an announcement coming over the speaker—'Ana Bella Foundation, you have the award for social inclusion!'"

Telling the story now, years later, she sounded just as surprised as I could tell she was on that day. The award was €25,000. At the time, Ana Bella was balancing her own work, her family, and the launch of the Ana Bella Foundation. She was paying rent on the transitional houses for the women her foundation served. It would have been easy—and logical—to use the money to help with any one of those things. But Ana Bella didn't. "I used it to start a business to get a job for Elsa," she told me, laughing with delight.

The purpose of this new venture was to create jobs for survivors of domestic violence. The first contract they were able to get was cleaning buses at night. "Elsa had her baby and then started cleaning the buses," Ana Bella said.

But she felt like the work they were attracting was work for "victims."

It kept the women who did it in the shadows, and Ana Bella wanted them to be visible. She tried several different ventures, including a shop that sold organic produce and healthy food. The business struggled. One day, Ana Bella was asked if she could offer catering services using the fair-trade coffee products they sold. That put her workers, all survivors of domestic abuse, in front of the public, and that's when another wall fell.

"These were visible jobs, where people could see we were effective workers and not victims," she explained. The women were proud, and they wore T-shirts that read, *Survivor*. The first day of the catered event, following their coffee service, the women got a round of applause. "When does a victim receive an applause?" she asked me rhetorically. The recognition was important. It made the women feel like they were contributing to society.

That moment caused a significant realization for Ana Bella. "I didn't want to run a catering business," she said. "And I already had my idea."

Ana Bella had found a new wall to tear down—the wall that separated survivors of abuse from visible public roles. She closed the food shop and formed the Ana Bella Social School for Women's Empowerment, with the objective of training women to be public ambassadors for company brands and to help them develop skills that could serve them in public facing jobs. She called them "brand ambassadors."

In 2017, five years after I first met Ana Bella, I was again with her in Seville, Spain. She asked me to meet her at a grocery store, of all places, where she escorted me to the dairy aisle. There I was introduced to a lovely, vibrant "brand ambassador" at a display for Danone, a European multinational food products company. Rosalia was probably in her 50s and not an employee of the store, though she looked like she could have been. In the brilliant light of the dairy aisle, dressed in product-branded clothes and a blue apron, she enthusiastically greeted customers and offered to answer consumer questions about Danone products. I noticed her big smile and how tall she stood. Ana Bella was clearly enamored with Rosalia. "Look at how beautiful and alive she is," she said. And it was true.

"When she came to us, Rosalia was coy, and she was worried about her bruises," Ana Bella said. "Women like her usually are given jobs in the dark or in places where you don't see other people—they are maids,

house cleaners, hidden away." But Rosalia benefited from the partnership and program Ana Bella had co-created with Danone to help women
transitioning from abuse to build their confidence by developing their
presentation and customer-relations skills. "Our survivor women stand
in the light, and they come face-to-face with other people," she said, her
own face brightening as she spoke. "They get skills, like how to present,
and they wear the uniforms of important companies. You can see they
stand tall and proud."

I watched Rosalia again with this in mind. I saw that she not only
represented her products effectively, but she also worked with the store's
staff to help customers with other needs. She was skilled and flexible in
relating to customers, Danone representatives, and store employees alike.
She was working confidently in a team-of-teams environment.

"They will leave these jobs because they get recruited," Ana Bella
said. That's another benefit of the job—demonstrating their skills to
new contacts. "We just had a woman who was an ambassador only two
months who was recruited to a major advertising company."

Today, the brand-ambassador program that Ana Bella began as a
partnership with Danone has been extended to more than 80 companies. "We look for a business need, and we offer a social solution that pro-
vokes a paradigm shift," she explained. "It is a co-created program with
the company, where our women are positioned at the end of the value
chain. They are the image of the company, in front of the client—one of
the most valuable places in the value chain."

Ana Bella continues to expand her network of survivors across the
globe, helping women tear down the walls that enclose and separate
them. She says an estimated 1.2 billion women suffer abuse worldwide,
and that the best antidote to domestic violence is to bring women who
survive it out of the shadows and into the light. It's an idea that she believes
spreads in much the same way transformative ideas always have—from
one empowered person to another, one changemaker at a time. "But
there are more and more of us every day on the task," she added. Each
one of the thousands of survivors in her network get the training and
tools to make valuable, visible contributions in their communities. They
are empowered to help others.

"What we do is transform the suffering into expertise and empathy to support others," she explained. "They are contributors to social and economic progress in their local communities. So, women, instead of being victims, become changemakers."

The Courage to Jump In

Expertise has a shelf life, and in a world of rapid, accelerating, omnidirectional change, no one can claim to be an expert for very long. In the new game, perspective is more valuable than conventional expertise. Everyone must be respected for who they are and the points of view they bring. Diverse perspectives and a 360-degree view is what keeps teams nimble, creative, and ahead of the curve. But we're sometimes hesitant to form this new sort of team because we're still attached to the old way of working.

Dr. Javier Solana knows about this challenge because he has experience tearing down walls and bringing people together—literally. Dr. Solana is a Spanish diplomat who served as the Secretary-General of the Council of the European Union for more than a decade, beginning in 1999, and as the Secretary General of NATO before that. His tenure at NATO, which ran from 1995 to 1999, came during a time of great change in Europe and, hence, the world. The Berlin Wall began to come down in 1989, East and West Germany were reunited into one nation in 1990, and the Soviet Union collapsed in 1991. All of these developments generated great excitement, as well as great uneasiness. Western European leaders were confronting difficult questions, including how to approach relations with countries that had once been under Soviet influence. The old geopolitical map had changed, new relationships were being formed, and old ones were fracturing.

I asked Dr. Solana for his advice on bringing people together during times of change, especially when they're still attached to the old teams and old ways and more interested in preserving those than making new, emerging teams work. After all, alliances and coalitions of nations are defined and separated by political and strategic barriers—in other words, walls.

"It was a very different world after the fall of the Berlin Wall," he said. "Things were uncertain, and you have these big personalities—Bill Clinton and Gerhard Schröder and Tony Blair and Jacques Chirac among them—and I have my own charge as the leader of the alliance. I am not the leader of these leaders, but I must get us all going the same direction."

"What did you do?" I asked him.

"It wasn't easy," he confided. "For us to be a 'team of teams,' to use your vernacular, we had to be a team together and not representatives of our disparate interests. We ultimately decided we had to jump into the pool."

I was surprised by his comment. I expected a much more technical diplomatic response adapted to a changing world. "That's it?" I asked. "The leader of NATO says, 'We need to jump into the pool?'"

"Exactly that!" the Spaniard said with a gesture that showed he was passionately sincere. "It was a guiding principle." Of course, he was speaking figuratively. Dr. Solana had painted an image for me of everyone standing alongside the pool, studying the situation from their place and their point of view. Perhaps one or another may jump in at a certain point, but it is only when you are all in and taking that risk together that you can work and communicate as a team. Just jumping in is an equalizer. It is key to embracing the change instead of standing by and studying it. "You will never have the perfect situation," he said. "And if you wait too long, your moment will likely pass."

As the old order gave way to the new, everyone involved was trying to make sense of the changing strategic landscape. By jumping into the uncertainty as a team, they were forced to figure it out together as they went along. In such situations, one can't hang onto pretenses or prior configurations. There are no experts. Everyone must simply cut their moorings and let go of the expectations placed upon them as political leaders or experts, because those expectations would only weigh them down.

Dr. Solana emphasized the importance of reaching a consensus that works for the betterment of all. "You have to be brazen," he said. "We have seen for years the consequences of our leaders choosing to stand aside and take the decision not to engage. Jumping into the pool is an act of courage."

The 1990s were delicate. The world had changed suddenly, and there was contention about the role of NATO, which had initially formed as a defensive response to the Soviet threat. With the fall of the Soviet Union, it wasn't clear what NATO's role would be going forward or even whether it was useful any longer. Dr. Solana had a "jump-in-the-pool" moment, working to reorganize NATO and expand its influence in a post–Cold War world.

In 1997, he engaged Russia over a delicate matter to create a pathway for the former Eastern Bloc countries of Poland, Hungary, and the Czech Republic to join NATO. Dr. Solana credits Russian Foreign Minister Yevgeny Primakov for his role in advancing this effort. "He was a courageous man," Dr. Solana said. He recalled a meeting between the two of them in March 1997 and the personal connection they formed—each working at really hearing the other. "I still can visualize it," he remembered. "We'd had lunch and then he suggested we take a walk. Two and a half hours later, as we talked through the issues, I thought, *This is really possible.*"

Dr. Solana and Primakov had formed a bond and become a team, but the Western leader also kept his NATO team apprised of and engaged in the process as it developed. Dr. Solana next helped establish a groundbreaking dialogue between Russia and the US, as well as other key leaders within NATO. This led to an historic new agreement for the three formerly Soviet-allied nations to join the Western alliance in 1999.

"The things that can happen when you respect the other," he said with a hint of delight. "It was difficult, but three months after that lunch, we were all in Paris to sign a new agreement with Russia. [Russian President] Boris Yeltsin was there with myself and Bill Clinton, President Chirac, and other leaders."

Relations between Russia and NATO were on a new course, and the organization that had originally been chartered for the purpose of defense was now pursuing a mandate of cooperation. All of this, Dr. Solana says, required courage from the NATO leaders to upend the status quo by opening up the alliance to former Eastern bloc countries and from the Russian leaders as their country's relationships evolved.

Dr. Solana hadn't fully completed his mission at NATO when he was tapped to be the Secretary-General of the Council of the European Union. Here, there were even more opportunities to jump into the pool. He said it was a chance to come together to co-create and redefine Europe.

Ironically, by not holding on to pretenses and letting go of the trappings of traditional political leadership, Dr. Solana came to be recognized as one of the most able diplomats of our time. And he didn't do it by pulling rank or asserting his expertise. Instead, he cultivated an ethos of equality and championed the value of different points of view. He got everyone to "jump into the pool together."

Whenever we speak, Dr. Solana always brings our conversations back to the subject of change. He recently commented to me that in 1992, when Barcelona hosted the Olympic games, mobile phones and other related technologies barely existed. "Only three decades ago, the world was so different," he said. "Today's world requires something uniquely different from all of us: the ability to adapt to fast change and the capacity to create the conditions for change. You cannot wait for things to happen."

He concluded on a hopeful note: "Today, we can combine our abilities with our technology to truly make the world better."

Superpower for Social Change

Most of the changemakers I have known have made big change with very little. They often don't rely on big Twitter followings or muscular communications shops. Yet they still change mindsets at huge scales and move large systems. I find it remarkable that even in the age of social media, when reaching millions is as simple as hitting *Send*, the greatest impacts and the strongest impetus for change still come from breaking down silos and tearing down walls that separate potential powerful collaborations. The superpower for social change is bringing together unlikely players.

Kendis Paris exemplifies this with the organization she co-founded, called Truckers Against Trafficking (TAT). It does exactly what it sounds like it does—recruits truck drivers as unlikely soldiers in the fight to end human trafficking. That's a remarkable flipping of the script, since truckers have been widely viewed as part of the human trafficking problem, which is widespread and intractable.

The program was originally launched in 2009, with her mother and sisters inside their family's ministry, Chapter 61, to raise awareness of human trafficking and to enlist truckers as active players in recognizing and reporting abuse. Later, in 2011, Kendis formed Truckers Against Trafficking as a separate organization.

The idea grew from a recognition that truckers were largely uneducated about the elaborate schemes used to manipulate and trap young women into the commercial sex trade. Many people in prostitution are victims who have been lured, kidnapped, or extorted into forced labor. In fact, Kendis says that what we might have once called "prostitution" could in fact be classified as forced commercial sexual activity. And these truck drivers, who had been the targets of continuous shaming campaigns, she believed could be part of the solution to human trafficking if educated on the problem and given the opportunity.

Kendis succeeded in bringing together an unlikely team of allies in the fight to end human trafficking, which included transportation professionals, law enforcement, and victim organizations. Through TAT, truckers and industry workers are trained to spot signs of sex trafficking, especially trafficking of underaged girls. In just over 10 years, Kendis built TAT into a national organization and she says that as of early 2019, the National Human Trafficking Hotline reported that truckers' calls had helped identify 1,230 victims. In addition, nearly a million people have received TAT-training and are participating in this broad-based movement to stop human trafficking. TAT didn't gain support by propagating an Internet meme that went viral, it was through Kendis' networked-leadership approach of gaining trust and focusing industry resources on her goal. The idea is wall-busting.

The first big leap came when Travel Centers of America, one of the nation's largest truck stop chains, stepped up to partner with TAT to ensure that every one of their employees became TAT-trained. Their 200-plus locations nationwide also became points of distribution for TAT materials, educating countless truckers about the realities of human trafficking and how they could get involved to help end it. One of the nation's largest trucking companies, Ryder, followed suit shortly thereafter. They not only trained their drivers but also their entire 24,000-person workforce, as they believed that everyone in their company needed to know about this issue. Then, thanks to the Iowa Attorney General's Office, Kendis connected with Chief Dave Lorenzen of Iowa's Motor Vehicle Enforcement unit, where the two created a model to activate troopers and state agencies to combat this crime. Today, 48 states have adopted this model in part or in whole.

Kendis is now taking her model into new industries, including busing, shipping, and energy. In fact, while the future of trucking in an automated world is an open question, Kendis says that modern-day enslavers are not confined to any one industry. For example, the North Dakota oil boom created an environment for the sex industry to explode and for human trafficking to follow. When new oil rigs pop up, men are recruited away from their families for extended periods of time to follow jobs that put a lot of cash in their pockets. "Pimps follow the money," Kendis explained. "This isn't a truck-stop problem."

Traffickers are also very clever when it comes to finding markets for their trade, whether it's in a distant destination or right in your own neighborhood where brothels are disguised as homes, and storefront businesses are a front for forced labor. Company executives, management professionals, and everyday workers at all levels engage with the underground sex economy, but where there is a financial sexual transaction between two people, Kendis points out, there is very often an unseen third party involved.

When human traffickers need laborers to meet their market need, they prey on people, and a large percentage of victims are women and children. The "recruiter" can be very savvy, telling their victims what they want to hear, often promising a better life or an end to their problems. They are slick hucksters. It's no surprise that victims are commonly recruited at bus stops, schools, online, and in shopping malls.

Human trafficking is an unseen problem that is happening right in front of us, but Kendis has found a way to tear down walls and connect a mobile army to stop it, using her networked leadership model to work into and then inside large, influential systems—equipping and mobilizing partners to use their expertise, resources, and power to make meaningful change. "Everyone is a changemaker," Kendis said, "with a phone in their hands and the tools to engage around the problem and save a life."

The Last Wall

Kendis' story is remarkable, but you don't have to be a social change superhero to put these insights into practice in your everyday life. To illustrate this point, meet Princess Laurentien of the Netherlands. Yes, she's a princess, and she is very down to earth. My kids certainly think so.

Princess Laurentien believes that the traditional hierarchical walls between young people and adults should be torn down so that kids can own their full potential. I learned this lesson at an event she hosted at The Hague, called the Social Innovation Carousel. It was held in conjunction with the fifth anniversary of her organization, Number 5 Foundation, which incubates initiatives for a more inclusive, just, and sustainable society.

One of her most impactful projects is called the Missing Chapter Foundation. It fosters intergenerational dialogue between children and decision-makers from the public and private sectors. As a result of her work, more than 100 companies and citizen-sector (nonprofit) organizations in her country now have a Kids Council, which is an initiative of the Missing Chapter Foundation, to give children a role in decision making.[2] The princess once told me that it was her deep belief that having the uniquely wonderful role of being the stakeholders of our future society, children bring an important and distinctively different perspective to the table that should be welcomed by adults.

As my family arrived at the event, the princess greeted us warmly at the door. She then immediately turned her attention toward our boys, whom she had never before met. "Dante, Zane, I want to know if you will help me tonight." Ten and nine years old, respectively, they froze. She continued, "We will be hosting two conversations between adults and children, where grown-ups learn from kids. I want to know if you boys can lead the discussion and share your viewpoints."

Princess Laurentien explained that there would be a guide for the conversation, so all they had to do was share their thoughts on a few topics. She finished her pitch without once looking to my wife or me for permission.

There was a pause. I could feel their cold feet chilling the floor beneath us.

"I'm in," Dante said.

"I'm in," Zane said.

That evening, Dante and Zane led two sessions attended by nearly 50 Dutch adults, both lasting about 30 minutes each. They were asked for their ideas on topics ranging from school and education, to work and government. It was astonishing to see what open intergenerational dialogue could look like. There was genuine curiosity about Dante and Zane's perceptions. A schoolteacher rushed over to the boys after one session to ask follow-up questions. The boys had made the point that they thought school was hard for kids because it was abstract, and that learning was easier when it was connected to "real life." That opened up a whole discussion about how kids like to learn.

"How do you think math should be learned?" the teacher asked.

"Maybe we can learn it the way we will use it," Dante began.

I didn't hear the rest of his answer, but I did notice the confidence and a new kind of swagger that the boys had gained after the intergenerational walls had been breached. As the evening went on, they also played with the other children there, despite being foreigners and having only just met them hours earlier.

Back at home, a few months later, Dante became an advocate for the youth voice in his school. Writing for his school newspaper, our fifth-grader reflected on his experience: "After seeing the Dialogue Sessions in the Netherlands for myself, it made me wonder: What if kids really did serve a major role in the world some day? Would rules and laws become more interesting and fun? Would kids overrule adults, or would adults overrule kids?"

I agree with Dante and Princess Laurentien. What if kids found their natural place on the team of teams as co-leaders and co-creators in this age of dynamic, disruptive change? What would we learn from their inclusion? What impact would they have on social change? Even as we're growing more accustomed to seeing and hearing youth leaders like climate-change activist Greta Thunberg or gun control advocate and Stoneman Douglas High School shooting survivor Emma González, these are still radical questions. All that's preventing us from learning the answers are the intergenerational walls that continue to keep children's voices quiet. But in an everyone-a-changemaker world, these, too, may yet come down.

CHAPTER EIGHT

Changing Minds Changes Behavior

W HEN OUR CHILDREN were small and money was tight, we learned we could pass an afternoon at the airport, where we had unlimited access to escalators, moving walkways, and elevators. Each time they entered one, their eyes would widen, and their smiles would explode, often accompanied with a nervous hum punctuated by giggles. Their favorite was the elevator, especially if it had a windowed view. Somehow, our kids understood the magic and risk of the elevator that adults could no longer see.

We've forgotten that riding in elevators was once a dangerous prospect. Up until the mid-nineteenth century, the public was afraid of them—and for good reason. The ropes or cables from which elevator cars were suspended were prone to breaking. Similar cable breaks in heavy hoisting equipment caused horrific accidents and injuries in factories. Elisha Otis, the new founder of the Otis Elevator Company in 1853, had invented a safety brake that could catch the car and prevent it from falling if the cable broke.[1]

In 1854, at New York City's Crystal Palace, site of World's Fair the year before, Otis did something bold to allay those fears. Spurred on by the great showman and expert marketer, P.T. Barnum, he stepped off a ledge overlooking the large crowd below him, onto a flat wooden lift platform, intending to demonstrate the safety brake he had invented. With the crowd looking on, the lift was carefully hoisted high up to another platform where an attendant was waiting with an ax. He swung, severing the lift cable. The crowd gasped. The elevator fell! But it dropped mere inches. The safety brake caught the elevator and held it.[2]

This was game-changing. The dramatic image of a man cutting the cable and escaping harm altered public perceptions. As attitudes changed, so did the market, and Otis began selling elevators. A whole new world of possibilities opened up. Skyscrapers eventually transformed the cityscape as innovators were unleashed behind this game-changing breakthrough, and the top floors of buildings would become the priciest and most sought-after real estate. The ascent of the elevator also created the new profession of elevator operator, skilled workers—notably including African Americans looking for work in the post–Civil War era—who manually aligned car stops at floor ledges and who gave riders confidence in elevator technology.[3]

Today, we trust elevators without even thinking about it. The days of the elevator operator are gone, and elevators are now controlled by a button panel so simple that my children could operate them. Perceptions have changed radically since that day in 1854, when Elisha Otis showed us that a grand demonstration like his cable-cutting can shift mindsets. And when mindsets shift, promise is released, and big changes follow.

Shopping for a New Perspective

A much more modest demonstration of this same principle made a lasting impression on me and shifted my own views. It was 2013, and I was at an innovation competition, where teams of young people presented their ideas—a kind of *Shark Tank* for university students. One in particular struck me. It was a simple idea, but as I was a father of small children at that time, Fruit Buddi got my attention.

An attachment to a grocery cart, Fruit Buddi had three colorful pockets for different kinds of fruit. The idea was to get children to match fruits to the corresponding compartments, thereby gamifying shopping for fresh produce. The inventors wanted to help end childhood obesity, so they conceived this device to encourage kids to touch and interact with fruits and vegetables. They also proposed that stores should offer children one piece of fruit to eat as part of the shopping experience.

Now that's a game-changing idea, I thought. As these young creators pitched it, they invited their audience to put themselves in a child's shoes. When walking mindlessly alongside their parent's cart and viewing the lower shelves from that eye-level perspective, what comes into focus are a range of sugary products full of unhealthy ingredients, whose branding and marketing is designed to appeal to kids.

Fruit Buddi was an engagement strategy for children, but it was also an awareness vehicle for parents like me. From that day on, I began making shopping a more interactive activity for my children. I don't believe Fruit Buddi ever hit the stores, sadly, but it became part of my thinking, and I became more sensitive to advertising directed at children as a result.

Lady with a Spade

When mindsets shift, behavior change follows. Fruit Buddi made me more aware of all the ways in which products are marketed to my children, and that altered my own shopping choices. On a much larger scale, a working mom from the South Side of Chicago devised a way to shift attitudes about childhood nutrition and well-being to meet the nutritional and fitness needs of an entire generation.

She started by planting a simple backyard kitchen garden at her new home in 2009, after relocating her family. She had a section of the back lawn plowed up, which caused a bit of a ruckus with some of her new neighbors. Then, she invited two dozen grade-school children over to participate in the planting, which garnered additional attention and made news. Her garden quickly took on an iconic status. Images were beamed across the country and it captured national attention. Such an event would not typically be newsworthy, but the mom in this case was Michelle Obama, and the backyard she had plowed to make room for the garden was the South Lawn of the White House.

It was just weeks into the new administration, and the country was still getting to know the new First Lady. Michelle Obama had appeared occasionally on the campaign trail but had mostly avoided the limelight and was guarded about her privacy, primarily for the sake of her two young daughters. Her reputation was primarily that of a successful attorney and career woman. Now, we watched her digging in the garden with a bunch of kids.

There was nothing contrived about this image. I have known Mrs. Obama since the earliest days of the campaign, and this was the kind of thing she did when there were no cameras rolling. When we moved into our new campaign headquarters, before we even had any campaign posters or signs, she convened a meeting of the staffers' children to produce artwork that was used to dot our bare office walls.

But if the media eventually came to present the First Lady as the nation's *First Mom*, it was also no accident; she had illuminated that aspect of her identity. When her family delivered items from the White House garden to a local food pantry serving the homeless, the media was there. When Mrs. Obama was the first customer at an open-air produce market launched just outside the White House grounds, the media also reported on it. With recess and play vanishing from the childhood experience, even as food portion sizes and snacking increased, the First Lady would deliberately use her voice to spark a national dialogue about children's health and fitness through her Let's Move! campaign. Like Otis' cutting of the elevator cable, the First Lady's backyard garden created a striking image that resonated and made people take a fresh look at our plates.

One key opportunity to focus a spotlight on the issue arose just days after planting the garden, at the annual White House Easter Egg Roll, when some 30,000 children and their parents would spill onto the South Lawn for a grand play date of sorts. It was the 131st running of the event, dating back to 1878, and I was the co-chair. But this year's Easter Egg Roll was different from years past. Instead of the traditional Sunday-best attire, the kids were encouraged to wear sweatpants and sports gear— Michelle's idea. "Tell them to wear their tennis shoes, Henry!" she gleefully shouted as I left one of our planning meetings. "We want them to know we're coming to play." Her theme for the event was "Let's Go Play," a precursor of her signature "Let's Move!" The next Easter, the theme was "Ready, Set, Go." Painted on each wooden egg was a bunny in running gear.

On February 9, 2010, the First Lady formally launched Let's Move!, her initiative to raise national awareness in support of healthy, active children. That same day, at the kickoff event, President Obama issued an executive memo calling for a Task Force on Childhood Obesity to develop a national action plan to achieve Mrs. Obama's goal to end childhood obesity within a generation.[4]

As changemakers do, the First Lady understood the power of bringing unlikely stakeholders to the table, and she built a team of teams with diverse members all working together, including Big Soda representatives, big-name food retailers, social entrepreneurs and advocacy groups, and importantly, a cook—not just any cook, but her family's chef from Chicago. Sam Kass had helped Mrs. Obama craft her plans for the initiative back in Chicago at her kitchen table. Now, he was a part of the White House Kitchen Corps and also daylighting as a policy advocate for the First Lady's ideas. Reminiscent of Wellington's story of joining medical teams in the operating room, policymakers in the Department of Agriculture, Education, and the White House Domestic Policy Council were sitting across the table discussing policy with the guy who put food on the First Family's table.[5] Sam eventually became the executive director for Let's Move! and the president's Senior Policy Advisor for Nutrition Policy, and he was an effective promotor for healthy eating and ending childhood obesity. Michelle Obama wasn't content to simply connect traditional issue advocates to the relevant policymakers; she broke silos, jumped hierarchies, and invited outsiders in—or perhaps insiders out, in this case.

Mrs. Obama did more than champion a First-Lady agenda item; she personally embodied and fundamentally expanded the role and what someone in that role could do. She became known for her personal vivacity, from dancing with kids to digging gardens with them. She was often seen and photographed alongside citizen innovators, including some of the social entrepreneurs described in this book, to draw attention to how their contributions were advancing young people's health and empow-erment. As a parent, she embodied a new imperative for kids' health and well-being, and that enabled her to inspire a reconsideration of our collective views of nutrition and obesity. Once she accomplished that, changes in practices, policies, behaviors, and whole systems inevitably followed.

Two years after she planted the White House kitchen garden, the beverage industry began voluntarily featuring nutrition information on packaging—something that had seemed unthinkable in 2009.[6] Olive Garden and Red Lobster were in the vanguard of high-profile restaurant chains that reduced sodium and replaced fries with fruit and green veg-etables in children's meals.[7] Walmart made commitments to dramati-cally cut sugar, fat, and salt in its product line, which in turn affected the broader supply chain. Congress caught the wave, passing a law in 2010 that transformed the meals on the lunch trays of more than 21 million kids. School vending machines swapped out junk food snacks for healthy alternatives.[8]

Barack Obama was a changemaker on the campaign trail, but he wasn't the only one in that family. Michelle Obama certainly personified changemaking in the East Wing. Like all highly effective changemakers, she didn't wait for a debate in Congress or a federal agency regulatory process. To get traction, she had to be creative and resourceful. The office of First Lady doesn't come with a large staff or budget, and the role is often hemmed in by confining public notions of the kinds of activities a president's spouse should or should not engage in. Still, Mrs. Obama used what she had available to her, and she added unlikely players onto her team, forming teams of teams around various elements of her initia-tives. She used her influence instead of formal authority to work fluidly and across different systems to change mindsets, which in turn led to scaled behavioral and systemic change.

At the end of his tenure in the White House, when President Obama was asked how he wanted to use his role in his post-presidency, he said that he would look to his wife's example of how she had leveraged her role as First Lady.[9] The president indicated he will be using the changemaker playbook.

Lady with the Lamp

Florence Nightingale was the founder of modern nursing, and she was a world-class changemaker. During the Crimean War in the mid-1850s, she not only changed the way medical care was delivered to the soldiers, she also changed the minds of military officials, which led to an overhaul of the whole system of nursing. Florence spent just 2½ years at the front, but by the end of her tour, she had exposed a broken system, created a new way to deliver care that would become a model for modern nursing, and shifted aspects of procurement, which was a strategic and administrative function of the war operation itself. Her work in the Crimea laid the foundation for her distinguished career as a reformer and public figure, and for the outsized impact she would have on public health and sanitation around the world.

Like many changemakers, Florence possessed a strong sense of self-definition as a child. She knew that she was drawn to medicine at a very young age, recalling that a clear early desire from her youth was nursing the sick. At 9, she began carefully documenting family ailments, shades of her statistical forte.[10] She later dreamed of studying under a physician at the nearby infirmary and establishing a school to prepare women for nursing work. However, the social expectations of her time and her family's well-to-do status weighed against this. Nursing was considered work for women of much lower standing. Her father and others close to her discouraged her from this plan. They saw her as a lady, destined for a life of balls and galas and perhaps suitable charitable works. But Florence wasn't content to hand out books and blankets, as she had often done with her mother throughout her childhood. She was pulled toward service and career.[11]

Florence found that she could appease her family by acting ladylike by day and secretly pursuing medicine at night, when she retired to her room and devoured health reports and statistics.[12] The oppressive feelings of not being able to pursue her calling preyed on her spirit as a young adult. A trip to Rome in 1847 with family friends, ultimately her personal allies, would fortify her purpose when a nun counseled her to be strong in the face of her family's resistance, lest she disobey God's will for her.[13] On that tour, she also befriended the statesman, Sidney Herbert, who had just finished a term as Secretary of War. They formed a lifelong friendship.[14]

Two years later, Florence was off again with these same friends, this time traveling through exotic Egypt and far from home; still clear on who she was but not allowed to be. Then, after a planned stay in Greece, her friends agreed to allow her two weeks at a nursing institute in Germany. Florence had set her path.[15]

There was no suppressing her passion over the next five years, and when the Crimean War broke out in 1853, less than a year before Elisha Otis cut the cable, Florence found herself both motivated and experienced enough to seek an appointment in the war effort. She sought out Sydney Herbert, who was once again serving as Secretary of War, and the letter she posted may have even crossed his seeking her support to lead a company of female nurses into the war zone. She was appointed "Superintendent of the Female Nursing Establishment in the English General Military Hospitals in Turkey," which was something unheard of in British military hospitals to that point in time.[16]

When her team arrived at the front, they found gruesome conditions. Sanitation was woefully inadequate. Kitchens served unfit meals, facilities lacked proper eating utensils and personal hygiene resources, and the soldiers' dirty clothes and bandage-dressings were imbedded into their wounds with dried blood. The living environment was shared with bedbugs, flees, lice, and rats.[17]

Florence also faced negative attitudes toward her that she would have to change before she could succeed. She was mostly shunned by her male counterparts, who thought the front lines were no place for a lady. But she began to make her mark by changing the minds of those directly around her. She worked hard to establish credibility and gain acceptance from the men. Whenever she was invited to help, she jumped in, proved her competence, and earned personal credibility.[18]

She used that credibility to appeal to influential people about the need for reforms, going all the way up to Queen Victoria.[19] She was highly regarded for her knowledge of statistics and had a talent for representing data visually. In fact, she was an early pioneer of infographics, and she used this ability to convey complex, data-driven findings to influential officials and civil servants who otherwise might not have understood them.[20]

Florence was a talented communicator, who could write clearly and simply so that wide audiences could understand her. A mediagenic figure, she built relationships with reporters and newspapers, which the advent of the telegraph and other recent advances in technology had transformed into faster, more powerful means of disseminating information and moving public opinion. Reporters who once needed weeks to get copy back to their home office now only needed hours. Headlines from the front on the other side of the continent exploded in Western Europe with a new level of immediacy and fascination. In a way, it was the nineteenth-century version of a reality show. Florence soon became sought after as a source of real-time insights into the horrors of war. As awareness of her work and ideas spread, so did public demand for reforms in medical care.[21]

As she fired the imaginations of newspaper readers, charitable donations poured in. Her media connections helped her access *London Times*-organized charity funds. The money freed her from the bureaucratic morass in which the government procurement system was mired.[22]

By the time her service in the Crimea ended, Florence had achieved sweeping, system-wide reforms. She renovated the procurement process to meet sanitation needs; she reformed the kitchens so that they served clean, nutritious meals that helped patients regain their health; she innovated the laundries so that soldiers had clean clothes; she established a money-order office so that soldiers at the front could remit some of their pay to their families back home; and she organized reading rooms as a healthy alternative to drinking for bored convalescents. Florence even wrote condolence letters to families.[23] She did all this in a two-and-a-half-year stint at the front, a kind of laboratory for change-making that served as an incubator for the rest of her career. Florence went on to create lasting, global-scale change.

Upon returning home, she received an outpouring of financial support, which she used to start a professional nursing school. Her 1859 book, *Notes on Nursing*, set the standard for nursing education, but it was also broadly popular with the general public as an aid for caring for the sick in the home.[24] It argued that sanitation wasn't just the province of medical professionals; it was something everyone should know about and benefit from. This was a groundbreaking view at the time, and it still reverberates today.

Florence Nightingale transformed nursing. Once regarded as a vocation where the poor served the poor, under her leadership, it became a recognized profession requiring specific training. She trained and mentored nurses who went on to lead and take on positions of responsibility at other hospitals and schools.[25] Florence had professionalized the field and democratized knowledge. Her ideas and influence were felt far and wide, including in India, where the reforms she advocated there reduced the death rate from 69 to 18 per thousand in just a decade.[26]

The key to the huge impact she made was in the way Florence first changed societal expectations and mental frameworks by convincing influential people to believe in her, finding effective ways to communicate her insights, and then disseminating those at an even larger scale. Like Michelle Obama and her kitchen garden, Florence relied on imagery—including vivid images from the Crimean front along with statistical charts—which were disseminated widely. These stuck and framed for people a new way of viewing things. Once that shift in perspective was underway, none of the formidable obstacles posed by a retrenched status quo could stop her. Like Elisha Otis, Florence Nightingale effectively cut the cable that tethered people to outmoded views—from restrictive social attitudes regarding gender and class, to parochial military practices, to ignorance of public health and sanitation. She also communicated a new vision for professionalizing nursing and modernizing the healthcare infrastructure. By shifting old mindsets, Florence transcended all of the old barriers and unleashed changes that affect virtually all of us, even today.

Creating a Dignity-Driven Economy

Anshu Gupta was following a story. As a young photojournalist in Delhi in 1991, Anshu had seen tragedy and hardship, but this was hardship of another kind. He watched as the older gentleman he was following gently picked up the dead body from the roadside—a man dressed in a thin shirt and trousers. It was obvious that this man had died of the freezing cold temperatures that mark a Delhi winter.

Anshu first met Habib, the body collector, after coming across his tattered rickshaw and noticing the words, "Picker of abandoned dead bodies," scrawled across the back in Hindi. Curious about his strange profession, Anshu began shadowing Habib over the next week. Habib's job was to pick up unclaimed, unidentified dead bodies in public places and cremate them. He was paid a bounty of about forty cents per body. Habib lived along the roadside, in poverty himself.

"In the summer, he collected four to five bodies over a 24-four hour period in the two-mile radius he worked in," Anshu said. "But that number spiked to 10 to 12 bodies during the winter months." The difference was unmistakable—people were unable to survive the cold winter nights while exposed on the Delhi streets.

Anshu shared another moment that stood out in his memory. It was Habib's 6-year-old daughter's unforgettable words: "When I feel cold, I hug the dead body and sleep. It does not trouble me. It does not turn around."

In this encounter with Habib and his work, Anshu noticed something that had been previously unseen, but which he could not now unsee. He realized that the man Habib had picked up didn't actually die from the cold. Anshu himself—and millions of other people in Delhi—survived the same cold every winter. No, this man died because he wasn't adequately clothed. "As a society, we are continually mobilized around providing food and shelter to those who need it," Anshu said, "yet we think of giving clothing only when there is a disaster: floods and earthquakes and the like. But on the streets of Delhi and many other cities across the world, there is a disaster every winter night that goes unseen and needs that go unmet."

Six years later, in 1998, Anshu left his corporate job to start Goonj. His main objective was to use clothing as a metaphor for society to understand the many neglected needs and dimensions of poverty. He and his wife, Meenakshi, started by eliminating their own extra clothing. "We went through our wardrobes to figure out what we hadn't been using, and we found 67 items between the two of us, including clothes and shoes," Anshu said. "This was quite striking because it made us realize the scale of underutilized material lying untapped across urban India when two people coming from a normal middle-class family had 67 unused clothes."

"So, that was the first day of Goonj," he added.

As a couple, they worked to make this organization successful. Meenakshi continued to work at her corporate job, while Anshu started to work on Goonj full-time. Theirs was a personal and professional partnership. Their home literally became a collection center and remained so throughout the organization's early years.

I first met Anshu around 2013. He had recently visited a secondhand clothing center in the San Francisco area. "I have an issue with how the material is being dealt with," he said reflectively. "While the bad-quality material is being treated as trash, the good-quality stuff is placed in the stores in the more affluent neighborhoods. You refer to it as a charitable gift, but it is really just cheap clothing sold to working families, while the poorest get the lesser-quality items as charity."

I had never thought of it that way, but if you look at the world the way Anshu does, you can quickly see his point. Anshu believes that clothing is not only a precious resource; it is also a basic human right. He believes that anyone who gives away their old material shouldn't call it "donating." " 'Discarding,' " he said, "would be a more appropriate term."

He continued, "Our clothes are also a symbol of our dignity and self. They add value to us." To make his point, Anshu reached for a photo album he'd brought to our meeting and opened it to an image of a child crouching on the ground and staring wantingly into the camera. He looked dirty, and he was without a shirt. It was the face of poverty that we see all too often on TV just before the word *DONATE* flashes across the screen. Next, Anshu pointed to another picture of the very same boy, this time handsomely attired and standing tall—almost at attention—with a confident smile. "Look here," Anshu said. "The boy in the first picture, you would not want to be seen with. The same boy in the second picture, you would proudly walk alongside into a school classroom." I understood his point.

He showed me two more sets of before-and-after photos. The first set was of an old man. In the "before" photo, he was shabbily clothed. "You might only call him out from afar on the street, even if he looked confused and in need of help," Anshu said. "In the second picture, notice the same man in respectable clothing. This is someone you would walk up to and offer a hand."

Next, he showed me photos of a young bearded gentleman. In the first, he was scantily clad. In the second, he was well-dressed, openly laughing, and looked joyful. "Here, see this one?" Anshu said, again pointing to the "before" picture on the left. "You wouldn't want to stand near him at a bus stop, while the same person in the right-hand picture you would eagerly approach and engage in a chat."

Not only did the perception of the viewer (in this case, me) change when these people's clothing changed, but the people's own confidence and sense of self also changed. In a simple yet powerful way, these images conveyed a transformation of mindsets.

A few years after our initial meeting in the United States, I visited Goonj in India. What had once been run out of Anshu's home was now a huge operation in a much-larger building. I went from room to room, seeing piles upon piles of what looked like an overwhelming mass of waste being sorted by hundreds of mostly female staff members into categories. I watched as these items—clothing, school supplies, toys, and hygiene products—were mindfully and carefully turned into beautiful packages for distribution to rural Indian families. There was even a whole section of Goonj's processing center dedicated to making cloth sanitary pads for women. This particular effort was part of a campaign to inform women in rural areas about menstrual hygiene and bring greater public attention to the culture of shame and silence around the subject, establishing menstruation as a human issue rather than solely a women's issue.

But Anshu's team doesn't give anything away as charity. They strongly believe that dignity, not charity, brings about sustained development. In rural India, Goonj offers these "family packs" as a reward for the efforts people take to solve their own community issues. "Goonj has always been about dignity," he said.

The most powerful images associated with Goonj's work are not the before-and-after pictures Anshu showed me; they are the beautiful pictures of whole communities mobilizing to work on a variety of issues, such as repairing their own roads, cleaning bodies of water, and building bamboo bridges. In these photos, everyone is respectably dressed, smiling, and appears to be vigorously engaged around a project that serves the whole community.

"People in the villages lack both in opportunities and resources, but they put a lot of value on their dignity," Anshu told me. "You don't find beggars in the villages. Begging is a city phenomenon. So, we had to find a way which addressed their needs of material and dignity, while also addressing their chronic neglected community issues." Anshu figured out that by valuing and honoring what people *did* have in the villages—their labor, their wisdom about their world, and their natural resources—he could create a barter item that would connect the community's assets and its basic needs. The clothing and family packs simply act as a mobilizing, motivating reward.

This became the basis for using clothing and other urban surplus materials as a new currency for development work—what Anshu calls Dignity for Work (DFW). His innovative model brings impact on different dimensions. Goonj mobilizes people in rural villages to identify a local need, and together, the community finds a solution and then collectively works on it. "The world calls them 'unskilled workers,' yet these same people create amazing roads, lakes, and sanitation systems," he said. "When people come together around a self-determined shared goal, we see ownership and pride come alive."

For those few days when the villagers work on this shared community project, they aren't working for money; they're working for themselves. Using Dignity for Work, Anshu has created two new currencies: labor and surplus material. He also created a new economic model that is based not on cash but on trash.

Anshu rejects using images of poverty—like the child in the photo he initially showed me—as a promotional tool for giving. "Why do we sell poverty to solve poverty?" he asks. His photographs are beautiful, and they draw the eye to the well-dressed people in rural villages proudly mobilizing around local projects. Those who might be otherwise viewed as charity recipients are shown more authentically as contributors. Anshu's images and his work illuminate the concept of dignity in action. More than that, they are a tool for him to change attitudes about giving.

"We often thoughtlessly cast off our old unwanted items without any thought to the receiver," he said. "We give what we have, not what people need. And we do this without realizing that people who reuse this stuff actually do a service to the world, because otherwise, it would end up in a landfill, further polluting our world.

"What if we made giving more about the receiver's dignity and well-being and less about the giver's pride and satisfaction?" he asked. "More importantly, what if we thought of the poor not as a liability or a burden on the world, but as equal stakeholders and contributors in the world? How would that change the way we see and respond to a fellow citizen in need?"

Picture-Telling

Salient imagery has impact. The key to mindset shift is not through logical arguments or lofty rhetoric. What we see in all of these stories of changemaking is that minds are best changed through the heart. When Florence Nightingale evoked the images of the Crimean War front, she stirred the public's imagination. When Michelle Obama wanted people to view youth nutrition and fitness differently, she didn't say it; she showed it. She appeared in a viral video dancing to a Beyoncé song at a high school Let's Move! event and again in news footage breaking ground for a new playground. But Anshu shows us that we don't have to be an icon or household name like Florence or Michelle Obama.

We should also recognize Michelle Obama was a working mom before she became First Lady, and Florence was a frustrated socialite before she became the Lady of the Lamp. The trails they blazed aren't just for an elite few. Anybody, regardless of circumstances, can do what they did and become effective changemakers. In fact, many people from all walks of life have done it, and increasingly, we all have to do it. In the era of accelerating, omnidirectional change, old hierarchies and elite structures are falling away, and the tools and knowledge structures they used to monopolize—mass communications, specialized research, influencer networks—are now at the fingertips of anyone with a smartphone.

There are many different gardens and gardeners from all walks of life who are cultivating change all over the world. When it comes to changing attitudes about youth, there were others before Mrs. Obama reshaping the landscape. We've met examples in this book—people like Molly Barker, who took 13 preteen girls on a run and sparked a national movement building girls' self-definition and self-esteem.

And there are others. Jill Vialet, a high school track star who went on to become the founder of Playworks, creating programs in public schools to reclaim recess and play as key educational experiences. Where some see a playground, Jill sees a training ground for kids to develop the skills to be inclusive, solve disputes, and create an environment of trust and self-leadership—skills that will serve them for life. Their impact stretched to 1.25 million kids in 2,500 elementary schools just last year alone.

Darell Hammond grew up with his seven siblings in a foster home in Chicago, and he went on to found KaBOOM!, an organization dedicated to ending "play inequity" by carving out child-friendly, vibrant recreation spaces in underserved neighborhoods, often by reclaiming barren or underused spaces. Where others see a play desert, Darell sees an opportunity for community-building. He created a model to bring local residents together to fund and design their recreational spaces themselves, with the kids taking the lead. As a result, they get access to high-quality play equipment at a low cost. They also work cooperatively to tend the new space, knitting together different elements of the community. For every new play space built or upgraded through this learning process, the cultivated knowledge is estimated to result in ten more built nearby.[27] In the past 23 years, KaBOOM! has engaged more than 1.5 million community members, improved over 17,000 play spaces, and brought joy to over 11 million kids.[28]

What Jill and Darell have done isn't all that different from what Michelle Obama did. They shift mindsets, and behavior change follows. We all have our own platforms and talents to bring to an opportunity.

Anshu not only used his abilities as a photographer, he created his own unique platform by collecting waste, and he invented local economic systems from nothing by using trash—not cash—as the currency. My son, Zane, made his own platform from nothing in his early school years by creating a lunch table with kids who didn't always have someone to sit with; it was diverse and it crossed grades. On one occasion, in third grade, he learned how to use his influence by mobilizing his schoolmates to sign a homemade card for a child who had suddenly and unexpectedly left for another area school. From a First Lady, to a photographer, to a former track star, to a third-grader, all our stories become part of the larger, beautiful changemaker mosaic.

The New Playbook for the New Game

We are now familiar with the essential skills and capacities everyone needs in order to play in this new changemaker game. First, empathy is foundational because we live in a world that is highly interactive, and rules can't keep up with the pace of change, making conscious empathy-based ethics fundamental for how we live and work together. Second, we need to cultivate self-definition in ourselves and others, because every player on the team must be an initiator—no one can be passive. Third, the requisite new leadership skill is tearing down walls and bringing teams together around challenges and opportunities. Finally, normalizing new behaviors for the good of all is best achieved when we are all able to see new perspectives and truly connect together. Changing mindsets leads to changing patterns and systems.

Changemaking isn't a game for only the rich and famous or the fabulously inventive. We all have the capacity for changemaking, but most of us either don't see it or don't value it. Whenever I have shared my stories about changemaking and the attributes of changemakers—now, in some 22 countries including the Philippines, South Korea, India, Brazil, Argentina, Spain, Sweden, and Mexico—people consistently recognize it within themselves. The most common response I get isn't "How can I do that?" but "They won't let *me* do that." People from all walks of life rightly recognize that they have the capacity to be a changemaker, but they often feel that they are not allowed to *be* changemakers.

The examples are myriad—the younger worker whose boss frowned on collaboration across departments; the student whose teachers and classrooms kept learning restrictive and hierarchical; the CEO who thought changemaking and having a changemaker workforce was important for the company's future but fretted that he was hemmed in by old-game KPIs (key performance indicators) imposed by his board. These are all examples of people ready to play the new game, who still find themselves on the old field inside a stadium designed for another time. Many of us have recognized or intuited that change has accelerated into the new constant and that changemaking and teams of teams are imperatives today. The problem is that organizational and social structures haven't caught up. They still carry the vestiges of the old game and suppress the new.

There is no putting the genie back in the bottle. We cannot and will not go back to a siloed, hierarchical world of a few telling everyone else what to do. We need a collective, societal awakening to the fact that we have already left the era of repetition and plunged irreversibly into the world of change. Old-game thinking attached to antiquated organizational and social structures may remain entrenched and resistant to the changes underway, but it's too late to stop these forces. In fact, they are already ramping up fast. The new game is here, and we all need to jump in.

That means nothing less than redesigning education, governance, how we run our organizations, and how we live and work together to accommodate a new reality. Changemakers can't function in the old system, and the old system can't accommodate everyone as a changemaker. To benefit from the new system that is emerging, we have to correct social imbalances and let go of vestigial attachments to the old system and the old mindsets it was founded on. We need social attitudes that recognize and value changemaking and embrace the capacities and structures that enable it.

So, how can we hope to accomplish that kind of sweeping social change? By doing what Florence Nightingale, Michelle Obama, Elisha

Otis, and many others have done—cut the cable, show people how to let go of outmoded thinking, and shift mindsets as the key precondition for big change. We need to design strategic systems for the everyone-a-changemaker world and educational systems that foster the development of all young people as changemakers. It's time for a new framework for playing in the new game.

SECTION THREE

Framework Change

CHAPTER NINE

The Changemaker Youth Apprenticeship

ARE CHANGEMAKERS BORN or made? This is a question I'm often asked, and it was the subject of a conversation I had with a representative of the Conrad N. Hilton Foundation, the charitable arm of the Hilton hotel chain. We were discussing Ashoka's Everyone a Changemaker™ and what I had personally learned from working with social entrepreneurs. It was a question I had certainly considered myself, particularly as a father thinking about my own sons' futures.

Based on my firsthand exposure to changemakers around the world and my research on some of history's leading innovators, I shared with the Hilton Foundation representative the clear patterns in their experiences while growing up, drawing on familiar names to help my case. Four things clearly stand out.

First, in a world where empathy is a foundational attribute that everyone must possess, every child must master empathy. It's clear that the years up to age seven are the ideal years for cultivating empathy. What I call the changemaker's "service heart" is formed in the early years, mostly modeled and cultivated by parents or other important adults in their regular orbits. Story after story of contemporary changemakers and history's leading innovators demonstrate this. For example, when Florence Nightingale was a child, she accompanied her mother to distribute blankets and support to the needy in a nearby community.[1]

The second major component of a changemaker's formation occurs between the ages of seven and eleven. This is when the young person begins to find themselves. They discover interests and passions separate from the influence of their parents. This is important because learning around their passions, they are motivated to explore what captures their imagination. Discovering a passion early in life is the beginning of self-definition, a critical attribute of the changemaker as a catalyst and full contributor in society. Changemakers must have a solid sense of self-definition in order to believe in themselves, collaborate effectively with other strong personalities, and give themselves permission to make full, unique contributions. Exploring one's passion is also the stimulus for self-directed learning at a young age, which is an ability that will serve the changemaker for life.

Florence Nightingale was destined for the lady's life of charity, but she knew at the age of 6 she wanted a fulfilling occupation.[2] Abraham Lincoln eschewed hunting and embraced books. He shot and killed a turkey when he was 8, as was customary for boys on the frontier. Then he made a vow that it would be the last time he would do that—a bold pronouncement of self-definition from a frontier kid.[3] Not surprisingly, the presidential tradition of "pardoning" the White House Thanksgiving turkey is actually traced to Lincoln himself.[4] Young Abe was also a self-driven learner and became engrossed in books at an early age. He worked hard when he wasn't reading, but he had a clear preference for the latter, which perhaps gave him an unearned reputation for laziness. Still, his uneducated father, as well as his mother and stepmother, protected him and indulged his passion for books.[5]

There is a third common pattern, and it occurs in the teen years, when the young person strikes out on their own and builds a team around their idea or venture. This is the phase when they begin to express their entrepreneurial spirit and collaborative outlook. Henry Ford, one of history's most recognizable innovators, was inventive and worked in teams, collecting other kids on the schoolyard to experiment with steam.[6] A current-day entrepreneur, Robin Chase, the founder of Zipcar, launched a philosophy club in college at age 19 to make being intellectual cool. At 16, Richard Branson launched a magazine, which included an interview with Vanessa Redgrave. The discount records marketed in the back of his magazine became the genesis of Virgin Records, which Branson would later sell for $1 billion.[7]

Finally, the fourth commonality is "leaving to learn" during one's youth and then throughout life. This can first occur in childhood alongside family events or activities, and it can be in the teen years, often as a marker of individual independence. Abraham Lincoln's family embarked on a two-week, hundred-mile move from Kentucky to Illinois when he was seven, and on arrival, he was immediately handed an ax as a tool for clearing away the dense tract of forest and brush on which his family settled.[8] When he was 19, he journeyed in a flatboat down the Mississippi River with a neighbor to sell farm produce in New Orleans. That's also where he got his first glimpse of a major city and the horrors of its slave market.[9]

I call this progression the *changemaker youth apprenticeship* (I also refer to it as the *startup of youth*), and when I had finished ticking off these four recurrent themes in what I believe comprise the changemaker's formation, my guest exclaimed, "Conrad Hilton was a changemaker! He got empathy from his mother through prayer and he had an idea in his teens that his family rallied around." She piqued my interest, and I researched his story further.

Putting a Team Around an Idea

Born to Norwegian immigrant parents in 1887, Conrad was the second of nine children, and the oldest son. Connie, as he was known, grew up on his family's homestead in the sparsely populated New Mexico territory, riding his pony to the local one-room schoolhouse and working in the family's general store, where he picked up entrepreneurial skills working under the watchful eye of his father.[10]

When he was 12, his parents sent him to boarding school in Santa Fe, and at 15, he announced that he was done with school. He wanted to be back at the store. By then, the family's corner in New Mexico was booming, complete with a post office, a telegraph office, a Studebaker dealership (they had just started making automobiles in 1902), and a lumberyard. Conrad argued that the emerging business community was where he was needed, not school, and his parents went along with his idea.[11]

In 1904, when Conrad was 17, the family made the trip to the World's Fair in St. Louis, Missouri, which was also home to that year's Olympic Games. The World's Fair was an astonishing event, lasting many months. Stepping past the new coin-operated automatic gatekeeper, the Hiltons entered an unimaginable world filled with groundbreaking inventions, all lit by new electricity.[12]

The family's rising fortunes took a sudden downturn during the 1907 recession, and they needed money, fast. Conrad came up with a plan to rent out rooms in their 10-bedroom house next to the general store. It would mean that the family would have to crowd together into fewer rooms to make space for paying travelers, but his parents again agreed to his idea, and it worked.[13]

Conrad put his father in charge of overall management. His mother and sisters worked the kitchen. Conrad himself handled baggage and general hospitality. Within weeks, the outpost was known as far afield as Chicago for its food and friendliness, and Conrad himself was recognized for his enterprising nature.[14]

That was the beginning of Hilton's empire. He purchased his first hotel in Texas in 1919,[15] and the business grew into a worldwide global chain. When Conrad died in 1979, he left the bulk of his fortune to the charitable foundation he established in 1944.[16] He connected his success to his early experiences and that first hospitality venture in the family home, saying "I wouldn't take a million dollars for what those days taught me."[17]

Educate for Change

It's easy to identify the key markers of the changemaker youth apprenticeship in Conrad's story. His "service heart" was developed as a child through his faith. In his preteen years, we see evidence of burgeoning self-definition and self-directed learning around his passion at the family store. In his teens, we see a leave-to-learn opportunity at the World's Fair. And as a young man, he had a bold idea and he organized a team to implement it. He didn't get those experiences through his formal schooling, yet his changemaker apprenticeship formed the cornerstone of his career.

As former Secretary of Education Arne Duncan said, "The key factor of success for any society going forward is what percentage of its people are changemakers. It's the new literacy."[18] Of course, neither he nor I would argue that budding changemakers should drop out of school. The most highly effective changemakers I have known and read about embrace their formal education experience, but they also recognize its limits. Hilton himself eventually obtained more formal education, attending what is now the New Mexico Military Institute, the Santa Fe University of Art and Design, and New Mexico Tech. But he always valued his informal schooling.[19]

It's not an either/or proposition. To prepare our kids for success in the new game, we should encourage them to succeed in school. But educators and parents shouldn't overlook other experiences and forms of development that young people need to become changemakers.

This is not a call to change education, but rather to educate students for change. My experience is that educators *are* changemakers—they are dedicated to service, empathetic, innovative, resourceful, and impactful. But they are operating in a system that was built for the world of repetition, designed to prepare students for a rigidly defined vocation in a world where vocations are fading fast. By one popular estimate, 65 percent of today's school-age children will hold jobs that haven't even been invented yet. And when they are, they won't be based on repeating a specialized skill over and over again.

To succeed, every child will need to be a changemaker. Educators must figure out how to help students practice and master empathy, learn around their passions, self-define, and work effectively in fluid, open teams.

And I know it's possible to do this in schools because I have witnessed it firsthand.

Learning From Our Littlest Learners

The best course in empathy that I have ever taken was at a public school in Toronto, Canada. The teacher was a baby.

His name was Patrick, and he came to the school once a month with his mother to help teach a program called Roots of Empathy. It was invented and scaled up by Mary Gordon, and today, it has reached more than 1 million children around the world.[20] When I dropped in on Patrick's session, he was working with fifth-graders, but infant Roots of Empathy professors like Patrick work with school-aged children up to 13. By interacting with babies, the children get to explore their own feelings and learn about each other's.

When Baby Patrick arrived in the classroom, the students got excited and quickly formed a circle on the floor around him. I was in that circle, too—an oversized kid. Patrick's mother stayed close, but off to one side. A program facilitator sidled up behind the baby, who laid on his back at the top of the circle, feet inside the circle, and she began asking the students questions. How do they think the baby might be feeling? What do they think he is learning at this stage of his development?

The students talked about the emergence of his first teeth. They also discussed how Patrick communicates, how his mom might understand and meet his different needs, and what it might be like for him when he is hungry. They explored together how they might react if they knew he was unhappy. These students were learning to put themselves in his shoes.

Both boys and girls in the class engaged with Patrick. In fact, they fawned over him and vied for his attention. Even when the facilitator asked questions or brought the mother into the conversation, most students never took their eyes off the baby. But there were a few kids who seemed uncomfortable and remained noticeably aloof. The baby seemed particularly keen to win them over. One student said that although she really wanted Patrick to notice her, she was glad to see him flirt with another student instead, because he "needed it more." This was quite an openhearted observation. Patrick was eliciting empathy in her, and she was passing it along to her classmate.

In between Baby Patrick's monthly class visits, the students have activities—discussions, play-acting, and art—designed to help translate their experiences with the baby into more empathetic interactions with each other, their families, and their communities.

I translated my session with Patrick into a deeper engagement with my own kids. I paid closer attention to what they were communicating through the art they brought home, and our conversations over it brought out important feelings. I also spoke to them and listened to them with more awareness. For example, when we talked about how Baby Patrick was getting his teeth, I learned that Zane was a little unnerved by watching his older brother begin to lose his. "What else will fall off Dante?" he asked in a moment of vulnerability.

Changemaking for Kindergarteners

My next lesson in teaching changemaking skills was in a kindergarten classroom in Jamaica Plain, a suburb of Boston, Massachusetts. This time, my instructor was an adult, Kathy Clunis D'Andrea. Her class was buzzing with 5-year-olds, all busy with different projects. In order to talk with her, I had to pull up a miniature chair that looked like it would break under my weight. We were regularly interrupted by the children, and I marveled at this gifted teacher's patience. There were other adult aides in the classroom that she could have relied on to intervene, but whenever a child approached her, Kathy stopped our conversation, looked at the child directly, and listened carefully to what they wanted. Sometimes, she responded by expressing her own feelings to the child, but she always did so empathetically and respectfully, never dropping her eye contact.

Soon after my arrival, it was time for recess, and then Kathy was able to give me her full attention. "These kids come into my classroom as someone's small child," she said, "but they leave as changemakers."

"Can you teach changemaking at age 5?" I asked, intrigued.

"When these students come to me, 25 percent have opted out of learning altogether—one in *four*," she said.

I found that extraordinary. Do kids really opt out of learning so early?

Not if they have a teacher like Kathy. Her primary focus during the beginning of the school year is building the students' trust, and she has found that playing and cultivating empathy are the most powerful ways to do so. "As the year progresses, we help the children to find their passion, and we help them learn around their passion. If one of them likes turtles, then she researches and learns all she can about turtles." The students end up combining their research with their artwork to construct a written narrative. The whole thing is packaged into a book that they then present to the town's mayor. "We find [the] mayor...wherever he is," she told me. "If he is at the waterfront, they present to him there."

By the end of kindergarten, Kathy's students have found a passion, researched it, written a book about it, and shared it with an elected official in a public presentation. They are experts in their subject. "This isn't just a curriculum for these children at 5," she explains. "It is a road map for self-learning that these children can use throughout their lives."

Children can and do start their journey toward being changemakers as young as age 5.

Teams of Teams on the Playground

Not only can schoolchildren cultivate empathy and learn around their passion, they can also practice open collaboration and teamwork. I witnessed this in one of Jill Vialet's Playworks programs at a New York City school. I initially met Jill at a small dinner party she gave at her home in Oakland, California. There, I listened to her describe what can happen on the playground when kids are given the tools, the reins, and the encouragement to include everyone. I had to see it for myself.

When I was next in New York, I visited a Playworks recess at a K-8 school, housed literally in a former storefront in Harlem. There was no dedicated schoolyard, but as fourth- and fifth-graders spilled out into the city street lined with trees and parked cars, it was magically transformed into an outdoor playground—like some idealized scene out of *Sesame Street*. Their laughter drowned out the sounds of the cityscape.

The teachers formed a human barrier closing off the street and guarding the invisible boundaries of the playground. They were available to supervise if needed, and a few joined the games, but they were definitely on the sidelines. This recess was organized and led by the kids, for the kids.

A small cohort of students had been trained to facilitate play. From the steps of the storefront, I could see perhaps six or seven different games going on—all interactive and all engaging everyone who wished to play. Some ran, some played basketball, and some played soccer, but it was all carried out so that no one dominated and everybody got to participate. A child in a wheelchair could find a central place in a jump-rope game by twirling one side of the rope. Others who were less physically inclined could huddle together to talk about a book. If disputes arose, the kids were trained to resolve them using a variation on Rock, Paper, Scissors.

I recognized the different recess activities as a collection of small collaborative teams, where the kids themselves took charge. Each team was autonomous, everybody was included, and everyone's contribution was valued. As Jill had described, the playground was no longer a breeding ground for bad habits like exclusion, dominance, or scapegoating. Instead, it was a training ground for building self-esteem and developing skills and healthy mindsets that would serve them well in the new everyone-a-changemaker world.

Seeing the Big Picture

A visit to Launceston Big Picture School in Tasmania, Australia, offered me a model for how young people can learn around their passion. Escorted by the principal and a student through the airy, open floor space, young people in grades 8 to 12 were busily working on their personalized projects.

At the beginning of the academic term, the students develop a project-based plan designed around their specific area of interest. My student guide, for example, had decided that he wanted to explore a career as a goods exporter to China. His learning plan had to include core requirements, including quantitative reasoning, scientific reasoning, social reasoning (getting other's perspectives), relationship skills, and communications—and it was co-designed with his family and an advisor. As part of his study, he was also responsible for finding an internship in the community that would advance his interest and study. Clearly energized by his education, he was particularly enthusiastic about real-life experience as the canvas for learning school subjects.

As we were speaking, another young man strolled up to the food bar nearby and madly jotted down notes on a writing pad. I was puzzled by this, since he wasn't ordering food. "Is he learning to be a manager?" I asked. "His learning interest is soccer," my student host said. "Caloric intake and healthy eating are part of his study."

Since my visit to Launceston Big Picture School, I have deployed this learning model quite casually at home with my boys. For example, when they learned soccer, we also applied mathematics as it related to the game, calculating ticket revenue and costs associated with running a team. After we'd have a Saturday afternoon practice, I customarily broke out my iPhone to interview and record them as a way to develop their public speaking skills. And watching my video recordings of their matches and games has been something they have done regularly from a very early age to learn their sports and notice how they interact with others on the team.

Sea of Strangers

Children can and should learn changemaking skills at home as well as at school. Conrad Hilton and countless others credit their early experiences at home—particularly the ways in which their parents instilled values of service, generosity, and empathy—with their later success.

But as a parent myself, I understand how intimidating all this talk of changemaking and throwing out the old playbook can be. Parents just want their kids to have happy, successful lives. How are we supposed to prepare our kids for a life of exploding, accelerating omnidirectional change that we hardly understand ourselves?

Not to worry. Whenever I tried to integrate different methods of cultivating changemaking into my own kids' lives, I found it surprisingly easy. Sometimes, it can be as simple as an earnest two-way conversation with your child. And sometimes, your child can teach you.

Soon after my session with Baby Patrick, I was preparing for a trip to New York City, where I was meeting Seth Godin, a best-selling author and popular blogger known for marketing and leadership. I was admittedly uneasy. My son Dante was a kindergartener at the time, and as I packed my bag, he asked me where I was going. I could have just told him that I was going to New York and left it at that, but I thought I could use this meeting as an opportunity to talk about shyness, because I sensed that Dante was on the shy side, like me.

In my case, having grown up shy may have denied me some things—like certain dates or social opportunities—but it wasn't a barrier to success in the world I had known. All you needed to succeed in the twentieth century was a good skill and only enough empathy to get along with others at work. But it would be different for my boys. They would be stepping into a future where work was intensely interactive. Shyness could interfere with their ability to contribute and thrive.

I sat down on the couch next to Dante, his legs stretching only to the edge of the cushion, the rounded tips of his tiny shoes pointing upward. I explained that I was going to New York City to meet someone and that I was worried about the meeting. I used my iPad to show him the picture of the man with whom I would be having lunch. He looked friendly enough, and Dante asked me why I was worried. I told him that I was shy and then asked, "Do you know what 'shy' means?"

He paused for a moment, thinking. "That you're angry?" he guessed.

I told Dante that it was a feeling I had when I was nervous meeting strangers, and that it made me not want to talk.

He sat motionless as he listened to my explanation, his gaze firmly fixed on his shoes. Then he announced, "Dad, I think I'm shy."

"I think you *are* shy, Dante," I said, excited at his breakthrough. "Maybe we can talk about the things that being shy makes you miss out on." We had an adorable bonding moment as we brainstormed a list together.

When we were done with the list, Dante said, "Dad, I have three things you can tell your friend." He had my attention. "First, ask him what his favorite tall building is."

I thought that was a clever idea given our New York meeting. "Okay, I will," I agreed.

"Next, ask him what his favorite food is."

Also good. I typed his ideas into my phone. "What's the third question?"

"Ask him how he is doing."

This was an amazing breakthrough. My son was relating to me and giving *me* strategies I could use to help me overcome my shyness. Shyness doesn't preclude empathic connection. It's more the other way around. Empathy trumps shyness.

Armed with my icebreakers, I met Seth at a Midtown restaurant. When I approached him, he closed his laptop and began to stand to greet me.

"Don't get up," I said as I took my seat. "I have three questions for you. What's your favorite tall building?" He hesitated before settling on the Chrysler Building.

"Great, now, what's your favorite food?" He quickly named his dish.

"And my last question—how are you?"

"Okay, what's up?" Seth asked wryly.

I told him about my conversation with Dante. He enjoyed the story, and it jump-started our own conversation about changemaking.

The next day, colleagues at work were dying to know how my meeting went. They were big fans of Seth. I told them that I had found it hugely enjoyable and shared some of his advice on leadership and marketing. But they seemed oddly disappointed by that report, as if they were looking for more. I apologetically asserted that the depth of a connection might not be revealed right away, but clues come with time.

"He wrote a strange blog post this morning," one of my colleagues said, an indicator as to the source of the disappointment, "something about strangers and being shy." Wait. What?

His piece was entitled "The Sea of Strangers." It read like a kind of mentoring letter to my son—or perhaps to me. "Everyone is at some level shy," Seth wrote. "The connected person is no different from you, they've merely made a generous choice. When we weave together strangers and turn them into a tribe, we create real value, value that lasts."[21]

This is a team-of-teams view, and Seth was articulating how introverts and extroverts alike can join and weave teams. I loved the insight, and it built so nicely our conversation from the day before. A week later, I received a package from Seth, a large box which included copies of his works, and autographed books and notes for my boys—a gesture of genuine thoughtfulness; a connection had, in fact, been made.

Today, Dante is not shy. He is an introvert, to be sure, but he is also very social, makes friends easily, and has a well-developed capacity for kindness.

Leaving to Learn

As with 17-year-old Conrad Hilton in St. Louis or 17-year-old Abraham Lincoln in New Orleans, leaving home (or at least stepping outside one's usual circles) at a young age to discover new, formative experiences is a common thread running through many changemakers' biographies. Whether it's discovering life outside your neighborhood as a child or participating in an exchange program in your teens, exploring new environments is key for developing changemaking skills. Or, as Mike Marriner, co-founder of Roadtrip Nation once told me, changemakers learn outside of their comfort zones.

When they graduated from college, Mike and his friends felt like they were on too-settled a life track, with their careers and future expectations all mapped out. They decided to take a road trip, seeking out people from different walks of life and a broader view of the possibilities available. They pooled their money, bought an old RV, and hit the road.[22]

Their road trip experience became the basis of a book, a PBS series, and an expansive program to help young people explore their own lives by reaching outside their habitual boundaries. "We needed to get away from where we knew to find ourselves," Mike told me. "But even if you can't pile into an RV, just getting out of your zip code can go far."

I met Mike in 2014, and through him I came to understand the concept of *leaving to learn*. About a year later, when his story was still fresh in my mind, a unique personal opportunity arose in Tasmania, an island state of Australia. I had been offered a short-term visiting scholar position at the new Peter Underwood Centre for Educational Attainment at the University of Tasmania in Hobart, where I could help build changemaking into the culture and curriculum.

I made the case to my wife, Sine, that our family should go. We didn't have much in the way of savings, so cobbling together the money we would need to travel there wouldn't be easy. It would also mean taking the boys, who were 8 and 6, out of school. But I argued that this was a leave-to-learn opportunity for them, a chance to cultivate some change-maker skills at a young age. Sine was game. "We need to build those empathy muscles up," she said.

We spent nearly three months in Tasmania in 2016, and I quickly realized that it is a changemaker island. There is a sense of individual agency and devotion to community that made it feel like a natural incubator for my ideas on parenting and educating changemakers. It's also a bit of a frontier society, civilization's last stop before Antarctica. When we arrived in Tasmania, our host, Elaine Stratford, challenged me to consider what could be learned from this island community on the edge of the world.

The first thing I noticed was that it was disorienting for our boys. They got on the plane during the winter and flew into summer. The sun made its way through the northern sky, not the southern. People spoke a form of English that they couldn't understand. Unfamiliar exotic animals came out at night.

So, we worked at adaptation and focused on the learning part of the leaving-to-learn equation. We went off-grid for a week on Bruny Island, a pristine, exotic island just south of Tasmania, clinging to the edge of the world. We visited all the local museums and made a point of accepting every invitation to meet new people and join community activities. Everyone in Tasmania—from our neighbors and churchgoers, to restaurant owners and tour guides—engaged with our kids. But the one who had the biggest impact on them was the man they still refer to as Bob the Zookeeper.

They encountered Bob at the Bonorong Wildlife Sanctuary, which has a night feeding tour. It was the perfect activity to help the boys learn about the area's animals and also practice the care and nurturing of these exotic night critters. We were the only ones to step through the gates the evening of our tour, and the boys must have felt a little like Conrad Hilton at the St. Louis World's Fair. The sanctuary was a magical place filled with animals we had never seen and even some we had never heard of. It was dry and wooded, and shadows were falling across the park as sunset approached. Kangaroos and wallabies grazed around us.

Upon our arrival, we were greeted by Bob, a burly man with a salt-and-pepper beard, wearing thick boots that we would later learn were attractive to Tasmanian devils. He would drive his boot into a den, and out would come a snarling devil, its jaws and teeth locked onto the toe. A man who could pull off a trick like that quickly assumed heroic dimensions in my small boys' minds.

As soon as Bob joined us, Dante and Zane ceased to notice us; they were locked onto Bob, almost like a pair of Tasmanian devils themselves. Our photos from the outing show a stream of images of them looking up adoringly at him, despite the incredible animals they engaged. Sine and I just trailed along behind as Bob took them under his care, putting them in charge of the feeding rounds. The experience felt surreal. We pet a koala bear, scratched the chests of wallabies, dropped food down the throats of tawny-mouthed owls, held a wombat in our laps, and even fed the devils (don't try this at home). It was as if we'd broken into the zoo at night, pet all these exotic animals, and gotten away with it unscathed.

As the boys fed the animals, Bob told stories about each one they met. Randal the echidna, or spiny anteater, had lost a leg, and the boys nursed him with a peanut-butter mix. The albino possum they fed had been rescued from his dead mother's pouch after a road accident. Being nature's anomaly, he would not have been allowed to have a full life had she not been struck down. The Tasmanian devils had a disease that had turned them into an endangered species. Fred, the sulpher-crested cockatoo, was 102 years old, outliving his devoted owner by more than a decade.

It was more than a night feeding we were witnessing; it was care-giving. Bob exuded empathy in the way he described and treated the animals, and in how he interacted with the boys. What they remember most about Bob is that he made them feel important. We had many amazing experiences in Australia, but for Dante and Zane, that evening with Bob—and interacting with animals in a way they never had before—was the highlight. "Bob gave me my love of animals," Zane later remembered.

I noticed subtle changes in the boys as a result of our time in Australia. For example, they lost interest in their *Star Wars* light sabers. When I came home at the end of my work day, they charged to the door to give me a hug—a routine that had stopped happening back home quite some time before. They were interested, even curious, in their new surroundings. When they returned to their life in Virginia, the process of settling back into their familiar friendships wasn't a seamless one, in part because they had experienced a social and mental growth spurt that their friends couldn't relate to. When they summed up the time in their own words, both boys told me that our extended leave had taught them how to cope with an unfamiliar place. "It's important to get to know people who are different from you because they might not be what we expect," Dante said.

Those are key lessons for future changemakers. Children might learn them at school, at home, and on the road. They might learn them from parents, teachers, babies, mentors, Tasmanian devils, or each other. Each child's experience is unique, but there are two principles that apply to all children and to all those who care for them and strive to prepare them for the future. First, every child needs to master the basics of changemaking—conscious empathy, being of service, self-definition, building a team to implement an original idea, and getting out of one's zip code or comfort zone to learn. Second, these things can be learned at surprisingly young ages and can even be taught by other children and teens.

Every child must grow to be a changemaker, and the world is the changemaker's classroom. That means adults at home, in schools, and in our neighborhoods have an obligation to create those enabling conditions for all young people to practice and master the core skills for thriving in today's world. The blueprint for practicing empathy young, learning around a passion and developing self-definition as a preteen, and leaving to learn throughout youth and even into adulthood, are easy to integrate into the growing-up experience.

There is one more element of the changemaker youth apprenticeship that requires special attention: the teenage years are prime for practicing and mastering changemaking.

CHAPTER TEN

Lead Young

BILL DRAYTON IS widely credited with popularizing the term "social entrepreneur" and pioneering the field, and he is considered by many to be the preeminent expert on citizen entrepreneurship directed to social good. My former professor, David Gergen, has called him the godfather of social entrepreneurship.[1] So what does Bill think is the most critical cohort that needs to be empowered in order to usher in the "everyone-a-changemaker" world?

It's young people. Bill is passionate about making the case that they must find their power early in life so that they can become confident contributors to society in an era of unprecedented accelerating and explosive change. In an ever-changing world, to be able to play, everyone must be a changemaker. And today, changemakers must start young.

"Once a young person has had a dream, built a team, and changed her own world, she has what is required for a good life," Bill says, "the power to be a contributor in the wider world. And she knows it. That is the breakthrough that empowers that person for life."

Bill found his own power young. Too small for contact sports and bored by school memorization, he found inspiration in starting things. This is what drove him forward. He started a newspaper in the fourth grade. "People were surprised and even back then, they were puzzled by who I was," Bill says. "Many thought I would become a journalist. I was 100 percent committed to the paper, as any entrepreneur would have to

159

be. But it was really about being a changemaker, an entrepreneur—about mastering the change-the-world superpower."

As Bill dove into building his paper—the writing, the advertising, the sales revenues, and the production and assembly—his fascination with how the world works likewise grew, and it fueled a subsequent life-long love of history and geography.

In the fifth grade, Bill experienced game-changing technological innovation: he upgraded from carbon copy sheets to the mimeograph—a low-cost duplicator. "With this new machinery, I was unstoppable," he recalls.

He saw new opportunities and built a team to tackle each—expanding his paper from four pages to 32, and on up to 50. This required turning out more writing to fill it, using new forms of advertising, and extending to other schools. In more ways than one, he was breaking out of the boundaries of his school and breaking through to his real passion, which was entrepreneurial—turning an idea into something excellent and big, and something that changed everyone's sense of what was possible.

He had a secret champion in this, but Bill didn't discover that until many years later. When he went through his mother's papers after she died, he found correspondence between her and his school principal. Since the newspaper kept him so busy, he was often not at home and sometimes not in class. "You can imagine my mother was more than a little worried," Bill says. But he was grateful for the principal's reply: "Trust him—don't even show him you are anxious."

That seeded Bill's view that preparing young people to become changemakers is a job for all of us and that they need adult allies, like Bill's principal—or like his mother was to him. Bill says she provided encouragement and support, without interfering or taking over. He points out that the benefits of such relationships are often a two-way street, since he believes a change among children is transformative for adults. Fostering young changemakers' development isn't just good for them; it's critical for all our futures.

"Any employer with an interest in helping their company have a future should be alarmed if the school down the street is not send-ing changemakers into the world," Bill says. "It should be the central question for every household, every school, every community, and every organization—how many of our young people know they are changemakers?"

Greening the Food Desert

Because changemaking is the new imperative for a rising generation, and young people must be protagonists in their own learning journeys, I've made it a personal mission to find and witness young changemakers in action and to share their stories so that others can learn from them. That was the purpose of my visit to West Oakland, California, nearly 10 years ago. An industrial town on the edge of the San Francisco Bay, it possessed a bleak landscape. Even my cursory Google search of West Oakland only pulled up headlines about the ravages of crime and poverty. According to the coverage, this community offered little opportunity or hope for young people. Driving through, my first impression matched the headlines; it had the look of a community in crisis.

After spending a day there, I came away with a very different picture. I met with local teenagers working on various neighborhood projects; some worked on adaptive reuse of abandoned spaces, while others were building community around mural-art projects. These young people were making a significant impact, and they had pride in where they lived, love for their families, and hope for the future. Seen through their eyes, West Oakland was the opposite of the way the media depicted it.

One team in particular captured the spirit of the neighborhood as I experienced it that day. Comprised of four teenagers—three young women and one young man—the team was part of an afterschool community-activism group called WYSE (West Oakland Youth Standing Empowered). Taking me on a tour to show me their project, they led me to a corner liquor store. I was a little puzzled at first, but then they explained the story and logic behind our destination.

There were around four dozen liquor stores in a 30-block radius, but no grocery stores providing access to healthy food—what is known as a "food desert." Liquor stores inside the neighborhood did sell some food, but primarily low-quality, unhealthy snacks. The whole area lacked access to fresh produce and other healthy food options. Since most local residents didn't have cars and the walk to the nearest full-service grocery store could take an hour for some, these local stores had a captive market, and their prices were exorbitant.

Food insecurity—the lack of access to healthy food, which leads to malnutrition and hunger—has a big impact on neighborhood public health. Diabetes and other diet-related diseases were common in the lives of these teens' parents and those of their friends. It was as if there was a wall around their neighborhood keeping good food out and bad health in. They decided to tear down that invisible wall.

As we stepped into the corner liquor store, I was immediately greeted by a large shelving unit in the entryway, well-stocked with a variety of neatly organized fruits and vegetables. Of course, people came to stores like these for alcohol and unhealthy snacks, and you could still find them. But first, you'd have to navigate around the large display of tomatoes, onions, radishes, carrots, bell peppers, apples, bananas, lemons, and other items.

Jamelah, the group's marketer and spokesperson, stepped in front of the display and explained their project. They wanted to educate the community about healthy eating and living using food displays in participating stores—like this one—to get attention, make healthy food available, and enable some different choices and behaviors. The initiative was called the Healthy Neighborhood Store Alliance (HNSA).

To create the HNSA display, Jamelah and the team had partnered with the Mandela Foods Cooperative and the liquor store owner—a team of teams. Thanks to some ingenuity and an elaborate bicycle transportation system, they managed to keep it stocked with fresh, organic fruits and vegetables from local producers. I asked these WYSE team members how they'd found the confidence as teenagers to try to shift the behavior of adults and whether they were taken seriously. "It doesn't matter how old we are," one said. "We can be the change right where we are right now."

I peeled away to chat with the store owner, asking him why he had chosen to partner with the WYSE teens. "They take care of their business, and it's good for mine," he said. "And what they do is good for all of us." He spoke of these young people both admiringly and matter-of-factly, as if they were partners or allies, and as if there was nothing particularly unusual or remarkable about what they were doing or how young they were.

But in truth, I hadn't fully understood just how remarkable their work was, as the tour wasn't over yet. I followed the team out of the store and onto the sidewalk in front. "Do you see this corner?" one of the young women asked, gesturing around her. "If you came here on a Saturday morning, you'd see that we turned this walkway in front of the store into a pop-up health clinic, with educational materials and health-monitoring services." They had partnered with community medical caregivers to bring health services to their neighborhood. Another team of teams.

Then, once they had established their presence on that street corner, they saw a new opportunity. "Look down that street," one of the team members said, pointing. "We think people—particularly elderly people—should be able to walk in safety from there to here." So, they had organized local youth to team up with law enforcement to keep the area safe.

That's three connected ventures this group had generated—the produce display, the pop-up clinic, and the protected walk, all working together to bring nutritious food, health services, and security to the block. It was a kind of hybrid approach to improving the health and well-being of the community.

We went to a local spot to have lunch and talk more. The young man in the group prepared our lunch. I was too engaged in our conversation to remember much about our location. It may have been a training facility for aspiring chefs, since becoming a chef was his ambition. I recall we had the place to ourselves, and he had all the resources needed to cook a delicious meal in our direct view. He served salmon and asparagus, and as our young host tended to us, he offered nutritional facts about our meal throughout the service. It was clear he was learning around his passion, while also working as part of a team to solve a social problem. His changemaking skills would not only be an asset in any kitchen, but also in any community he might engage with as a restaurateur in the future.

Jamelah was interested in business and marketing, which is why she was the group's public face. I thought this was an interesting choice on her part because she seemed somewhat shy; however, when I saw her again a year later at a public event, she was brimming with confidence and was completely unreserved. She told me that the team had struggled at the outset and that their first store had failed. "We just didn't know what we know now," she said. "It took time for us to work out some of our ideas."

These young people were already practicing the key elements of changemaking that would serve them for life—starting young, defining themselves, finding passions, serving others, launching ventures, building teams, seeing opportunities, and solving problems. They saw themselves as "West Oakland Youth Standing Empowered," and they had stepped into their BIGness by choosing to see themselves as bigger than the limitations of their neighborhood or the afflictions their families faced. And they were equal to the task of overcoming them. They identified a problem, pursued a solution, and succeeded because they weren't afraid to learn from failure. They had adult allies and teammates, including an unlikely ally in that liquor store owner. But they remained in charge of the produce shelf and their other projects, and they truly were empowered to pursue their own ideas and passions.

Like Michelle Obama's White House kitchen garden, the WYSE teens couldn't feed the whole neighborhood with that shelf in the liquor store, but it served as a salient image. They could and did change mindsets with it. Today, West Oakland is no longer a food desert. Just last year, environmental justice advocate and social entrepreneur Brahm Ahmadi opened a full-service grocery store to serve some 9,000 residents in the McClymonds, Hoover-Foster, and Clawson neighborhoods of West Oakland. It was the first time they'd had a grocery store in more than 40 years.[2]

Headwinds in Patagonia

WYSE started as an after-school program, and it's an impressive example of what changemaking can be in the teen years. During a visit to

Argentina, I witnessed another effort that was more closely connected to the school context.

I flew 2½ hours from Buenos Aires to Bariloche and then drove through the stunning Patagonia landscape to QMark (stands for *question mark*), a school tucked away in remote, hilly terrain. I was told the school's curriculum integrated nature and learning to promote scientific thinking, as well as problem-solving skills. You could have easily missed it if you weren't looking for it. From the outside, it seemed unremarkable, even a little sloppily constructed. But inside, there were young changemakers at work.

After a brief tour, I entered a high school classroom where about 25 students, between 15 and 17 years old, sat at desks arranged in a large circle. They were designing and building an app for smartphones that would help travelers in the area enjoy their backcountry experience safely. Out-of-town hikers in Patagonia are often lost or have accidents, and this app, they said, would help prevent that by providing hiking maps, local information, and emergency contacts. The app would also have a planning feature that hikers could use to plan routes. It would then also suggest what food, clothing, and gear they should take.

The students worked in different teams. They were divided up based on areas of interest—marketing and communications, geography and the environment, math, and coding and back-end development, among them. Each group had a plan and regularly updated the others on their progress. For example, the communications team pitched news stories about their work to local journalists and appeared in television and news interviews, while the finance-oriented group worked on fundraising. Adults affiliated with the area National Park and a local mountaineering organization also offered support to the students.

These young people were all learning around their different interests and working collaboratively in a team of teams. They were clearly excited by what they were doing. I asked them what skills they thought they were learning. They spoke about empathy, teamwork, the chance to learn through doing, and building relationships. They certainly thought they were getting valuable workplace skills. But there was a problem.

"We are not respected by students at the other schools in the area," one student told me in our group conversation.

"Their parents question our parents' decision to send us here," said another. "People think we are odd." Some also expressed worries about whether they could succeed in a more structured educational environment once they left high school and went on to university.

Clearly, these kids were friendly, engaging, smart, and charismatic. They valued their educations and felt lucky to be getting a unique experience in a school where nature was their classroom. But the world didn't value it the way they did. The message was that what was unconventional was somehow wrong.

My response to them was that not only were they getting a solid education but also an unusual grounding in the skills that success in today's world will require. I told them that my money was on them. In the long run, they were getting everything traditional learning offered, in addition to the benefits of experiential learning and the skills that go along with it.

That seemed to satisfy them, but their concerns speak to a larger point—the experience of being viewed as odd or outside the norm is a very common one for changemakers young and old alike. Even highly effective, established changemakers who are recognized for their achievements have to buck headwinds and negative perceptions regularly. In the world of conventional thinking, they are often thought of as outsiders or oddballs. They're given the message that their goals and/or behavior are strange, and they face resistance from colleagues, parents, and teachers whom they would otherwise count on for support. Some changemakers, like Wellington's clowns, embrace the outsider or oddball role and make it work for them.

The role seems to go with the territory for now, but as mindsets shift and the changemaker imperative is recognized more widely, changemaking must go mainstream. While it's not yet the norm, I've witnessed changemaking skills being taught in all kinds of schools—public schools, charter schools, private schools, educational cooperatives, and nonprofits. Schools play a powerful role in shaping and conveying societal norms. One of the most important things schools can do to prepare students for the everyone-a-changemaker world is to counter the perpetuated resistance to it, embrace changemaking as a norm, and ensure that every student possesses changemaking skills.

Changemakers Pass It Forward

Malcolm Asher knows all about encountering resistance. At age 18, he has already founded and scaled up two major international organizations, and he got his share of pushback along the way.

Malcolm began to feel this resistance at age 7, when he found his passion and set his heart on becoming a doctor. Ironically, it came from his parents and family members, even though his family was steeped in the medical profession. Those closest to Malcolm worried that the sacrifices he would have to make were too great, and perhaps some were worried he was making a choice simply because it was what he had been most exposed to. Headwinds come in different forms. His grandmother, a therapist, encouraged his interest, and Malcolm didn't give up.

When he was 14, he wanted to learn about patient care, but he was too young to take on a paying job or internship. Instead, he started volunteering at the local hematology and oncology outpatient clinic in his hometown of Portland, Oregon. No one at the hospital could imagine a role for him, so Malcolm determined he would do whatever was asked of him to get an inside look at medicine. Malcolm was learning to push back against the pushback.

What he didn't expect was to be working on a unit where the children were in treatment on his very first day. In fact, he was actually being trained for the library and computer room, when he got the call that he was needed in the playroom. It was here that Malcolm realized the importance of empathy in guiding his interactions with patients.

Upon arriving, he sensed the gravity of the circumstances surrounding these children. "It was tense. You could feel the tension," he said of his arrival to his new assignment. "The parents were tense. The kids were tense. I felt the heavy pressure."

What struck him most was the fear the young patients felt. "These were small children and I just wanted to do whatever I could to alleviate the pain and help them."

Malcolm decided to help these children in treatment and recovery stay occupied through art. He brought in art supplies and organized art projects to help the kids take their minds off their fears, fight off boredom, and stay busy. The children typically made art for their parents or to hang in their own rooms, but something unexpectedly happened when a 7-year-old girl working at his table suddenly leapt to her feet and marched away.

"There was a little girl who had been peering our way just off the playroom, but she was clearly nervous about joining us when we offered," Malcolm remembers. "After a while, a girl at our table took her own initiative to engage her." After having made a piece of art, Malcolm says she quite purposefully walked it over to the other girl who had resisted their previous overtures.

There was something tender in that exchange. Malcolm had noticed the girl who created the artwork seemed quite mature beyond her years— her dry sense of humor and conversational skills certainly stood out— but she also had an extra sense of pride in the interaction. The recipient was also noticeably affected. The giver felt empowered; the receiver felt invited and supported.

Malcolm knew he had come upon an idea for a serious art therapy program to help children engage each other, but initially he couldn't seem to get a listening ear or any meaningful support. Sure, he was young and only a volunteer, but Malcolm didn't think those were prohibitive factors on their own. On the other hand, it's hard when you are young and a volunteer. The dense hospital regulations and limited attentions of over-stretched staff are also complicating. Again, Malcolm pushed through and eventually found support from a team in the outpatient-treatment unit, and after that, from the hospital administrator. He requested and got more room to work on his idea. Art exchange, he reasoned, could change a child's hospital experience. It countered fear and isolation with creativity, connection, and community.

At age 15, Malcolm began taking steps to start his own nonprofit organization. To get it off the ground, he began asking peers for advice. "I knew some kids a couple years older than me who had started their own organizations," he said. "I also connected with a classmate wanting to start a pen-pal program. So I asked a lot of questions of others and I worked with her to integrate our ideas, and we created ArtPass."

Malcolm also looked for support from established CEOs and executive directors in Portland, to learn as much as he could about starting an organization. He cold-called and emailed any top executive whose contact information he could track down, which was not easy given that LinkedIn and other online avenues were not accessible to him as a young person. This led to helpful, in-person meetings, but it also led to a fair number of awkward moments when those leaders welcoming him discovered that the visitor seeking executive management advice from them was, in fact, a 15-year-old.

Sometimes the pushback was inexplicable and extreme. On one occasion, a resident on Nextdoor, a neighbor-to-neighbor online platform, reacted angrily to the young executive director's request for donations to to purchase art supplies for his new nonprofit. Forcefully asserting that Malcolm was pulling resources from other needy organizations, he was lectured that such work should be left to adults. It was memorably disheartening, but momentum was now on Malcolm's side, and the outpouring of support he received from other young people becoming involved carried him through.

ArtPass' leadership was composed entirely of young people because Malcolm wanted them to know they can make a difference. "We are not always invited to lead in a meaningful way," he said. "I thought ArtPass could have a dual purpose to empower children through our initiative, and to develop young people as leaders using our organization as a vehicle for involvement."

Sharing leadership with his peers wasn't always easy. Malcolm had to give up some of the ownership of his ideas to others who were less invested due to competing activities like schoolwork, sports, and after-school jobs. Still, Malcolm can see that their views and energy improved ArtPass and gave it vitality. They helped it get traction as a local program.

ArtPass' initial mission was to create a new form of art therapy that incorporated the exchange of art between patients, but its mission morphed and eventually grew after an experience Malcolm had in Ghana that changed his perspective. It happened the summer he turned 16. As part of a program to assist on health system strengthening projects, Malcolm was introduced to the poor state of Ghana's hospitals. He remembers his astonishment at the difficult conditions he witnessed. He also happened to notice the lack of resources for emotional support during hospital stays, which he said was contributing to a taboo associated with hospitalization. Adults were wary and kids in particular were hiding their symptoms from their parents until they were critically ill. Children were dying. "I knew that any money that was available in terms of aid had to go to improving the conditions and care," he said. "It couldn't go to a program like mine. But I also knew that my program could help children in a new way I hadn't before considered."

When Malcolm returned home, he evolved his organization to have international 501(c)(3) nonprofit status, with a multidimensional mission to transform how children perceive and experience hospital care by collecting and distributing art supplies, establishing art therapy programs in hospitals, and raising international awareness about the need to destigmatize hospitalization and improve hospital infrastructure. Then, powered by more than 150 student-led chapters and 500 Global Ambassadors around the world, ArtPass International helped 30,000 children in over 72 countries. "Our global impact and expansion was all youth led," he said of the young people involved. "But the added benefit was that ArtPass had become a kickstarter for their leadership journeys."

When he was 18, Malcolm decided to reposition his leadership to expand his impact. He handed off ArtPass and formed EmpowerMed to create a new standard for medical education in countries with a critical shortage of physicians. Beginning in Ethiopia, his goal is to mitigate the talent drain caused by burnout and a lack of support for healthcare providers and to create more effective, innovative, and empathetic clinicians through systemic improvements in medical schools.

Serial Changemaking

ArtPass going global didn't happen by accident. Malcolm was deliberate about helping other young people own the idea and lead it in their own contexts. Having found his passion and his power young, he encouraged other young people to find theirs, too, and to run with his idea. That is also what Jeroo Billimoria has done throughout her career. Jeroo is a serial social entrepreneur who has founded seven impactful social change organizations reaching tens of millions of young people worldwide. She started young, became a master at finding solutions to complex social problems, and then scaling those solutions so that they could spread across society.

I met Jeroo in India in early 2017, and when she tells her story, three things stand out—the support she had from adult allies in her youth, her conscious choice to enable other young people as changemakers, and her collaborative outlook. For her, the key to impact is collaboration. "I changed a system through collaboration at a young age," she said. "After that, I could do it again. And again. And yet again."

Born in Mumbai in 1965, Jeroo found her power when she was 11. That's when she organized the domestic workers in her neighborhood to set up bank accounts as a way to achieve financial literacy and improve their lives.[3]

Then, at 16, Jeroo confronted her mother, a social worker in a poor Parsi school system and a professor at the prestigious Tata Institute of Social Sciences, over her approaches to raising India's level of educational attainment. Jeroo believed that the data indicated students struggled most in math and English, and she was convinced that helping students with their studies was the solution, while her mother was focused on nonacademic issues such as conditions in the home.[4]

Jeroo's mother encouraged her daughter to develop her idea more fully, and then she introduced her to fellow faculty colleagues at the Tata Institute. That led Jeroo to Gloria de Souza, an advanced social entrepreneur who was pioneering a "schools without walls" approach to experiential learning. It was a model that eschewed repetitive classroom memorization in favor of real-world problem-solving skills fostered in the real-world environment. Around the time of meeting Jeroo, Gloria was elected one of the first-ever Ashoka Fellows. With Gloria's help, Jeroo created an experiential curriculum intended to make learning academic subjects fun and real. She took her idea to the head of the Parsi school system where her mother worked, and it was adopted and spread successfully.[5]

That was the first of many successful ventures that Jeroo launched to empower young people. In 1992, she returned to Mumbai after getting a master's degree in nonprofit management at The New School for Social Research in New York City. While in New York, she joined the Coalition for the Homeless and helped organize homeless men to overcome isolation and improve their lives by working together. Her approach was simple—help them appreciate their own capacity to help themselves where the system was failing them. When she got back home, she turned her attention to Mumbai's street children.

As she worked with street kids locally, Jeroo recognized that these children were inventive and had a spirited, can-do attitude. She also saw that they were unable to get full medical care when sick, and they feared being abused by the police. There were certain social services they could access during the day, but they felt especially vulnerable after dark. So, she began giving out her home phone number in case of an emergency.

Her phone rang constantly. These children had many unmet needs. The existing system that adults had built to protect them had failed. Jeroo couldn't meet their needs by herself, so she applied the insight she had gained through her work in New York—that homeless people could be empowered to help one another. From that idea, she launched Childline India in 1996. It was the world's first emergency hotline for street children, and it was staffed *by* street children. When a street child dialed the free phone number, another trained, friendly, and sympathetic street child would answer. With every call to the 24-hour service, immediate help was dispatched, and a new data point was registered to help the Childline India team map the holes in the existing safety net. Support services improved. Police exploitation dropped.

Since that first proof of concept, the organization Jeroo founded has handled 90 million calls and spread to 579 Indian cities and districts (covering 77 percent of the country) through more than 1,000 partners.[6] How was she able to accomplish this when she couldn't even keep up with the calls to her own phone? Through collaboration. "We expanded our influence through partnerships," she says. Where most look to scale a product inside an organizational vehicle, Jeroo would expand it by letting go of her idea. Even as she organized the first cohort of street kids, she began cultivating partnerships with established organizations who could adapt Childline India within their own operations.

Then, rather than expand her existing service internationally, Jeroo created Child Helpline International in 2003 as a global network of child helplines to leverage collective knowledge in support of expanding or launching new services within countries. Today, more than 180 child helpline members have fielded more than 20 million contacts from children and young people globally.[7]

Jeroo has gone on to start other globally influential organizations, including Aflatoun International, which teaches young people life skills by linking self-belief and financial literacy. She also launched Catalyst 2030 at the World Economic Forum in 2020, to create a movement of social entrepreneurs, social change innovators and practitioners, and funders to achieve the United Nations Sustainable Development Goals by 2030. "If you collaborate, you can change the system," Jeroo said. "You will see exponential change."

That's the key to creating social change for the good of all on a large scale. Instead of doing it through a large organization with a lot of staff and overhead, changemakers often scale their ventures by letting go of them, letting others run with them, and then starting new ones.

While Jeroo's level of global impact may seem beyond reach, in many respects, her story is not so unusual. She's only doing what most changemakers do. Most young changemakers find an adult ally (Jeroo had two—her mother and Gloria de Souza). Many learn early, as Jeroo did, that they can advance a game-changing idea by building a team and community around it. But there is also another important dimension to Jeroo's outlook. She understood early in her career that anyone can be a changemaker. Whether it's homeless men in New York or street children in Mumbai, she demonstrated that marginalized or at-risk people can often do for themselves what the existing support systems failed to do. The trick is empowering them to do it.

"I have always encountered someone or some group taking the position of what the marginalized can't do for themselves," she said. Drawing on the lessons from her youth, Jeroo is the first champion for those at the margins to tap that inner-changemaker—to find the agency within—when others insist that they are unable to. "The key to change begins with a belief in the goodness of people to give and share, even if they have nothing," Jeroo said. "That I have always believed. If that is your starting point, you can achieve anything you want."

There's a generous, empathetic, joyful dynamic in this approach. In Malcolm Asher's story, when one young patient gave her artwork away to another child as an act of kindness and connection, everything changed. She had received the gift of art's therapeutic effects, and she wanted to pay it forward. When Malcolm built a program around that simple idea and then gave it away so that other young people could run with it, it scaled up globally.

Once Jeroo had found her own power at age 11, her work became largely about helping others find theirs. She built a peer-to-peer system in which changemakers empower the people they're working with to become changemakers themselves. She's far from alone in that; it's an impulse and an ethos that many effective young changemakers share. Through collaboration and partnership, she extended her impact to a global scale by giving her ideas to others to run with.

"You will make a lot of mistakes," Jeroo says of learning to be a changemaker. "I know I did. Just follow your heart, use your head, and be happy."

Your Kid

What Jeroo did is in many ways typical of what changemakers do. But, in fact, anyone can do what she did. Anyone can collaborate. Any young person can cultivate empathy, learn around their passion, find their power, recruit an adult ally, build a team around an idea, and start another. Increasingly, these are things all young people will need to do, including the children in your life.

As Bill Drayton likes to point out, 80 percent of Ashoka's network of nearly 4,000 leading social entrepreneurs started their first organizations or initiatives before they were 20. In that sense, the stories in this chapter aren't exceptional. In fact, there are many thousands of such inspiring, astonishing examples of young people becoming effective changemakers all over the world, with more young people stepping into their BIGness every day. But learning and practicing changemaking must become the norm for every child everywhere.

To succeed in the new world young people are inheriting, with changing rules that continue to evolve rapidly, every young person needs to become a changemaker. They must start young, and their parents, teachers, and employers need to learn how to support their development as changemakers.

It's the new imperative of our time.

CHAPTER ELEVEN

Getting Changemaker-Ready

ANYONE CAN MAKE and lead meaningful change that brings every-one along, just like Jeroo and Malcolm. And everyone *must*. Unlike in the old game, playing fully isn't limited to a few. All of us must capably, confidently, and positively contribute to the forces of change all around us. This imperative also exposes the new great challenge of our time—correcting society's structural imbalance, as our old mindsets, organizational systems, and institutions, which were built for repetition, are at odds with the rapidly emerging, everyone-a-changemaker world.

Enabling everyone to freely and fully contribute across society will require a new framework for living and working together. To lead us through this transition, we must rely on those with the greatest stake in the future—our younger generations. But this new urgency is also colliding with a breakdown in youth employment and engagement that long predates the job losses of the coronavirus crisis and risks perpetually sidelining Millennials and Gen Z. In fact, the future of work and the plight of youth in a disrupted labor market were major topics of discussion wherever I traveled during the past decade. All around the world, youth unemployment has been at crisis levels for many years now. In 2016, during a visit to Spain, I was told that 45 percent of young people between the ages of 15 and 24 were unemployed in that country. Numbers for Australia around the same time put the combined youth unemployment and underemployment at nearly one-third.[1] In preparation for a speech at the Asian Leadership Conference in 2016, I was asked to frame my comments to address the challenge being faced there: "In (South) Korea, more than 90% of high school graduates go to university, and 50% of university graduates become unemployed. What do you think is the most appropriate solution to this problem?"

Everywhere I visited—including the US—there was policy discourse about helping young people navigate the changing economy, but it seemed mostly limited to traditional ideas about STEM education and worker training programs—measures that are important but that really only address the symptoms of the crisis, not the cause. They entirely miss the fundamental, volcanic, cross-cutting nature of how work itself has changed. In a world of rapid, accelerating change, by the time a young job seeker completes a training program and acquires a new skill, it could already be obsolete.

At the same time, stories regularly surfaced of employers complaining that young job candidates lacked people skills (empathy), teamwork capabilities, creative thinking, and leadership skills[2]—all of which are core changemaking attributes.

The New Strategic Landscape

The world is speeding up, yet younger generations wired for change aren't keeping up. Those we are counting on to lead the way in confronting the most complex, challenging problems in history are the very ones being left behind. This became apparent to me a decade ago, when I emerged from my White House bubble. The news frequently featured stories about the plight of US Millennials living in their parents' basements, saddled with high college tuition and mounting student debt, and struggling to find work after graduation or accepting jobs with low wages. Despite getting a college degree, working hard, and playing by the rules, this was the first generation to do worse than their parents and the first for whom the American dream seemed out of reach.

Both Millennials and Gen Z now find themselves caught in the historic dilemma of having been educated for the old game just as the new one emerged. Millennials entered a disrupted twenty-first-century economy with twentieth-century educations, only to find that the careers and norms they had prepared for were evaporating. It is a generation that came of age amid the cascading, dynamic changes brought about by 9/11, the Great Recession, the rise of social media, and endless technological disruption. Regarded as the first generation of digital natives, Millennials also received the education and training that effectively handed them the same old playbook that had been passed down for generations—the one that was designed for the vanishing world of hierarchy and repetition.

In 2016, Millennials became the largest generation in the US workforce,[3] yet they have experienced slower economic growth in their professional lives than any preceding generation. Millennials suffered disproportionately from the Great Recession of 2008, and since then, they have been unable to regain ground in the way their predecessors did. More recently, the coronavirus pandemic exacerbated this problem. As the eldest Millennials hit 40—an age where they should traditionally be wielding economic clout—they suffered more job losses in the two months after the pandemic hit than either Boomers (born 1945–1964) or Gen Xers (1965–1980). In fact, Millennial job losses during the pandemic were so severe that they are now teetering on the edge of yielding their majority status in the US labor force back to Gen X.[4]

For their Gen Z successors, or "Zoomers," the dilemma is similar—and potentially much worse. Born between 1995 and 2015, they have less economic status and workforce representation than Millennials. They are graduating and entering the workforce in the teeth of an economic crisis in which job scarcity and slow growth could last 15 years or more.[5] But even before the pandemic hit, they faced a daunting future.

In his 2016 book, *There Is Life After College*, Jeffrey Selingo describes youth unemployment rates not seen in decades and significantly reduced wages, even for college graduates. A bachelor's degree today still gives new workforce entrants an edge, but for barista and clerical jobs, rather than prestigious or professional-track jobs. In that sense, college diplomas are now more like the high school diploma a generation ago. Employers complain that college degrees are an increasingly unreliable indicator of workforce readiness. These slow-to-launch generations are seeing delayed career, marriage, children, home-buying, and other milestones previous cohorts reached at younger ages. Compared to the trajectories of their parents, today's youth are lagging well behind.[6]

Many young people know this intuitively. They sense a profound disconnect between the old paradigm they were trained for and what they're actually experiencing. They are left with unsatisfactory options—either trying to shoehorn old-game approaches into the new game or improvising by making it up as they go along and attempting to navigate uncharted territory without help or guidance from the preceding generations.

Emerging generations ought to be an engine lifting up the rest of society, yet they are being impeded, in part, by competition with their elders. Boomers are living longer, working longer, and holding on to well-paying jobs. Even in retirement, older workers are downgrading into lower-level jobs that would otherwise have helped build younger workers' careers. As a result, not only are Millennials in particular less well-off than their Boomer parents, but there is an increasingly untenable trend toward fewer younger workers supporting more retirees.

The resulting intergenerational social tension and clash in outlook is shaping our culture and economy. Denied a stake in the economy—unlike their parents at the same age—Millennials and Zoomers are unsurprisingly less consumer-oriented and more politically disaffected. They are slow to embrace consumer and political brands, preferring ride-sharing to car-buying, tiny houses to McMansions, and insurgent candidates to establishment candidates of either party. As their numbers rise, their attitudes are increasingly felt in the marketplace and at the polls. As economic inequality and job losses increase, so do social tensions around these intergenerational fault lines. Without judging whether the impact of their rising influence is positive or negative, it's fairly clear that their preferences could lead to a dramatically shrinking economy.[7] This risks further exacerbating intergenerational tensions.

It's also not hard to see how the clash of attitudes and values feeds into trends of disaffection and eroding confidence in our institutions, which has been on a clear decline since the turn of the millennium. Confidence in the presidency and the Supreme Court alike—around 50 percent 20 years ago—fell to 38 percent in 2019.[8] Faith in Congress hovered between 24 percent and 30 percent between 1998 and 2004. In recent years, it has rarely topped 10 percent, sinking as low as 7 percent.[9] That's not good news for the functioning of our democracy.

Nor is the news good for our educational institutions. When my dad started teaching in the early 1970s, confidence in public schools was at 58 percent. By the time he retired in 1993, it was at 39 percent, and by 2012, it was at 29 percent.[10] Confidence in higher education continues to fall as Gen Z students attend college and hit the job market with a thud. Between 2015 and 2018, it slipped from 57 percent to 48.[11] In 2013, 70 percent of American adults surveyed said college was "very important." Today, it's 51 percent.[12] Most still think college is valuable—88 percent of American polled said so—but 42 percent say it's not worth the high cost.[13] And that was before the coronavirus pandemic disrupted the field of higher ed and sent colleges and universities scrambling to put courses online and reinvent themselves amid declining enrollment.

The New Framework for the New Game

Because our education system and other institutions remain geared toward the old siloed, hierarchal, and repetitive system, a disconnect has emerged that risks undermining civic health and leaving young people further exposed to the cascading changes coming their way. But there is another trend, which is not quantifiable, that may prove to be more important than all the others combined. I have introduced it already— the *changemaker effect*. Individual agency is rising. We have tools at our fingertips that can empower any one of us as agents of transformative change. Silos and hierarchies are increasingly falling and making way for democratization of leadership across our society.

Bastions of power, privilege, and exclusion are being challenged like never before, from #MeToo to #BlackLivesMatter. But these are more than struggles to resolve the inequities from our past—reckoning the last mile of the old game—we are seeing the pioneering of the first mile of the new game through these same movements to ensure *everyone* is enabled as changemakers in this new team-of-teams world. This is the flip side of negative, disruptive change. Old structures are being swept aside, and the old world of hierarchy and repetition is quickly diminishing, which causes pain and uncertainty. At the same time, positive opportunities to build anew are everywhere and available to everyone.

The rise of changemaking and its aggregated impacts can often be surprising and unpredictable. At the time of this writing, the changemaker effect is shaking the foundations of deep-seated institutional racism, as protestors around world demand and lead change. By the time this book is published, it will no doubt have disrupted further barriers to transform in ways we never imagined would change in our lifetimes.

Everyone can participate in the changemaker effect, and to navigate this time in history successfully, everyone must—especially young people who have the greatest stake in the changes taking place. To avoid being left behind, to turn this turning point in history to good account, and to master the new strategic landscape, young people need to overcome the historical and demographic trends working against them and seize the changemaker mantle. The world today requires a new kind of citizenship. Even as our emerging generations are being disproportionately challenged, the great opportunity for young people today will be to get the world changemaker-ready.

Unbundle Learning

"What the world needs is twenty-first-century citizens who can solve for twenty-first-century problems," Abby Falik, the founder of Global Citizen Year, told me. "Meeting the unique challenges of today will require a generation that is defined by its courage."

Abby believes that equipping every young person to meet contemporary challenges is a great need in society, and not one traditional school environments are embracing. That's why she created Global Citizen Year—to launch a generation of leaders with the skills and outlook to solve today's most intractable global problems.

Abby has long had a propensity for starting things. At age 7, she demonstrated a certain entrepreneurial flair when she began selling her father's neckties door-to-door around their neighborhood. At 12, she organized a neighborhood camp for kids, with field trips and a range of learning and recreational activities, then handed it off to her sister. Later, in high school, she persuaded the administration to make community service a graduation requirement, and to ensure that students weren't just "ticking the box," she linked the service program to the freshman year writing course so that everyone would have an opportunity to reflect on their experiences. Ultimately, she embedded service into the education curriculum.

With every project Abby launched, the rhythm of changemaking came more clearly into focus. She had a methodology—perceive the unmet need, find a solution, experiment, and find a way to embed the evolved solution into an existing structure.

Her development as a changemaker was also marked by deep, immersive, global experiences that formed her into a global citizen and crystalized her ideas for preparing a new generation of social change leaders. The first was during the summer of her seventeenth year, when she lived with a family in a rural village on an island in Nicaragua. It opened her eyes to the reality of extreme material poverty. At the same time, Abby was struck by the fact that her host family members were more resourceful, generous, and industrious than anyone she had ever known. "When you see things you can't unsee, and your heart breaks with the profound inequity of a world where talent is evenly distributed but resources are not—there's no going back," she told me.

Abby came to fundamentally believe that sending young people straight from high school to college missed a crucial opportunity to help them develop as adults and to learn about themselves and the world around them. She sees the transition out of high school as life's most formative moment—when a young person has the maturity to leave home but hasn't yet fully formed a fixed identity or value set and is wide open to new experiences.

"I viscerally remember finishing high school and craving another experience that would stretch and challenge me before continuing with my higher education," she said. "I'd been a good student and checked all the boxes—it would have been fair to call me an 'excellent sheep.' But my identity had been as a student, and my sense of purpose was to simply get into college."

Abby wanted to go to college ready to declare a mission, not just a major. She wanted to find an opportunity to discover that mission and learn more about herself and the world before setting foot on campus. But such opportunities didn't exist. If she wanted to live abroad, she could perhaps have joined a religious mission or the military, but there was no secular, civilian program designed to leverage this formative moment after high school.

Today, her organization, Global Citizen Year, fills that gap—though Abby prefers to call it a *purpose* or *launch year* instead of a *gap year*, as is customary. "A gap sounds so deficient, doesn't it?" she asked. "It's like this thing you have to make an excuse for."

Each year, Global Citizen Year recruits a cohort of diverse, exceptional high school graduates from around the world, and uses a learning model that wraps coaching and curriculum around real-world experience to ignite a lifetime of purposeful leadership.

For the equivalent of an academic year, Global Citizen Year Fellows live with a family in Africa, Latin America, or Asia, apprenticing in communities and supporting local efforts to improve education, health, and sustainability. They develop insights and skills that shape their character, equip them to find cooperative solutions advancing the common good, and inform their college choices.

"We are preparing young people in ways that classroom learning alone cannot," Abby said. "The power skills of the future—adaptability, agency, empathy, courage—cannot be taught in a classroom. We need a new paradigm for preparing the citizens and leaders who will shape our shared future."

College is the single biggest financial investment we make in young peoples' future, but when they arrive to campus, Abby says many are not ready to make the most of the experience. A launch year can change that, helping young people develop the mindsets and skillsets that will prepare them to thrive in higher education—and beyond.

She also believes that in a fast-moving world, where social media pulls young people's attention away from the wider world and glues it to their screens, a year away is a chance to carve out space for introspection and connection. Invented online personas carry the risk of becoming false identities, but a launch year can help young people find out who they really are and focus on what really matters.

"The empathy gap is immense—and it's growing," Abby said. "What if we could help young people learn to reflect deeply and aspire to a purpose beyond themselves?" Immersing oneself in service of a purpose beyond themselves for a year does more than just clarify one's sense of self, she argues; it recasts it. "Global Citizen Year was never about giving young people a memorable growth experience. We offer a transformative experience that gives them a new sense of themselves."

This sort of self-discovery and self-leadership is not something most colleges and universities are set up to do, but it's something young people need and are wired for. Abby sees the launch year as part of a bigger opportunity to unbundle education from four-year institutions and empower young people to be protagonists in their own learning. "There was a time not that long ago when we had to buy a whole CD even if there was just one song we wanted to hear," she said. "In the same way that we can now subscribe to iTunes or Spotify to hear songs on demand, I am convinced that education will come unbundled from traditional four-year campus experiences. Increasingly, students can access courses, internships, and learning opportunities on their own terms—without needing to commit to the traditional path."

Walking Through the Tough Stuff

Abby Lindsay followed Abby Falik's path after high school. Seminal moments in her life had already distinguished her own journey of self-discovery. One occurred two years before she enlisted in Global Citizen Year. Helped by her participation in Best Buddies, a program that works to build greater inclusion for people with intellectual and developmental disabilities, Abby stormed into her father's home office to announce that she had discovered her power—she had an ability to connect with kids with disabilities in ways that even trained professional adults couldn't.

"That's a gift," Abby remembers her father saying.

The second such moment occurred the following summer, when her family was preparing to spend two months in Colombia. Their visit would include a stay at an overnight camp for Abby and her brother. "I didn't want to go," she recalls. "I was just getting friends at my new high school—it had taken me almost two years to find my footing—and I didn't want to be pulled away from them. At the end of my sophomore year, I was finally beginning to find myself and my place... and my people."

Her hard-earned sense of belonging interrupted, Abby found solace in the camp experience by looking after her brother during that time away from their parents. "He didn't speak Spanish, and I did, so I was able to watch over him and help him. There was something fulfilling about that—something empowering," she remembers.

Two years later, Abby was off for Ecuador for her own six-month immersion experience with Global Citizen Year. This time she was going alone but now she was well versed in learning outside her comfort zone. She lived with a host family and volunteered as a speech therapy assistant at a rural clinic that served people with disabilities. She was chasing a dream, but it was still unsettling to go to a place where she didn't have friends or a safe space.

"I found out who I really was," she recalled. "I was no longer able to hide behind my labels. Nobody there cared about them. Back home, I was a daughter, an athlete, a Bostonian, and a Best Buddy," she said. "None of that mattered in my new village."

In Ecuador, for the first time, Abby had the chance to really reflect on herself and work out who she was, away from the noise. "Back home, I'd had this armor on with all my labels, and suddenly I felt so vulnerable without it," she told me.

Abby showed me some of her online written reflections from her time in Ecuador. She described taking a leap into an unknown place, trying to find familiar faces, and communicating in a new language. "I know that there is no going back," she had written, "but I have faith that I will re-find comfort and stability here if I give myself the space and patience to settle and be okay with the discomfort. I think that this is something I'm going to get really good at, or at least that I will try to get better at... being okay with losing control of my situation and embracing that discomfort."[14]

When I met Abby in 2017, it had been three years since her launch year, and she was quite comfortable with herself. "I am not the type who has the big world-changing ideas, but I know my value," she told me. "I love to learn, I am a great team player, and I am good at making connections. I am good at using what I have to solve challenging problems."

After finishing her undergraduate degree at Georgetown University, Abby set off to work with people with disabilities in the Seattle area. She recently returned to Global Citizen Year as a staff member. What does she say about herself today? "I enjoy giving my time and walking with people through the tough stuff of life," she says.

Abby sees big impacts in small, everyday interactions.

Protect Your Courage

Impact is what Eric Glustrom is all about. With a fresh vision for a new kind of education that enables young people to emerge confidently as changemakers in today's world, learning has always fascinated Eric. Ask him when he discovered his power and Eric recalls two moments in particular. The first was sometime around age 7, when he developed a knack for candle-making. "I had these molds," he said. "And out came these big beautiful, colorful candles that I'd created." Eric remembers that his parents were supportive, but never took over. "It was a fine line," he said. "Our kitchen became a candle factory, but my parents never made their support conditional." Soon, he'd struck up a deal with a local crafts store to sell his candles. "I remember they gave me my own shelf," he recalls with pride. It was the first time he began to understand the possibilities for himself. While he credits his parents for being supportive of his entrepreneurship— they'd made the introduction to the local artisan—the relationship was his and the accountability was between him and the shop owner.

While Eric may be unclear what kindled his interest in candle-making, he was quite clear about that second defining moment—the one that brought him to Uganda at 17. Having already organized an Amnesty International Club to address real-world problems outside the bubble of his high school and community, Eric was determined to next make a film about a refugee encampment in the Congo region. He was encouraged by a mentor to apply for a scholarship through Amnesty International. Eric remembers the work he put into convincing his parents. They would only allow him to go if he presented them with a thoughtful proposal that considered all the angles, including personal safety and financing. He also had to prove through his conduct that he was mature enough for such an endeavor. "This was a motivator for me to change my behavior toward my sister and treat her more kindly," he joked.

His plans hit an obstacle when, at 17, Amnesty International turned down his application on the grounds he was too young and that the situation in conflict-ridden Uganda was too unsafe. Eric took the rejection to his mentor. "She was quite direct about my best new option," he remembers. "She said, 'just go anyway.'" Thanks to the proposal he had written for his parents, his ideas were already fully developed. Not unlike Conrad Hilton arguing his way back to the family store after being sent away to school, Eric made his case and he was given their permission to go.

Eric lived, learned, and filmed in the Ugandan refugee communities for a month. He was astonished by the resilience, leadership, and determination of the people he got to know. At the end of his month there, he asked the small circle of young Ugandans he'd grown close to what he could do that would make the biggest difference for their people. Their reply was not what he expected. "The best way to help our community and our country is to help us receive an education," one said, "because with an education, we will be equipped to solve the challenges of our community and conflict-ridden country." Eric was struck by that idea.

"My view of education was changed by their words," he said. "Education in Uganda is primarily rote memorization—such as memorizing the regions of Germany—a model of learning that had little to do with solving the conflict right outside their classrooms."

Eric set out to do what his friends asked of him. When he returned home to Colorado, he hatched Educate!, with the aspiration to train generations of future leaders and social entrepreneurs in real-life problem solving, starting in Uganda. Through his program, students get to step outside the boundaries of their school grounds, identify a community need, formulate a solution, collect mentors, and put together a team around their idea. Eric proudly notes that from their first three students in 2002, Educate! has grown to work with over 46,000 students across Uganda, Rwanda, and Kenya as of 2020. The Educate! curriculum has also been integrated into the national secondary education curriculums of Uganda and Rwanda.

"This is now part of the curriculum for approximately one-third of all high school students in Uganda," he adds. "Uganda is the first country in the world with a curriculum that empowers young leaders and entrepreneurs to step out of their classrooms, identify community problems, and start initiatives that offer meaningful solutions."

Ten years after launching Educate!, Eric was challenged by a mentor to consider whether he should continue heading the program's day-to-day operations, or hand it off and reposition himself for his next big world-changing impact. It was a daunting prospect for Eric, but his reflection led him to realize that there was an unmet need in America for experiential learning and problem solving. "It was crazy!" he exclaimed. "Students in Uganda had more opportunities to create initiatives and to solve problems than I'd had while attending the best schools in the United States."

"The best education I got during my college years was not through my university studies, but it was the time I spent working on Educate! between midnight and 2 a.m., after classes and homework, and during the summers," he said wryly. "I'd had this amazing learning experience that was completely absent from my formal education, so I decided I wanted to import this model and the underlying principles to the US."

In 2013, Eric founded the Watson Institute, a four-month social-change accelerator program based in Boulder, Colorado. Students come from all over the world, bringing their social change ideas and hoping to learn how to make them a reality.

The Institute, he says, is a counterweight to an educational system and other societal systems that act like guardrails on the highway to mediocrity, guiding us all toward a default path for our lives. "Many elements of our youth and education system are actively pushing us towards a safe path, rather than a path in line with our deepest purpose," Eric said. "Most institutions don't have a learning-by-doing focus. They have an educate-through-thinking approach. I'm not saying we don't need that, but here we make learning around your idea the core 'active ingredient' of our education."

In its first five years, Watson Institute's 200-plus alumni from 53 countries have raised over $77 million for the social change initiatives they have led, created over 500 jobs, and impacted more than 150,000 lives. Watson alumni are showing up on the *Forbes* 30 Under 30 Social Entrepreneurs list. The Institute is also building partnerships with innovative universities in the US and around the world, including Florida's Lynn University, where students can earn a Bachelor of Science degree in social entrepreneurship.

One of the institute's key guiding principles is *Protect Your Courage*. Eric says maintaining courage is important for Watson students because they continually have to justify the uncommon decisions they are making to their parents, their peers, and even each other. "A life of change-making and a path of impact is oftentimes, if not by definition, the 'road less traveled,'" Eric says. "We talk at Watson Institute about how the road less traveled often isn't even a 'road' at all, but rather uncharted territory that requires true trailblazing. And taking a leap of faith to follow a road less traveled always requires great courage."

See Big, Think Big, Play Big

While Abby and Eric work to prepare young people to play in the new game by upending old systems, frameworks, and ways of thinking, it's not primarily about education, per se. Changemakers everywhere are revolutionizing the meaning of citizenship in today's world and what civic engagement requires of each and every one of us.

Isaac Marcet understands this, and he sees an opportunity of monumental proportions for young people today. "We are the *imagination generation*," says the founder and CEO of an online magazine aimed at Spanish-speaking Millennial and Gen Z audiences worldwide. Isaac launched *PlayGround* in 2008, when he was just 27. With 30 million followers and 100 million monthly video views, he is realizing his dream of helping the emerging generations lead global change.

While growing up in Barcelona, Spain, Isaac often wanted to make a significant social impact, but he faced significant pushback. He almost didn't overcome it. As a young boy, he was in and out of school with ongoing health issues, and he was very socially isolated. "My mom constantly exposed me to the ideas of Gandhi and Martin Luther King, Jr.," he said. "That is where my interest was. I watched hours and hours of MLK speeches during that time."

When he returned to school, Isaac organized his classmates to establish a recycling program—years before recycling took hold in Spain. Noticeably threatened by Isaac's energy and contribution to the school, a classmate belittled him and told him that he'd never be able to make any real change in the world—certainly not the kind he aspired to. This rejection deeply affected Isaac for many years. He never let go of his aspirations, but he did lose some of his self-belief. Later, he would remember this initiative as formative to his development as a changemaker.

Isaac was uniquely curious, and that didn't always serve him well in the world as it was. "Eleven is the age when you are confirmed [in the Catholic Church] in Spain," he explained. "That was when the priest went to my mom and told her that I couldn't be confirmed with the others in my class. He said it was because I had too many questions."

Isaac's curiosity also worked against him in school. He often found himself bored. Time moved slowly for him. "School wasn't a useful place for me," he said. "It wasn't where I learned. I sensed early what I could see with clarity later—that the classroom was where creativity and ideas died. I once heard it said that the mark of a successful school system makes people competitive. It was what groomed some to be the richest and the greatest. I was just not buying that game."

When he was in high school, Isaac's attention drifted to literature and film. "I shifted from Martin Luther King speeches to culturally oriented film. That was my new fixation." Isaac learned through his passions. Books and films fed Isaac's curiosity. And he learned by doing.

Isaac finished high school, but he lasted only four months in university before he knew that he needed to go in another direction. One day soon after he'd left college, Isaac woke up with an idea. He could see clearly how he could make the change in the world that he had always wanted to make—by putting people's words and ideas on the screen. More importantly, Millennials (and later Gen Z), who'd been endlessly told that they were a "lost generation," could have a place for making change—a playground. "After all," he said, "playgrounds are spaces where you can be imaginative, inventive, experimental, and interactive."

"The Internet is a marketplace of ideas that allows us to think forward—to imagine and use that creativity to re-create and, more importantly, co-create," Isaac reasoned. "In the past, the marketplace was based on finite things—commodities like oil, for example—and it could only accommodate a finite number of people. But ideas and possibilities are infinite, and the more of us who engage in that marketplace, the greater the opportunities are for an inclusive and creative future."

Isaac saw an opportunity to reimagine how institutions can work, and he believes that the younger generations can lead the way into this new world we are all entering. "Unique to our time, we literally can create things that don't exist. For example, why don't we create a Department of Youth? Or even better, a Youth Parliament? The tools are there. How might that look differently from our current governing bodies? My sense is it would be more imaginative; more inclusive."

"I appreciate that older generations want to give younger people a seat at the table," he said. "Sometimes, when we go to your power table, things are whitewashed. My feeling is that we should create our own table. How would that change the power dynamic? More importantly, how would that change the creativity dynamic?

"And yes," he said with a smile, "we will of course give older people a seat at our table."

In fact, Isaac is quite worried about the growing generational divide, and he wants to close it. But he believes that younger people must first find their voice and assert their own demands to change this power dynamic. He sees his platform, *PlayGround*, as a starting point for imagining and co-creating a new future. "We started in Spain, but now, we are all throughout Latin America, including Brazil, where we now have a Portuguese-language operation," he explained. *PlayGround* will premier in the US Spanish-speaking market in 2021.

When he first started his organization, Isaac thought *PlayGround* could make its mark in content creation, giving voice to a voiceless generation. He quickly realized that creating content that was passively consumed was the wrong approach. Today, he describes *PlayGround* more as a space for a community of action. "Our motto is: 'like, share, do,'" he said. "On the 'do' side, we empower our audience. There is a space to share and debate ideas, and we form Facebook groups around issues we discuss and do something about them. Every day, we give one or two tips on how to connect or create impact—kickstarting an action, for example."

When I asked him to share examples of his organization's impact, he didn't recite typical social media or organizational statistics. Instead, he told a story about how his platform brought people together. "Henry, I know you are familiar with Ana Bella Estevez and her work helping abuse victims to thrive as changemakers," he said. "We created a three-minute video highlighting her community, and it took off across Spain and Latin America—one hundred million views. She created a Facebook group, which she manages, and it has 25,000 survivors who come together to lift each other up. That's how 'like, share, do' works, and that is how we are proving that the future of change is in how we will engage differently."

"When changemakers have the information they need and a space to exchange ideas, they create. Microdonations, microvolunteerism, microgroups—that is the stuff good content is born from. Our job is simply to enable," Isaac explained to me.

This, he believes, is the historic opportunity for his generation. "The three-hundred-year-old bubble is bursting, and that is beautiful. We see what is happening in the US, beginning with race and feminism, but that is just the beginning. What can we imagine as we sweep away the old system?" Isaac believes strong democracies and empowered citizens are key to our new future.

It's time to go from old to new, and Isaac is showing how our rising generations can lead the way.

"Social Response Ability"

If there is a single factor affecting all age groups today, it's the firehose of social and economic change we're living through. But these changes are affecting young people disproportionately. To survive and thrive in this watershed of change, young people need to be changemakers. Bill Drayton is insistent on this point. "Henry, we must be clear about the question," he once said with conviction, "what percentage of our people are changemakers?"

This is the question that drives the Abbys and the Erics and the Isaacs of the world. Are we preparing rising generations to be changemaker-ready? Are we creating changemaker-enabling systems, beginning with education, but including the workplace and the larger community? These are the fundamental questions that every school principal, every employer, every elected leader, and every household should be asking themselves. The future of any nation depends upon the answers.

"Social responsibility" takes on a whole new meaning when anyone with a smartphone can make and lead change on a societal scale. Even as civic engagement is still evaluated based on old-game metrics—hours volunteered and charitable giving, for example—we all now have the tools to contribute to societal well-being and to reach and organize vast numbers of people. Not that long ago, this was an ability reserved for an elite few. This new reality is changing the very meaning of civic engagement.

We're all responsible for using our leadership potential and applying these tools to create positive social change for the good of all. I call this "social response ability"—a step beyond the *social responsibility* we know from the old game—and full citizenship in this century demands it. Everyone must shape the forces of change in a way that benefits all of us and all of our communities. As we enter a world where change is the only constant, we will also need to reimagine our systems and cultures to accommodate everyone seeing and creating opportunities together.

The world needs to get into this new game. But it's the rising generations in particular that must be courageous, overcome the obstacles of their historical predicament, and lead the way.

CHAPTER TWELVE

For the Good of All

"WE'RE JUST SQUEEZING the life out of our future," I recall Molly Barker murmuring under her breath during our cross-California road trip. We were talking about teen addiction and general well-being. "The addiction so prevalent in our younger population is really just the visible evidence of emerging changemakers having their souls crushed in a world that's holding them back and keeping them down," she added indignantly.

That was a powerful insight for me. *How many other populations and demographics can we say that for?* I wondered. It seemed to me like the brokenness extended as far and wide as the breadth of her statement. Molly was making a direct link between *being well* and well-doing.

We can see how unhappiness is contributing to an epidemic of smallness when we need everyone to be stepping into their BIGness. It is the root of great distress in the world. Discrimination against race, gender, sexual orientation, age, religion, and disability are rampant and deeply embedded in our old-game systems. Depression, homelessness, mental illness, food insecurity—a wide range of issues cause us pain, yet they are pushed to the shadows and dealt with quietly. We all have adversity in our personal life stories that we carry forward into our interactions.

This rapidly changing world is clearly exhausting. It's stressing us out. It is hard on us individually, and it is hard on our society generally. Adding to the complexity, we must all learn how to play in a new societal game that has shifted away from repetition-making to changemaking.

There is a new disparity that we must reconcile. It's the unnoticed yet growing gap between those who can see and play in the new changemaker game and those who cannot. Our ability to meet the challenges we face at home and in our communities is directly proportional to how quickly and effectively we close that gap. We can accelerate solutions to the problems we face when we address the changemaker deficit. Only when we all get into the new game can everyone contribute, feel included, and freely form teams to create opportunities and solve complex challenges. As each of us changes our own world, we also change the wider world.

Valuing Dignity over Status

Changing our worlds begins with a choice. Vishal Talreja made a choice when he formed Dream a Dream in India with the mission of lifting young people out of adverse circumstances and giving them the life skills to thrive in the twenty-first century. His program transforms the outdoor school landscape into a young person's dreamscape, offering a way for children to find identity, belonging, and confidence through play and art. It's helped over a million young people living in deeply adverse circumstances find their own way to thrive and contribute to society when they might have otherwise been shut out, left aside, or gone unnoticed.

When I first met Vishal in 2015, it was his personal history that most grabbed my attention. "Mine is a story of growing up in a poor, upper-caste, Hindu family and living with the advantages of having had truly exceptional parents," he told me. Raised in Bangalore and surrounded by poverty, his parents managed to rise above those circumstances through education. It was the path they encouraged him and his sisters to follow as well.

Vishal's father had lost his own father at a young age, but he worked hard to become a lawyer. His mother was the only one in her family of eight siblings to complete college, and she became a medical doctor. "My sisters and I didn't have a lot of things growing up, but our parents stressed consistently that education was the way to break the back of poverty. We saw this both in their words and their actions," he said. His parents often worked four jobs to ensure that their children had the best education possible. Vishal grew up with strong, empathetic role models.

Having attended the best schools and on track to becoming a banking executive, Vishal's life took a sudden turn when he spent three months in Finland as part of an exchange program after college. Leaving what he had known and grown used to upended Vishal's worldview.

"I don't think I could have found Finland on a map," he said of the experience. "But the discoveries from being in a place that was completely different from home were eye-opening."

Living in Finland challenged all of Vishal's biases. He became aware of his fixed prejudices about class that came with his upbringing and inherited values. "Fortunately, I also had the capacity to challenge these notions," he said.

Vishal befriended a woman during his stay in Finland who had spent six months volunteering in India. She was a bartender. "As soon as I found out what she did for a living," he recalled, "I determined this friendship could not continue. Having grown up in a deeply class- and caste-driven environment, I could *never* explain to my parents why a woman would want to work at a bar."

Vishal also remembers becoming acquainted with a security guard at a hotel and was surprised by the fine home in which he lived and the pride with which he talked about his work when he visited. "People doing service work could never have such a life back home," he said.

Vishal marveled at how people in this country could live good, dignified lives without judgment. The premium was more on who you were than what you did or the background you came from. "I did become friends with the bartender and as I got to know her better, I came to respect her as a human being and challenged my bias on her choice of profession," Vishal said. "I discovered the importance of valuing dignity over status."

Through his experiences in Finland, Vishal reflected on how he engaged with the world and connected with others. He realized that his life's journey had mostly been pursued along the surface—framed largely by his parents' worldview—and he determined that he needed to deepen his relationships. "It all came to this realization that I never really even got to know the people who were caretakers in our own home," he said with a hint of dismay. "These were people—I don't know—they just existed for me. The class and caste system in India was my identity."

For Vishal, when he returned to India, people didn't *just exist* anymore. He noticed the poverty all around him, and while it, too, "just existed," he was determined to not get used to it.

"I had another experience outside what I was used to, in Mumbai, and I had never been there before," he said. "And what I saw, the extent of visible poverty around me, you could easily allow to become background."

Vishal changed the entire script for his life. He was now committed to improving and supporting human dignity. He hopped off his bank-executive track and threw himself fully into helping young people reframe their lives. "I wanted a new script for myself, for my own life," he said. "I wanted to give kids dignity, particularly those who struggled to find their place in this world."

His focus began with children who were being cloistered in their homes during the AIDS epidemic in his hometown of Bangalore. The parents of children with this disease were shielding their kids by hiding them indoors or abandoning them to institutional care. Vishal's goal was to form a community around these children, rather than hide them away. He built a team around his idea, bringing together about a dozen of his friends. "None of us had any experience in social change," he said. "We formed a foundation, and we started working with kids who were not only shut out from school but also who were shut out of society. Literally."

Vishal's organization went on to work with schools across the region to give kids the life skills they need to thrive in today's world. About 10 years into this mission, Vishal and his team realized that learning begins with what is modeled by the dominant adults in a child's life—in this case, parents and teachers. They couldn't achieve the kind of personal-transformative results they wanted if there wasn't a change in the environment first. So, Dream a Dream began to work with teachers.

Vishal elaborated, "We see young people who come through our program, and they start feeling confident. They find something inside themselves, outside where they live. They couldn't find it when they were in their home or school systems." The inner capacity for dignity and self-worth often conflicts with external and environmental forces.

Vishal said that sometimes, these young people paid a high price for their newfound empowered selves. "It can be subtle, and it can be really quite extreme," he said. I understood what he was talking about—the pushback.

"In one case, we had a girl who was locked up and tied down and personally harmed when she attempted to make her own choice to pursue college," he said. "We have come to realize that dignity has to do with the personal *and* the cultural. To truly support the changemaker, you have to also deal with the systems around that person so that they can truly blossom in an enabling environment. If the first step is helping someone find their own power, the second step should be dealing with the rage against that empowerment. That requires a change beyond ourselves."

Vishal shared another example of overcoming adversity. He told me about another girl who came through the Dream a Dream program. "She'd been seriously abused at home by her father," he said. "She joined our football program, and she blossomed, and she was transformed from an insecure girl to a determined, confident woman." Four years later, she rallied people to address a problem in her neighborhood. Seeing that there was no playground for local children, she started a campaign to create a play space for kids. An individual made a land donation, and she got additional support from a local politician and other philanthropists.

Vishal recalled the day he went to her groundbreaking celebration. "Here was a young woman without any money or any connections, who'd taken an idea born inside her head and brought other people around it to make meaningful change," he said. "It was more than the play area for kids. This big beautiful playground was a monument to the transformation of the people involved—the community that was born from conceiving that playground."

Playing It Forward

Now, meet Lekha Sri, one of the many fortunate beneficiaries of Vishal's decision to leave his banking career and focus on opportunities for disadvantaged youth in India. Lekha was 14 when I met her in Bangalore. We were brought together for an on-camera discussion to exchange ideas on how young people today can thrive in a world of dynamic change. It was an intergenerational conversation that would have made Princess Laurentien quite pleased.

If I had seen Lekha on the streets of Bangalore, she would have blended into the masses. She is petite, but she sat up quite straight as she spoke, and her direct gaze communicated unmistakable self-assurance. Lekha has the confidence of a champion, and she credits that to her exposure to a Dream a Dream afterschool program that taught life skills using collaborative soccer play. In a safe, trusting space, the youngsters learn problem-solving, relationship-building, and modeling behaviors by teaching the game to their peers.

Lekha flashed a bright grin as she told the story of how she discovered her power. Lekha grew up in extreme poverty in Bangalore, where it would have been easy to give up and lose hope. She had all the burdens of a teenage girl, just as Molly had described, plus more. She was an only child until she was ten. That's when her younger sister was born, and she became jealous of all the attention the infant received. She began to harbor anger toward her parents. "I always had a wish of getting a baby brother, but instead, God gave my mom a girl baby," Lekha shared. "One of the reasons why I wished for a boy baby is because when I get married in the future, he will be there to take care of my parents. I had an illusion that boys will take care of parents." As the elder daughter in the family, Lekha already felt the burden of taking responsibility for her parents in the future.

Lekha worked hard at her studies, and in sixth grade, through her Dream a Dream afterschool sports program, she took a great interest in soccer. She discovered that she was very good at it. Watching her handle the soccer ball, I immediately knew that she was good enough to compete with the boys—and probably against many adults. "The thing is that my parents forbid me to go out and play with the boys after dark," she said. "They were reactive to the stigma associated with a young girl out after dark playing with the boys."

There's that "girl box," I thought.

She also felt judged by some of her neighbors for playing a game that was considered a boy's game. Lekha was determined to break that stigma by recruiting other girls in the school to join her. "There was a girl named

Harshitha, who was an inspiring girl and played football better than all the boys," Lekha told me. "I always wanted to be like her, but I was also thinking of becoming an inspiration to other girls in the community."

Lekha and Harshitha, another Dream a Dream graduate, started practicing with the boys, and as they did, they noticed the regular disapproving glare of one neighborhood man in particular. "As we played in the community, there was an old man who used to observe us so many days," she said. Lekha had a hunch that changing his mind might help her win acceptance in the neighborhood as a whole. "I would make sure the ball skipped away somewhere his way, and I would sometimes make him know I saw him—maybe a smile or just a glance," she said, her face beaming at the memory. Sometimes, she'd casually display a flash of her skilled footwork near him, as if she didn't notice his presence.

"One day, he came and approached us and asked—'Have you played at the state level?'" Lekha responded that no, she hadn't. Then, another day, he approached her again asking, "Why do you simply waste time by playing in this ground for many months?"

"This was an eye-opener for us," Lekha said.

Up to that point, Lekha had tried to blaze a trail by breaking into the boys' network and improving her skills. The older man had opened her mind to new possibilities. Lekha and Harshitha got the support of the boys to help them field a girls' team, and they surveyed the other classes in their school to get recruits. "The response was overwhelming," she said. "We had more than 30 girls participate in our initiative. Even our principal encouraged and supported it."

But there was a problem. The challenging part of running a girls' team was getting the parents' permission for their daughters to play. While the students were interested, many were denied permission. "I feel one reason they denied was the community where we lived was not safe for girls," Lekha said. "I used to get scolding from parents for running the session. I didn't give up. I prepared girls to face those challenges, which many did." Lekha was able to prevail, and she succeeded in breaking stereotypes with her friends. The two young women also found and enlisted the help of a certified coach, and their team went on to play many matches.

A wonderful bonus for their effort, Lekha and Harshitha were also selected to and played for BUFC (Bangalore United Football Club), a super-division club team. "This is when I realized that an old man indirectly motivated us to reach this far," she said proudly.

The experience of traveling with her soccer teams left a big impression on Lekha. She discovered a whole new world away from where she lived. She recalled one particularly defining moment: "Once I got selected for the state team to participate in the national championship game, and our whole team of 23 girls had to travel to Odisha. Being with the team was interesting, and the team had people from different backgrounds, cultures, and places. It was wonderful to learn about each other's journey and game. I heard heart-touching stories of their struggles to play football in their place."

She also recalled a trip to Delhi with the Dream a Dream program. "I saw many girls who had cut short their hair for playing football," she said. "I know that if they hadn't played football, they would've [been] married forcibly by [their] parents."

Lekha learned that she could be independent and that she could succeed on her own. She also saw the difficult conditions that other people lived in, and she would like to do something about it. Today, she aspires to become a journalist, because she is able to ask uncomfortable questions, but there is a caveat: "I always dreamt of becoming a journalist. But on the other hand, I want to play football on the Indian team and be the best player in our country. I have a few responsibilities in my life. I have only a younger sister, and as the elder daughter in the family, I need to take responsibility of my parents. I also want to be an inspiring girl for others who take up football as their passion. I want to join or start a woman-empowering organization. I will be very happy if at least 100 girls are happy because of me."

The Club Nobody Wants to Join

Vishal helped me see that we all bring our adversity forward into our interactions with others. We can become victims of our story or we can deny or hide it. We can also turn the adversity we have faced into an asset in our lives by owning our story, and not letting it define us—by changing the script. That is exactly what happens at The Dinner Party, an organization cofounded and run by my old California road-trip mate and former colleague, Lennon Flowers.

You'll remember that Lennon is from North Carolina, but on moving to Southern California, she met Carla, and the two discovered that they had both recently suffered a devastating loss. Lennon lost her mother to cancer when she was in her senior year of college; it was a battle that began when she was a senior in high school. An aspiring performer, Lennon had her first read through as a lead character in the student production of *A Midsummer Night's Dream* just days after her mom's passing. She kept that secret from the other cast members.[1]

It is not uncommon for young people to withhold their sad news. Others in their age group are not equipped to support someone suffering through an event that is unfamiliar to them. More importantly, it is an awkwardly timed occurrence at this stage in life. Just as many people are finding themselves and their power, the grieving young person is experiencing traumatic loss and struggling through something they may not have the tools to process. An estimated 5 million children in the US will lose a parent or sibling by age 18, and that number explodes to 13.2 million by age 25. This means 8 million young Americans will experience painful loss just as they are graduating, starting careers, getting married, and beginning families of their own.[2] But this is often a secret that is only brought to light behind the closed doors of therapists and other professionals.

Not Lennon. She made the choice to throw a party. Months after our road trip, she and Carla prepared a dinner party to be held on Carla's back deck. This wouldn't be just any dinner party. It was a very special affair for the invitees to remember the loved one whom they'd lost in their lives. Their idea was that a caring community of people who had been through loss could better help each other through grief.[3]

Together, the participants discovered a safe space where they could share their experiences. No one felt like they were bringing a personal insufficiency to the conversation. In fact, one of the wonderful surprises that came out of this dinner party is that guests left feeling like they had found a new family.[4] More importantly, they celebrated the recognition that their loss was the catalyst for individual resilience.

A few months after that dinner on Carla's back deck, Lennon used the money from her mother's life insurance policy to create The Dinner Party organization. Today, there are over 400 twenty- and thirty-somethings who have hosted more than 4,000 participants who come together around Lennon's dinner table to talk about the experience of losing a child, a partner, a parent, a sibling, or another loved one, and they are supported as a community through her organization beyond that meal.[5]

Lennon's initiative shows how easy and uplifting changemaking can be, while also creating community to meet a vital need.

Changemaking Leads to Community

My wife's book group is another example of how we can easily bring our talents to meet a need right where we already are. Growing up in a rural community about an hour from Seattle, Sine was determined to take a stand against a school board decision to pull classic books from the shelves—a ban imposed by adults on young people without any input. By seventh grade, my wife had already long been reading at the twelfth-grade, nine-month level—the highest you could test at that time. Her friend Vanessa was also a book enthusiast. The two of them put together a plan to go to the next school board meeting to speak out against the ban. They were summarily dismissed by the adults. "They asked who we were and what grade we were in, but they had no interest in our opinions," Sine remembered.

The ban was upheld, but she gained confidence from her act of independence.

Two years later, her interest in politics led her to spend a week as a page at the state capitol, which was three hours from her home. "I'd heard about an older kid, a sister of a classmate, who had become a page in Olympia," she recalled. "I decided I was going to do that, but I had to do everything on my own to make it happen. There was just no support, and it was an activity really nobody knew about." The reward of this accomplishment—having her own goal and working to achieve it—was a game-changer for this girl from rural Washington.

Later, having grown up without a neighbor in sight of her house, Sine set out to chase her dream of being a radio personality, then moving to New York City and working for a startup coffee chain out of an office in the Empire State Building. One can see all the ingredients of a change-maker apprenticeship in her story.

Sine loves her rural roots, but she also knew loneliness in that life. She values community, which for her had always been a destination—at work, school, or some far-off gathering place. And she knew something about courage to overcome one's circumstances.

Twenty-five years later, after we returned to D.C. from Chicago in the wake of President Obama's successful campaign, we moved into a home in the Parkfairfax residential community in Alexandria, Virginia. It is 132 acres of World War II–era housing, making it one of the nation's largest concentrations of converted condominiums. It is a lovely undiscovered secret of the Washington, D.C., area, filled with trees and birds, and an inviting layout with shared green spaces and an inward-facing design that ensures you always pass neighbors while going to and from your car.

And that was the catch. We soon realized that many people whom we passed went home after work and shut themselves inside. The nearest playground, just out our back door, looked dangerous, with steel chains and big drops, and it largely went unused, amounting to a "play desert." For whatever reason, there was no community in our community.

Being a "White House widow" with two toddlers, Sine again felt the pangs of isolation. She read an article claiming that over 40 percent of people in the United States suffer from loneliness. Sine decided to try to get to know our neighbors. She explained to our young boys that 4 out of every 10 people they passed in our neighborhood were feeling lonely, so she did what Florence Nightingale's mom did for her—took them along with her as she knocked on doors. It was an act of courage, and even though she wasn't leaving her zip code, she was straying well outside her comfort zone.

Sine and the boys discovered an abundance of friendliness but also a lot of brokenness. One neighbor was living alone and struggled with the early stages of an unusual form of dementia. Others were shut in with children, like her. Yet almost everyone she talked to felt a desire to be connected. "We had a lot of loneliness living just outside our door," she said.

Sine immediately began recruiting co-leaders to host a book group—a natural fit for my wife, given her long-standing love of books—as a way to bring women in the neighborhood together once a month. That lasted for about a year. Then, while it was still called a book group, it candidly evolved into a wine and cheese social group.

The point is, a couple dozen women of diverse ages came together monthly and started socializing. Soon, the abandoned backyard "play desert" became the center of our community. People began organizing activities around their individual interests. We had kids' birthday parties featuring pop-up petting zoos, our own Easter Egg hunts, yard sales, and regular neighborhood cookouts. We all went trick-or-treating together at Halloween. Even the men started socializing more frequently. That once-a-month book club organized by some changemaker women in our neighborhood anchored a beautiful community and cultivated an environment of belonging for everyone.

When one of the women in our neighborhood was in the late stages of cancer, Sine visited her every day. She had grown close to this woman who was a few decades her senior, and because the dying woman's children lived far from her, Sine was with her when they couldn't be. "She would have been all alone," Sine said. "And how did I know I would be the one person who would visit her every day of the final days of her life? It was because of that book group that I got the opportunity to know her."

Sine's story illustrates that changemaking can happen right outside your door. The opportunity for changemaking is always right in front of us. Sometimes, it just requires seeing a need and putting a team on it. It is the secret weapon in our quest to thrive where we are.

The Generous Choice

I was sitting on the edge of a stage alongside Vishal from Dream a Dream in 2019, microphone in-hand, before an audience of 200 global leaders at his organization's annual Change the Script conference. It is a forum for leaders across sectors seeking to enable cultural and organizational environments where changemakers can flourish, with particular focus on youth and education.

Vishal asked me to share the story of Dante's strategies for my meeting with Seth Godin six years earlier, as he'd heard me tell it before. He listened intently, then I got to the moment in the story when Dante offered his advice to first ask Seth about his favorite tall building and then his favorite food. "And then, Dante must have run out of ideas for questions," I said to Vishal, but facing the audience, "because his last question seemed out of order—perhaps it should have been his first. Dante said: 'Ask your friend *how are you?*'" That got a chuckle from the audience.

At the end of my story, Vishal took up his own microphone to offer a reflection but respectfully paused to let the story set with the audience. The silence felt unusually long from the stage, but I'm sure it was just my discomfort.

"Can I offer what comes to my mind?" he began. "It seems like Dante, who was five, actually had the perfect flow of inquiry that perhaps a child quite naturally senses. We adults would go straight to asking, 'How are you?' But asking first about a favorite tall building and then a favorite food gives one a way to engage this stranger lightly and less directly before getting to such a deeply personal and direct question."

I loved that insight. Vishal's message was that Dante had made *the generous choice*. This was the very theme of Seth's blog post the next day after I met him: "The connected person is no different from you, they've merely made a generous choice, confronting their innate fear instead of hiding from it."[6]

There are many dimensions to Vishal's work, but at its core it is all about making the generous choice. It was his choice to ultimately look at his biases rather than accept his attitudes toward his bartender friend. It was also the reason he left his life as a banker to bring shut-out children into the community as changemakers.

Making the generous choice is the starting point for changemaking. Lekha liked playing soccer with the boys. She grew stronger as a player, and she was blazing a trail by breaking into the boy's system, but she ultimately wanted the other girls in her neighborhood to be involved as well. She made the generous choice to break away from the boys' team to form a girl's club. The old man who initially frowned on her neighborhood play also made the generous choice to encourage her to think bigger for herself and to push beyond the boundaries of where she was.

When my wife learned about the prevalence of loneliness in our society—something she understood—she made the generous choice to knock on doors in our neighborhood and form a club to combat loneliness. Molly took 13 girls on a run. Malcolm noticed when a brave small girl took her art to another hurting child, and then he devoted his teen years to spreading that therapeutic idea. Wellington walked away from his Broadway career to be a clown. Ana Bella used the proceeds from an award to create a business that would give Elsa a job. Katherine hugged the man who ran over her 3-year-old son with his automobile. These are all examples of the generous choice. As Stefan said, life is filled with opportunities to make that choice.

There is a critical next step after the generous choice and that's acting on that choice. Here is where using the changemaker capacities we have been introduced to in *Changemaker Playbook* come in. With every story and every example, we saw changemakers using their own unique talents and abilities to tear down walls and bring people together around a problem or opportunity. When walls come down and two or more sides connect, transformation happens. That is why tearing down walls to form a team of teams is the requisite new leadership skill for today's world. It's the new value premium.

Change begets change. Keeping up with the speed of innovation, and staying at its front edge, requires teams of teams working in spaces of trust. Changemakers build communities of trust that fuel a beautiful kind of change—change for the good of all.

Bill Drayton adds another perspective on why this new leadership capability is critical for thriving in today's world, at work and in our communities. "With everything in the environment changing, and the work going through changing phases rather than repetitive cycles, fluidity is key," he says. "One must find whatever individuals and groups are most important to the team of teams—which requires going beyond the existing structures and people. And yet, all the pieces must work together in a highly integrated fashion because there are a lot of pieces all moving and changing very quickly. And connected to many other teams of teams. Because everyone has to see and seize ever-changing opportunities, the new organizational model must be a fluid, open, integrated team of teams."

"This has implications for how we think of leadership," Bill added. "It's not a few people telling everyone else what to do. New leadership for today's world helps everyone see together, think together, and build together."

Today's leaders often miss this connection, managing people and events rather than facilitating everyone working together as changemakers. I'll occasionally hear a civic leader say something along the lines of "I can't focus on what you're talking about while we have this crisis in my city." The logic seems to be: *How can I work on changemaking when my house is on fire?*

Embracing changemaking is *how* to put out the fire—it's how to combat loneliness, and exclusion, and grief, and addiction. At work, it's how to keep missions relevant and workers agile in a shifting strategic landscape. At school, it's how we make sure every child enters the world with the tools and skills to confidently command the new world and play in the new game. The key performance indicator for every household, every neighborhood, every business, and every nation going forward should be: "How many of our people are changemakers?"

The biggest divide we face is not Right versus Left, or rich versus poor; it's the growing divide between those who can see and play in the new game and those who can't. Put another way, it's those who understand and practice changemaking as a new form of citizenship—a new way of living and working together in the world—and those who don't.

"What you are talking about Henry, is the new inequality," Bill once told me. "It used to be that being good at your skill and diligently following the rules made you welcome. This is the first generation where that formula no longer applies. In this new game, the urgency of mastering conscious empathy becomes clear. Anyone who does not have this learned ability and is not constantly improving it is going to hurt people, disrupt groups, and become unwelcome. And that's before even getting to how critical this foundational ability *is* to the other abilities that each of us must have to be an effective player in an everything changing, inter-connected world."

The challenge before us then is to close that gap and equip everyone for the new era of changemaking now dawning. This begs the question—if parents see changemakers in their home and not just *their children*, if schoolteachers see changemakers coming into their classrooms and not just students, if the mayor of a city sees changemakers in the city and not just taxpayers, and if a CEO sees changemakers walking through their stores and not just customers, how should their mindsets and organiza-tions change to respond to this? Aligning our perspective and systems for the emerging changemaker world must be the starting point for each of us, and as a society to get everyone into this new game—this is the imperative of the new global *everyone* a changemaker movement.

Dr. Solana says we should begin by jumping in—that standing on the sidelines and studying the landscape only leaves us on the sidelines. So take that leap. You now know that the *Changemaker Playbook* used by Wellington, Molly, Ana Bella, and others we have met really just comes down to three simple interconnected components—it's one part making the generous choice, one part putting your changemaker capacities to work for the good of all, and one part creating changemaker-enabling environments that facilitate everyone working in a team of teams.

The Big Breakthrough

My greatest discovery from my Obama campaign laboratory wasn't a political one at all. It wasn't about what we aspired to; it was what we tapped into that already existed in the citizenry that we then built a sys-tem to accommodate: innovative mind, service heart, entrepreneurial spirit, and collaborative outlook.

Jeroo saw the same thing when she said, "The key to change begins with a belief in the goodness of people to give and share, even if they have nothing. If that is your starting point, you can achieve anything you want."

This is the awareness that can fuel our future. This is fundamental in Anshu's communities of dignity, and it is how Ana Bella has built communities of changemakers from those who have been cast aside as society's *victims*. My friend Suchetha Bhat, Vishal's wife and the CEO of Dream a Dream, says it elegantly: "When we have changed together—once we have been transformed—there is just no going back to who we were."

That is the beautiful kind of irreversible change that transforms homes, neighborhoods, communities, workplaces, and humanity. It is the power of changemaking, and what Bill characterizes quite simply as love and respect in action.

FINAL WORD

Anousheh Ansari carried a dream in her heart from the time she was a little girl—perhaps as young as 6. Growing up in Iran, she often slept outdoors on a large balcony, where she could gaze up at the stars and wonder what it would feel like to be among them. When she was in her teens, Anousheh's family immigrated to the US. Then, in 2006, she became the first person of Iranian descent—and the first Muslim woman—to travel into space. For the 11 days from takeoff to touchdown and the nine months of training before that, this American business entrepreneur and technology executive put her career on hold for her own leave-to-learn experience that was literally out of this world. She boarded a Soyuz rocket in Kazakhstan, which delivered her to the International Space Station (ISS), where she lived and worked for nine days. But she almost didn't make her flight.

"I wasn't scheduled to be with this crew," she said. "I was a backup. Three weeks before launch, they made a switch, and I was going." Unlike the crew she joined on the ISS, Anousheh wasn't an astronaut by profession, but she underwent extensive training for her mission and agreed to carry out experiments as part of her assignment. Her story reminded me of my clown-friend Wellington, who had found his way into hospital operating rooms as part of the medical team. I wondered if she was welcomed or if her presence was viewed as an intrusion.

"It went as you might expect," she said in response, referring specifically to her training prior to the flight. "As a technology executive, I can say there has always been a high barrier of entry for women. There is always a natural resistance. Then, when you take into account I grew up in Iran, I was an entrepreneur and not an astronaut, and I was thought of as some kind of commercial traveler, it took a while for people to get to know me for who I was. But they saw I was passionate about the opportunity and dedicated, and that got me in good stead."

"But what about on the actual space station?" I asked, referring to the five people she worked with and lived alongside while in space. "Were you welcomed?"

"There was an American, a German, and a Russian cosmonaut already on board," she said. "We became close. But remember, I had been training with two others for three weeks, getting ready for our flight.

"I'm sure my crew put in a good word for me in advance," she added with a smile in her voice.

Anousheh very specifically refers to herself as a "space explorer." "People described me as a 'space tourist,'" she said. "That sounds like someone who just bought a ticket one day and got on the plane to a new city and ate the food. It is a label that undermines the longing and the passion that defined my purpose—and the hard work, preparation, and training. If you climb Mount Everest, you aren't an Everest tourist. You are an explorer. The same should apply here." Anousheh says characterizing herself as an explorer highlights her curious nature and her interest in applying what she learns to other aspects of her life and career.

Aside from her obvious desire to fulfill a lifelong dream, Anousheh also had her own agenda: she wanted to encourage young girls to take more of an interest in math and the sciences, and she wanted all children to pursue their dreams. As a result, she was particularly driven to connect with students in classrooms and auditoriums here on Earth using advanced communications technology. She also kept a detailed account of her experiences on her blog, making hers the first blog written in space. Her website was viewed by millions of people throughout the course of her journey.

Anousheh summed up the experience in a single word: "one." The team was internationally diverse, yet national interests, prejudices, or rivalries were not brought aboard the ISS. The overriding attitude was that they all had different backgrounds, responsibilities, and perspectives, but they all came from the same planet and were one crew. She described conversations over meals as inquisitive, with everyone being genuinely curious about others' opinions, ideas, and lives.

"One" was also what Anousheh saw out her window. When describing the stunning views of Earth from above, she emphasized: "Really, what you notice is one planet—no boundaries or borders."

In reflecting upon the skills Anousheh used in space that best serve her as a business and social entrepreneur here at home, her list is short and very specific: "empathy and teamwork."

Matters for Chatter

I began writing *Changemaker Playbook* in earnest while sheltering-in-place with my family at the outset of the 2020 coronavirus global pandemic. Our family was immediately confined to our home, which is quite small, and frankly not well suited to co-working. It felt cramped, as I imagined living on the space station might feel. It brought my mind immediately to Anousheh's experience living and working with strangers in unique circumstances.

I say "strangers" because living with your wife and kids is one thing; co-working with them is something very different. We had to learn to commune differently in our contained unit. We also needed a new perspective and organizational system that aligned better with our new reality. Our traditional hierarchical family structure wasn't ideal for these new circumstances. Dante and Zane were 12 and 10, and their supervisors were their respective teachers with whom they communicated all day. My wife's team at work included a range of personalities who showed up regularly on her computer screen, made possible by recent technological innovations. I was working on this book. Like Anousheh, we were balancing our responsibilities together as a core team, and all busily using the technologies of our time to communicate outside of our own makeshift workstation.

I also took inspiration from another changemaker, Jill Vialet, the Playworks founder who puts children in charge of school recess. Just as people everywhere were scurrying indoors for safety from the virus, Jill shared a new article with me that she had just written cleverly titled, "Meet Your New Coworkers: Your Kids." It read like a blueprint for how to manage your home space as a workplace.

Jill offered specific advice that my wife and I immediately put to use—plan your day together, check in regularly, and be available to help when needed. Her words helped us to envision a more appropriate system for living and working at home in these unusual times. By day, our familiar familial hierarchy was suddenly collapsed. There weren't bosses in this system. We were all equal, and we all had accountabilities outside our four walls. We transitioned our family structure into a team-of-teams system.

One of the first things we did to improve communication was to introduce the *family staff meeting*. As parents, we were suddenly accountable for our kids' hour-by-hour learning, which meant we had to be more engaged with their instruction. The *family staff meeting* gave our children space to plan their school objectives with us and to share teacher feedback. Routinely coming together again at lunch and dinner also kept us attuned to each other. Reviewing goals and schedules helped the boys get good at organizing themselves without the constant direction of their teachers, which they had grown accustomed to at school.

As part of our morning-meeting routine, we gathered around the kitchen-table-turned-boardroom-table at 8:30 a.m. and began with a five-minute podcast called "Little Star Café," by Dipti Kothari. Dipti is a mom in India who produces children-oriented news, so her broadcast eschews the kind of personality-based reporting we see on TV (which our boys find completely unappealing), to instead focus on issues. She helped our kids understand the stress on supply chains during isolation by reporting on the unnoticed bamboo shortages affecting pandas in zoos; she illuminated the pending challenge of equitably distributing vaccines worldwide when only a handful of primarily wealthy countries funded the research; and she shared a quirky story of how Supreme Court business in the US was being conducted over the phone during the pandemic.

With hierarchy having been eliminated in our new system, the boys were the first to give their opinions on what they heard in her newscasts, and they could express themselves in a safe space without judgement as they attempted to make sense of a world that was increasingly nonsensical. Their confidence levels noticeably increased as they learned to talk thoughtfully with adults about the news of the day, and they began to spontaneously express their opinions through different communications mediums—for example, Dante began creating professional-looking PowerPoint presentations to share with his peers and teachers.

As we scrambled to adjust inside our four walls to our new reality, it felt as if the world was suddenly unnaturally siloed again. Our most reliable connection to the world was no longer with neighbors, but through television, digital media channels, or online forums. Still, as we all went indoors, something else came into view. I could actually see what Anousheh had seen looking to Earth from space: one world.

For the first time in my life, the whole world faced the same threat at the same time. Like so many others, my revenue stream quickly dried up, and our family's physical health and financial security were immediately precarious. There were times when we didn't know how we would come through this unscathed, but each day, we gave thanks for what we had and for the fact that we were safe—and together. Our hearts were moved for anyone who lost a loved one, or a home, or a business, or a job. This virus did not discriminate, even if it exposed ways society had. It did not pick one country over another, and it did not favor a demographic. It was a dangerous, ravaging super-spreader. This moment called on everyone to come together, and to be mindful of each other as we made decisions for ourselves. It required an unusual response from us as a family, just as it required an unusual response from us as a nation and as global citizens. Like Anousheh, who saw the borders of Earth melt away the further from it she traveled, I similarly sensed that same melting of the boundaries.

This pandemic has ripped the Band-Aid off a system that was sputtering to its end. It's a system that clearly wasn't working. An alarmingly high number of working households collapsed financially within days, exposing families as living mostly without savings. Tens of millions of people went directly to unemployment, and the crisis revealed the hidden millions who had long relied on revenue and work outside of the formal sector. This event brought to the forefront of our awareness a grossly underequipped healthcare system and government functions that are clearly unpracticed at working together. The world built for repetition was unable to respond effectively to a dynamically changing threat. It required a changemaker response.

The COVID-19 crisis is accelerating us out of the old game and into the new game. That's the opportunity. Sure, some will cling to the old-game systems we have known, like the football player at the beginning of the book. Others will freeze in place, unsure of what to do. I'm not saying that there is an easy road ahead. We are in a highly complex world that requires a mindset dedicated to learning, growing, and understanding new approaches that might otherwise be foreign to us. But more of us will be ready to play—we now see the game clearly and we have the playbook.

Changemaker in the Mirror

Whenever I see Wellington Nogueira, my clown friend, he always makes a point of reminding me that the clown was forced under the Big Top of the circus. "He used that time to experiment, to try new tricks, and to learn," Wellington says. "He incubated."

According to Wellington, the clown was always planning for his return to the wider world. My friend is the clown in the wider world—a doctor of joy—the beneficiary of those clowns before him who incubated and practiced new ideas inside the confinement of the Big Top.

This has similarly been our time to experiment with skills and ideas of our own. Just as my wife and I brought together the examples of Anousheh and Jill for our home-working time during the coronavirus pandemic, we all will have new experiences and inventions to take with us back into the world. Certainly, we have added life perspectives and skills that when brought together with others, will help us thrive in new ways. Perhaps now is a good time to take stock and define ourselves anew. We have all had to be changemakers during this time, whether we noticed it or not.

Wellington's fool in the royal court relied on the mirror as a prop to help a ruler see the world more clearly—to help him find the answer by first looking at himself. Are you ready to play the new game? Start by using the mirror. *Changemaker Playbook* is not simply about what you can learn from the world's most-recognized and highly effective self-identified changemakers, it's what you can see in them that you already do yourself. It's what you already do that you don't notice.

Changemaker Playbook is simply the mirror.

NOTES

Chapter One

1. "The Future of Jobs: Employment, Skills and Workforce Strategy for the Fourth Industrial Revolution," World Economic Forum, January 2016, 13, http://www3.weforum.org/docs/WEF_Future_of_Jobs.pdf.
2. "Artificial Intelligence, Automation, and the Economy," Executive Office of the President, December 2016, 15, https://www.whitehouse.gov/sites /whitehouse.gov/files/images/EMBARGOED%20AI%20Economy%20 Report.pdf.
3. Maximiliano Dvorkin, "Jobs Involving Routine Tasks Aren't Growing," Federal Reserve Bank of St. Louis, January 4, 2016, On The Economy Blog, https://www.stlouisfed.org/on-the-economy/2016/january/jobs-involving -routine-tasks-arent-growing.
4. Kristen V. Brown, "Self-Driving Cars: Bumpy Ride for Insurance Industry?" *government technology*, April 13, 2015, https://www.govtech.com/fs /Self-Driving-Cars-Bumpy-Ride-for-Insurance-Industry.html.
5. "The Unlonely Planet: How Ashoka Accelerates Impact," Ashoka, 2018, 8, 13, 16, https://ashoka-cee.org/austria/wp-content/uploads/sites/2/2019/01 /UnLonelyPlanet-Ashoka-Impact-Report-2018.pdf#:~:text=Ashoka%20is%20 being%20the%20%E2%80%9Cunlonely%20planet%E2%80%9D%20where %20I,network%20where%20I%20can%20constantly%20learn%20from %20other.
6. "Our Impact," Street Football World, accessed August 2, 2020, https://www .streetfootballworld.org/who-we-are/our-impact.
7. "Arnoud Raskin," Ashoka, accessed August 2, 2020, https://www.ashoka .org/en-us/fellow/arnoud-raskin.
8. "Every Procurement Is an Opportunity," *Citymart*, accessed August 10, 2020, https://www.citymart.com/.
9. Zack Quaintance, "New Orleans Digital Equity Award Goes to Youth Art Programs," *government technology*, Civic Innovation, December 4, 2017, Civic Innovation, https://www.govtech.com/civic/New-Orleans-Digital-Equity -Award-Goes-to-Youth-Art-Programs.html.

10. Aisiri Amin, "Mitt Liv: Helping Migrants Integrate into Swedish Society," *Inkline*, April 28, 2017, Go-getters, https://the-inkline.com/2017/04/28/mitt -liv-helping-migrants-integrate-into-swedish-society/.

11. "Mark Johnson," Ashoka, accessed August 2, 2020, https://www.ashoka .org/en-us/fellow/mark-johnson.

Chapter Two

1. Henry De Sio, *Campaign Inc.: How Leadership and Organization Propelled Barack Obama to the White House* (Iowa City: University of Iowa Press, 2014), 207.

Chapter Three

1. "Number of Active Users at Facebook Over the Years," *Yahoo! Finance,* October 23, 2012, https://finance.yahoo.com/news/number-active-users -facebook-over-years-214600186--finance.html.

2. "Number of People Using Social Media Platforms, 2004 to 2018," graph, Our World in Data, *Global Change Data Lab*, accessed May 21, 2020, https:// ourworldindata.org/rise-of-social-media.

3. J. Clement, "Hours of Video Uploaded to YouTube Every Minute as of May 2019," *Statista*, August 9, 2019, Online Video & Entertainment, https://www.statista .com/statistics/259477/hours-of-video-uploaded-to-youtube-every-minute/.

4. "Technology Adoption in U.S. Households, 1930 to 2019," graph, Our World in Data, *Global Change Data Lab*, accessed May 21, 2020, https:// ourworldindata.org/grapher/technology-adoption-by-households-in-the -united-states?time=1930..2019&country=Automobile+Cellular%20phone +Colour%20TV+Computer+Ebook%20reader+Internet+Podcasting+Radio +Smartphone%20usage+Social%20media%20usage+Tablet.

5. "How Do You Know When You've Revolutionized an Industry," Ashoka, November 2013, https://www.ashoka.org/sites/default/files/2019-11/2013 -impact-study-final-web.pdf.

Chapter Four

1. "George Washington's History and Background," US History, America's Place in the Global Struggle, accessed August 10, 2020, https://www.ushistory .org/us/8c.asp.

2. "Ten Facts about Washington and Slavery," George Washington's Mount Vernon, accessed August 10, 2020, https://www.mountvernon.org/george -washington/slavery/ten-facts-about-washington-slavery/.

3. Daniel Wolff, *How Lincoln Learned to Read: Twelve Great Americans and the Educations That Made Them* (New York: Bloomsbury USA, 2010), 138.

4. "Henry Ford Biography," Ford Motor Company, accessed June 8, 2020, https://corporate.ford.com/articles/history/henry-ford-biography.html.

5. "Henry Ford: Founder, Ford Motor Company," The Henry Ford Museum, accessed April 6, 2017, https://www.thehenryford.org/explore/stories-of -innovation/visionaries/henry-ford/.

6. Henry Ford and Samuel Crowther, *My Life and Work* (New York: Double-day, Page, & Co., 1922), 247.

7. Daniel Wolff, *How Lincoln Learned to Read: Twelve Great Americans and the Educations That Made Them* (New York: Bloomsbury USA, 2010), 157–59.

8. Ibid., 159.

9. Ibid., 142–59.

10. Sarah Cweik, "The Middle Class Took Off 100 Years Ago ... Thanks to Henry Ford?," NPR, January 27, 2014, Economy, https://www.npr.org/2014/01/27 /267145552/the-middle-class-took-off-100-years-ago-thanks-to-henry -ford.

11. "Popular Research Topics: Henry Ford Quotations," The Henry Ford Museum, accessed March 29, 2020, https://www.thehenryford.org/collections-and -research/digital-resources/popular-topics/henry-ford-quotes/.

Chapter Five

1. "125th NCCU Baccalaureate Commencement Exercises," North Carolina Central University, YouTube video, streamed live on May 9, 2015, https:// www.youtube.com/watch?v=NhXSxS7HHy4&feature=youtu.be#t= 1h57m56s.

2. Ibid.

3. "Gwyneth Paltrow Joins Think It Up at the 2015 Telecast!," *Think It Up*, YouTube video, November 23, 2015, https://www.youtube.com/watch ?time_continue=38&v=fpUpfzgjvGI.

4. Ibid.

5. Peter Baker, "In Court Nominees, Is Obama Looking for Empathy by Another Name," *New York Times*, April 25, 2010, Politics, https://www .nytimes.com/2010/04/26/us/politics/26memo.html.

6. Paul Taylor, "Court of Public Opinion Sides with Women on Empathy," Pew Research Center, May 21, 2009, https://www.pewresearch.org/2009/05/21 /court-of-public-opinion-sides-with-women-on-empathy/.

7. "Older People Projected to Outnumber Children for First Time in U.S. His-tory," United State Census Bureau, March 13, 2018 (revised September 6, 2018 and October 8, 2019), Release Number CB 18–41, https://www.census .gov/newsroom/press-releases/2018/cb18-41-population-projections.html.

Chapter Six

1. Kim Parker, Anthony Cilluffo, and Renee Stepler, "6 Facts about the U.S. Military and Its Changing Demographics," Pew Research Center, April 13, 2017, FactTank: News in the Numbers, https://www.pewresearch.org/fact-tank/2017/04/13/6-facts-about-the-u-s-military-and-its-changing-demographics/.
2. "The Tapestry of Black Business Ownership in America: Untapped Opportunities for Success," Association for Enterprise Opportunity, accessed July 26, 2020, https://aeoworks.org/images/uploads/fact_sheets/AEO_Black _Owned_Business_Report_02_16_17_FOR_WEB.pdf.
3. "Census Bureau Reports the Number of Black-Owned Businesses Increased at Triple the National Rate," United States Census Bureau, February 8, 2011, Newsroom Archive, https://www.census.gov/newsroom/releases/archives /business_ownership/cb11-24.html.
4. Erin Duffin, "Millionaires in the United States—Statistics & Facts," *Statista*, February 6, 2020, Economy, https://www.statista.com/topics/3467/millionaires -in-the-united-states/.
5. Ellen Sheng, "This Underfunded Female Demographic Is Launching the Most Start-Ups in America, Far from Silicon Valley," CNBC, February 25, 2020, Invest In You: Ready. Set. Grow., https://www.cnbc.com/2020/02/25 /underfunded-female-demographic-is-launching-the-most-start-ups-in-us .html.
6. Sheena Ashley and Joi James, "Despite the Racial Wealth Gap, Black Philanthropy Is Strong," February 28, 2018, Urban Wire: Nonprofits and Philanthropy, https://www.urban.org/urban-wire/despite-racial-wealth-gap -black-philanthropy-strong.
7. W. K. Kellogg Foundation, "Cultures of Giving: Energizing and Expanding Philanthropy by and for Communities of Color" (Michigan: W.K. Kellogg Foundation, 2012), https://www.giarts.org/sites/default/files/Cultures-of -Giving_Energizing-and-Expanding-Philanthropy-by-and-for-Communities -of-Color.pdf, 5.
8. Jo Jones and William D. Mosher, "Fathers' Involvement with Their Children: United States, 2006–2010," *National Health Statistics Report*, 71, December 2013, https://www.cdc.gov/nchs/data/nhsr/nhsr071.pdf.

Chapter Seven

1. Jennifer O'Neill, "Domestic Violence Statistics: The Horrific Reality," *Good Housekeeping*, Feburary 24, 2016, https://www.goodhousekeeping.com /life/relationships/a37005/statistics-about-domestic-violence/.
2. "OECD: Coffees with the Secretary-General: H.R.H. Princess Laurentien of the Netherlands," 2018, 5, https://oecdobserver.org/files/coffeessg /LAURENTIEN_Brochure.pdf.

Chapter Eight

1. "History," Otis, accessed June 25, 2020, https://www.otis.com/corporate /our-company/history/.

2. Mark Bushnell, "Then Again: Cities Rise Thanks to a Vermonter," *VTDIG-GER*, April 16, 2017, People & Places, https://vtdigger.org/2017/04/16/cities -rise-thanks-vermonter/.

3. John C. Abell, "March 23, 1857: Mr. Otis Gives You a Lift," *Wired*, March 23, 2010, https://www.wired.com/2010/03/0323otis-elevator-first/.

4. Caitlin Simon, S. Lawrence Kocot, and William H. Dietz, "Partnership for a Healthier America: Creating Change Through Private Sector Partnerships," US National Library of Medicine—National Institutes of Health, April, 24, 2017, https://www.ncbi.nlm.nih.gov/pmc/articles/PMC5488065/#:~:text =Creation%20of%20PHA%20and%20Early,launched%20on%20 February%209%2C%202010.

5. "Chef Sam Kass of the White House—Biography," *StarChefs*, accessed June 25, 2020, https://www.starchefs.com/cook/chefs/bio/sam-kass.

6. "Front-of-Label Beverages Arrive on Shelves," *Packing Strategies*, February 12, 2011, Packaging News, https://www.packagingstrategies.com /articles/85689-front-of-label-beverages-arrive-on-shelves.

7. "First Lady's Anti-Obesity Campaign Ignites Change in Food Industry," *The Christian Science Monitor*, February 27, 2013, https://www.csmonitor .com/The-Culture/Family/2013/0227/First-lady-s-anti-obesity-campaign -ignites-change-in-food-industry.

8. Krissah Thompson and Tim Carman, "A Healthful Legacy: Michelle Obama Looks to the Future of 'Let's Move'," *Washington Post*, May 3, 2015, Food, https://www.washingtonpost.com/lifestyle/food/a-healthful-legacy -michelle-obama-looks-to-the-future-of-lets-move/2015/05/03/19feb42c -b3cc-11e4-886b-c22184f27c35_story.html.

9. Jeff Stein, "Barack Obama Has a Plan for the Trump Era," *Vox*, VoxMedia, March 13, 2017, https://www.vox.com/policy-and-politics/2017/3/13 /14750528/barack-obama-trump-post-presidency.

10. Catherine Reef, *Florence Nightingale: Life of the Legendary Nurse* (New York: Clarion Books, 2016), 14.

11. Ibid., 35–36.

12. Ibid., 38–39.

13. Ibid., 45

14. Ibid., 44.

15. Ibid., 48–54.

16. Ibid., 84–87.

17. Ibid., 90–98.

18. Ibid., 90–95.

19. Ibid., 125.

20. Ibid., 100–29.

21. Ibid., 97–107.

22. Ibid., 97–104.

23. Ibid., 98–117.

24. Ibid.,122–140.

25. Ibid., 147–56.

26. "Florence Nightingale," Famous Scientists, August 15, 2016, https://www
.famousscientists.org/florence-nightingale/.

27. Lloyd I. Sederer, "From Mission to Movement: 'KaBOOM!' and the Renais-
sance of Play in America," *HuffPost*, May 12, 2011, The Blog, https://www
.huffpost.com/entry/kaboom-playgrounds_b_858958.

28. "Working to Achieve Playspace Equity," KABOOM!, accessed May 23,
2020, https://kaboom.org/playspace-equity.

Chapter Nine

1. Catherine Reef, *Florence Nightingale: Life of the Legendary Nurse* (New
York: Clarion Books, 2016), 17–18.

2. Edward Tyas Cook, *The Life of Florence Nightingale—Volume I* (London,
UK: Macmillan, 1913), 280.

3. Daniel Wolff, *How Lincoln Learned to Read: Twelve Great Americans
and the Educations That Made Them* (New York: Bloomsbury USA, 2010),
102.

4. "Which President Started the Tradition of Pardoning the Thanksgiving Turkey," accessed July 26, 2020, https://www.whitehousehistory.org/questions
/which-president-started-the-tradition-of-pardoning-the-thanksgiving
-turkey.

5. Daniel Wolff, *How Lincoln Learned to Read: Twelve Great Americans and
the Educations That Made Them* (New York: Bloomsbury USA, 2010),
95–105.

6. Ibid., 137–38.

7 "Ashoka Launches 'Great Changemakers Start in Their Youth'," Ashoka, August
12, 2016, https://www.ashoka.org/en-us/story/ashoka-launches-%E2%80%9
Cgreat-changemakers-start-their-youth%E2%80%9D.

8. Daniel Wolff, *How Lincoln Learned to Read: Twelve Great Americans
and the Educations That Made Them* (New York: Bloomsbury USA, 2010),
100.

9. Ibid., 113.

10. J. Randy Taraborrelli, *The Hiltons: The True Story of an American Dynasty*
(New York: Grand Central Publishing, 2014), 13.

11. Ibid., 13–15.

12. "X-Rays, 'Fax Machines' and Ice Cream Cones Debut at 1904 World's Fair:
Washington University in St. Louis and the 1904 World's Fair," *The Source*,

April 7, 2004, Humanities & Society, https://source.wustl.edu/2004/04/xrays
-fax-machines-and-ice-cream-cones-debut-at-1904-world-fair/.

13. J. Randy Taraborrelli, *The Hiltons: The True Story of an American Dynasty*
(New York: Grand Central Publishing, 2014), 13.

14. Ibid., 16.

15. Ibid., 20–21.

16. "A History of Hilton Family Philanthropy," Conrad N. Hilton Foundation, History, accessed May 24, 2020, https://www.hiltonfoundation.org/about/history.

17. J. Randy Taraborrelli, *The Hiltons: The True Story of an American Dynasty*
(New York: Grand Central Publishing, 2014), 16.

18. "125th NCCU Baccalaureate Commencement Exercises," North Carolina Central University, YouTube video, streamed live on May 9, 2015, https://www
.youtube.com/watch?v=NhXSxS7HHy4&feature=youtu.be#t=1h57m56s.

19. *The Hilton Legacy: Serving Humanity Worldwide* (California: Conrad N. Hilton Foundation, 2009), 18, https://www.hiltonfoundation.org/wp-content
/uploads/2019/10/Hilton_History_Book_6_4_09.pdf.

20. "Why Donate?" Roots of Empathy, data as of August 6, 2020, https://root
sofempathy.org/donate/.

21. Seth Godin, "The Sea of Strangers," *Seth's Blog*, July 3, 2013, https://seths
.blog/2013/07/the-sea-of-strangers/.

22. Mike Marriner and Nathan Gebhard, *Road Trip Nation: A Guide to Discovering Your Own Path* (New York: Ballantine Books, 2006), xii–xv.

Chapter Ten

1. David Gergen, "The New Engines of Reform," *U.S. News & World Report*, December 12, 2006, Money & Business, https://web.archive.org
/web/20091012000716/http://www.usnews.com/usnews/biztech/articles
/060220/20gergen.htm.

2. Ali Tadayon, "West Oakland Neighborhoods Welcome First Full-Service Grocery Store in Decades," *East Bay Times*, updated June 2, 2019, Business,
https://www.eastbaytimes.com/2019/05/31/west-oakland-neighborhoods
-welcome-first-full-service-grocery-store-in-decades/.

3. "Great Changemakers Start in their Youth," Ashoka Innovators for the Public, 2016.

4. Ibid., 4.

5. Ibid., 4.

6. "Your Call For Help Will Never Go Unanswered," Childline India, Presence, accessed July 31, 2020, https://www.childlineindia.org/a/about/childline
-india.

7. Child Helpline International, "How We Got Started and Where We Are Today," History, accessed July 31, 2020, https://www.childhelplineinternational
.org/about/our-story/how-we-got-started-where-we-are-today/.

Chapter Eleven

1. Helen Davidson, "Third of Australian Youth Have No Job or Are Underemployed, Report Finds," *Guardian*, March, 26, 2017, https://www.theguardian.com/business/2017/mar/27/third-of-australian-youth-have-no-job-or-are-underemployed-report-finds.

2. Megan Elliott, "11 Job Skills Employers Wished Young People Had (and How to Get Them)," *Showbiz Cheat Sheet*, December 4, 2017, Money & Career, https://www.cheatsheet.com/money-career/job-skills-employers-wished-young-people-had-how-get-them.html/.

3. Richard Fry, "Millennials Are the Largest Generation in the U.S. Labor Force," Pew Research Center, April 11, 2018, FactTank: News in the Numbers, https://www.pewresearch.org/fact-tank/2018/04/11/millennials-largest-generation-us-labor-force/.

4. Andrew Van Dam, "The Unluckiest Generation in U.S. History: Millennials Have Faced the Worst Economic Odds, and Many Will Never Recover," *Washington Post*, June 5, 2020, Business, https://www.washingtonpost.com/business/2020/05/27/millennial-recession-covid/.

5. Hannes Schwandt, "Recession Graduates: The Long-lasting Effects of an Unlucky Draw," *Stanford Institute for Economic Policy Research*, April 2019, https://siepr.stanford.edu/research/publications/recession-graduates-effects-unlucky.

6. Jeffrey J. Selingo, *Life After College: What Parents and Students Should Know About Navigating School to Prepare for the Jobs of Tomorrow* (New York: HarperCollins, 2016), ix–xix.

7. Daniel Mahler and Paul Laudicina, "America@250: Four Possible Futures for the United States on Its 250th Birthday in 2026," *A.T. Kearney*, April 2016, 7–10.

8. "Confidence in Institutions," Gallup, Inc., accessed May 24, 2020, https://news.gallup.com/poll/1597/confidence-institutions.aspx.

9. Ibid.

10. "Education," Gallup Inc., accessed May 24, 2020, https://news.gallup.com/poll/1612/education.aspx.

11. Jeffrey M. Jones, "Confidence in Higher Education Down Since 2015," *Gallup Blog*, October 9, 2018, https://news.gallup.com/opinion/gallup/242441/confidence-higher-education-down-2015.aspx.

12. Jeremy Bauer-Wolf, "Report: Shrinking Share of Adults Thinks College Is 'Important,'" *Education Dive*, January 2, 2020, Brief, https://www.educationdive.com/news/report-shrinking-share-of-adults-thinks-college-is-important/569701/.

13. Joel Anderson, "Is College Worth It? 42% of Americans Say No," *GOBankingRates*, April 16, 2019, Student Loans 101, https://www.gobankingrates.com/saving-money/education/americans-regret-college-survey/.

14. "Abby Lindsay—Ecuador," Global Citizen Year, accessed March 5, 2020, https://www.globalcitizenyear.org/updates/taking-a-leap-of-faith.

Chapter Twelve

1. "Lennon Flowers," Ashoka, accessed July 3, 2020, https://www.ashoka.org /en-us/fellow/lennon-flowers.
2. "Childhood Bereavement in the United States," Judi's House / Jag Institute, accessed August 2, 2020, https://www.judishouse.org/cbem.
3. "Lennon Flowers," Ashoka, accessed July 20, 2020, https://www.ashoka.org /en-us/fellow/lennon-flowers.
4. "The Dinner Party: Changing How We Approach Life after Loss," The Dinner Party, YouTube video, December 1, 2013, https://youtu.be/Tyka7IrZhXU.
5. "Lennon Flowers," Ashoka, accessed July 3, 2020, https://www.ashoka.org /en-us/fellow/lennon-flowers.
6. Seth Godin, "The Sea of Strangers," Seth's Blog, July 3, 2013, https://seths .blog/2013/07/the-sea-of-strangers/.

ACKNOWLEDGMENTS

First, a huge hug to my mom, who asked me often as a child, *How do you think they would feel?* She taught me to value kindness and to practice acting on my empathy. I love you, Mom. My dad taught me to be comfortable with the uncomfortable, and I am grateful to him for consciously giving me the capacities of a changemaker beyond what my schooling provided. My parents were both public school teachers, and my youth was filled with education professionals who, like them, were excellent role models and champions of mine. My brother, Mark, was my best friend throughout our growing-up years, and Three Rivers, CA, was our playground for experimenting, creating, and interacting with nature. My friends and I were raised in a community of caring adults—and my values and appreciation of community certainly sprang from those rural roots. I loved high school and the many new friends I collected there, 30 minutes from my home.

My first leave-to-learn experience was in Sweden as a summer exchange student when I was a rising senior in high school. My late Swedish brother Håkan, my host family (who became my family for life), and the friends I made taught me to see the world through a new lens. Håkan was also a longtime collaborator on these ideas, often in the role of critical friend who would then try them out in his own work and life. I learned from my Swedish mother, Barbro (my kids call her Farmor), that I could have more than one mother who would love me unconditionally in this life. It was a beautiful discovery for me about humanity at an early age.

Linda Konnor is my literary agent, and she is a changemaker. She immediately *got* these wild ideas I presented to her and then had the courage to stake her reputation on a little-known author, writing about a topic that still seemed unripe. She has been a great source of support and everything I had hoped for in a partner on such an audacious endeavor.

Linda connected me with Jonathan Shipley at Hachette UK, and I knew immediately this book had the right home. I am grateful to Jonathan for all he did to promote this idea inside a prestigious brand. I quickly came to trust his judgment as the reader's advocate and have leaned on his wisdom throughout this process. I am also amazed at the operation he puts around an author. The team is fantastic to work with—Michelle Surianello has been indispensable in getting this book ready for launch and is excellent at guiding all of us on her team of teams, and Brett Halbleib's amazingly detailed review and skillful polish of the draft manuscript got it up a level and to the finish line right at the point I was frankly out of gas. I also want to send my thanks to Alison Hankey for pulling my proposal out of the stack.

It takes a team of teams to weave together lessons and stories like the ones included in *Changemaker Playbook*. This was a labor of love for me. I was able to attract incredible individuals to this project, beginning with a team of writers who contributed significantly in different ways. Lynn Griffin was an important early influencer on this project. My writing coach throughout the development process, her series of helpful exercises became the basis for a marketable proposal—no small feat—and our early work together made her a co-architect of the structure and the larger themes.

Next, when it was time to go to work, Steve Kent, my longtime writing collaborator, made a herculean contribution. We have been experimenting with these ideas in op-eds for years, learning to take what could be viewed as abstract concepts and using them to make sense of current events. Collaborating on a long-form project gave me a new appreciation of the many dimensions of Steve's abilities. He knows my thinking as well as anyone, and he helped me untangle the mess of concepts in my head to turn these complicated ideas into meaningful themes inside powerful stories. He was particularly skilled at pulling out the central premise in each chapter and keeping the focus where it needed to be. Steve is a master at his craft and a pleasure to work with.

For the final phase of the manuscript's development before it got to

ACKNOWLEDGMENTS 233

Jonathan, I was reunited with Elisabeth Chretien, who was my editor at the University of Iowa Press for my first book, *Campaign Inc.: How Leadership and Organization propelled Barack Obama to the White House*. Elisabeth knows my voice, and she has proven twice how to make it better. I think she's amazing at what she does.

Finally, my wife, Sine, looked over every word of this manuscript at least three times, just as she did on my first book. She is not only my biggest booster, but she is my de facto final editor. She is smart and she loves books—she knows how words should be put to work for readers.

Barack Obama changed my life, and if you liked chapter two, featuring my time supporting his campaign for president, you should go deeper and have a look at *Campaign Inc.* I am grateful to University of Iowa Press for allowing me to write so freely featuring material from that first book. Obviously, the lessons from that campaign were not what you might expect, and they were game changers for me.

Bill Drayton changed my life again. *Changemaker Playbook* picks up where *Campaign Inc.* left off, and this book is, in part, a tribute to my time working with him. It was truly an honor to collaborate so closely and creatively with a man who has left such a significant and indelible scratch on history. He generously shared his wisdom and knowledge. I learned every day. Working with Bill was the closest thing to my old rock and roll days, jamming in a band late at night and discovering something cool in every session. Ours is a partnership—and friendship—I treasure.

On one hand, this book was hard to write. On the other, this book wrote itself. These amazing characters walked into my life, deeply impressed me, and at some point became words on a screen—and later on paper. I especially want to thank the Ashoka Fellows with whom I have worked over the years, particularly those featured: Jürgen Griesbeck, Arnoud Raskin, Sascha Haselmayer, Sofia Appelgren, Mark Johnson, Karen Worcman, Rodrigo Baggio, Anna Penido, Wellington Nogueira, Katherine Freund, Molly Barker, Trabian Shorters, Riccarda Zezza, Ana Bella Estevez, Kendis Paris, Mary Gordon, Mike Marriner, Anshu Gupta, Jill Vialet, Darell Hammond, Jeroo Billimoria, Abby Falik, Eric Glustrom, Vishal Talreja, and Lennon Flowers. But the many who are not in these pages also left an imprint on me, and you can dig more deeply into the work of this incredible community of leading social entrepreneurs at https://www.ashoka.org/en/ashoka-fellows.

Next, I am grateful to my former colleagues at Ashoka Innovators for the Public, who are too many to acknowledge by name. It is an amazing group of people working on Everyone a Changemaker™. My co-architects were Diana Wells and Anamarie Schindler, who were wonderful partners. Laxmi Parthasarathy and Samara Randhawa were my close teammates on the journey, and we learned from each other every single day (I do miss you both!). Vishnu Swaminathan and his team in India generously invited me into their learning laboratory from the outset, and we all really pushed each other's thinking as we piloted these ideas together—it was a dream team, as were all the country teams with which I worked. It was always heartbreaking to leave my family to travel, but my amazing colleagues made sure every minute of my time away was meaningful and they were awesome(!)—every single person I was with. This is a good place to note that Everyone a Changemaker™ is a trademark of Ashoka Innovators of the Public and is used in these pages with permission and deep gratitude.

Beyond the Ashoka social entrepreneurs, I am grateful for the changemakers who participated in this project–those who gave interviews and those who made key introductions or helped my interviews along. In particular, Emilia Ganem (my former colleague in Argentina) who reconnected me to María Eugenia Favret at QMark; Alexandra Mitjans (another former colleague), who years ago introduced me to her brother, Isaac Marcet, and helped me track him down for our interview when it occurred to me too late that I wanted his perspective; Annette Johnson, Danielle Kilchner, and Sara Jog at Ashoka; Irene Alba at Esade in connection with Javier Solana's wonderful contribution (and Maite Arango, who made the introduction to him many years ago); Kisha Evans from BMe, who was my partner in Trabian Shorters' involvement; Yvonne Moholt at Jeroo Billimoria's One Family Foundation, who was just on top of every detail; Rachel Rose at XPRIZE Foundation, who managed myself and Anousheh Ansari around competing demands and some difficult deadlines (thank you!); and my former colleague Darlene Damm—always so generous with her connections. Also, a special thanks to Dane Lowry, who made my visit with Baby Patrick at the school where he was the principal truly remarkable and insightful. Dane said something that has always stuck with me: "There is a lot we can learn from our littlest learners." It's because of Dane, Baby Patrick is part of this story.

Along with those already mentioned, this project has been shaped by social entrepreneurs and innovators who are friends that I also value as thought partners, and with whom I have shared important learning experiences. These include Per Heggenes, CEO of the IKEA Foundation; Nihar Kothari, Executive Editor and Director at Rajasthan Patrika; Vishal Talreja and Suchetha Bhat; Sascha and Julia Haselmayer; Torey Malatia— an invaluable thought mentor; Shashi Velath and the very talented people at Bridge Institute, who encouraged me around these ideas; and Brad Kiley (the Mayor in that Mayor's Office), Sonal Shah, and Neil Mulholland from my White House days, who each had a hand in supporting this project by supporting me in meaningful ways since. Neil also organized the moving Newseum tribute in support of the Flight 93 Memorial (which was completed and opened on Sept. 10, 2015) that led me to President Clinton. Mimi Goss, author of *What Is Your One Sentence?: How to Be Heard in the Age of Short Attention Spans*, was so helpful in connecting me to experts and influencers in the book business, who all contributed to my getting this chance—and her longtime support dating back to my days as a student of hers at Harvard's Kennedy School has been singularly impactful.

I am particularly grateful to Elaine Stratford and Sue Kilpatrick, who welcomed me to Tasmania on two occasions. Working with Elaine and Oliver Grant during my stay as the first visiting scholar at the Peter Underwood Centre of Educational Attainment at the University of Tasmania gave me an opportunity to push my thinking in ways that were immeasurable. I was proud to be a contributor to the Centre's launch, and to the *Education Transforms International Symposium*. The people I got to know in Hobart—Rosie Nash, Lisa Denny, Rose Martin, Adam Mostogl, Bernadette Black, and so many others—contributed to a changemaker support system that I still value today. We learned together.

I was also deeply impressed by my fabulous 2017 cohort of resident fellows at the Bellagio Center, focused on Youth as Agents of Transformative Change. I was surprised to find Anna Penido in that group (someone I'd long wanted to work with), and the unanticipated friendships that were formed alongside the memories we all made during our time together that I will long cherish. In addition to Anna, I am speaking of Esra'a, Monisha, Aya, Kiran, Khary, Joshua, Mark, John, Novuyo, Ananya, and Laurentien—and our spouses and families, who became linked through the friendship we formed. I know we opened one another's minds during our time together. I am grateful to the Rockefeller Foundation staff, who supported our stay and made it enjoyable, and for the invitation—for the space over several weeks to continue my work on the youth components in the book that were begun in Tasmania. It was an invaluable contribution to the finished product.

Seth Godin's influence on me is obvious. I appreciate his mentorship and valuable insights over the years, as well as his generosity. He allowed me to cite *The Sea of Strangers* passage from his blog (seths.blog) with permission, but more importantly, he contributed to my thinking in a way that unexpectedly inspired a key message in this book.

Our Blessed Sacrament community has been a source of great inspiration and support to us as a family during this time. Father Kelly's kind heartedness and generous spirit deepened our faith in ways I will always treasure.

Finally, this book has been a family affair. More than lessons in changemaking, this is Part Two of our journey together. Dante and Zane, you boys are spectacular—I am so proud to be your dad. Stay authentic and keep your hearts open to the blessings that await, and you will remain brilliant lights in this world. I love you both. Sine, you are amazing. I find you completely adorable, and talented in so many ways. All this, a demanding job, and you still found a way to complete your master's degree in Producing for Film on the same day I finished this manuscript. I love you and have treasured every single step we have taken together since we met. Thank you for letting me take big bets on myself (I am aware they don't always work out immediately as planned). I am looking forward to our next adventure together!

ABOUT THE AUTHOR

Honorable Henry F. De Sio, Jr., is a social-sector executive, leadership advisor, campaign strategist, and public speaker. As the 2008 Chief Operating Officer (COO) of Barack Obama's presidential campaign, and then serving as Deputy Assistant to the President in the Obama White House for two-and-a-half years, De Sio became intimately acquainted with a new emerging pattern of societal change. He has since followed his campaign-driven passion for *hope and change* to make *changemaking* a global phenomenon. Henry became a member of the Leadership Group and Global Chair for Framework Change at Ashoka Innovators for the Public, where he worked from 2012-2018, and he published his first book, *Campaign Inc.: How Leadership and Organization Propelled Barack Obama to the White House.*

Known as the global ambassador for changemakers, Henry has brought the powerful framework of new leadership and team-of-teams organization described in *Changemaker Playbook* to board rooms, newsrooms, community forums, university institutions, and governmental halls all over the world. De Sio has appeared on radio and television, including C-SPAN's 2012 Road to the White House. He was a featured speaker at the 2014 Global Child Forum at the Royal Palace in Stockholm by invitation of the King and Queen of Sweden, and he headlined Ben & Jerry's 2013 Social Entrepreneurship Summit. He has been a panelist and contributor at the Skoll World Forum on Social Entrepreneurship at Oxford and at the Asian Leadership Conference in Seoul, South Korea; and he delivered the closing keynote at the 2014 Cities Summit at London City Hall, hosted by then-mayor Boris Johnson and Citymart.

De Sio is a 2017 Rockefeller Bellagio Center Resident on Youth as Agents of Transformative Change; a 2016 Bankinter Innovation

Foundation Future Trends Forum Fellow on Harnessing the Power of Technology to Solve Inequality, in Madrid; and he was the first Visiting Scholar at the Peter Underwood Centre for Educational Attainment at the University of Tasmania in 2016. He has a master's degree from Harvard's Kennedy School, and he earned his B.A. from U.C. Santa Barbara. Henry lives in Arlington, Virginia, with his wife and two sons.

Visit henrydesio.com and follow on Twitter @henrydesio.

INDEX